Studies in Economic Transition

General Editors: **Jens Hölsher**, Reader in Economics , University of Brighton; and **Horst Tomann**, Professor of Economics, Free University Berlin.

This series has been established in response to a growing demand for a greater understanding of the transformation of economic systems. It brings together theoretical and empirical studies on economic transition and economic development. The post-communist transition from planned to market economies is one of the main areas of applied theory because in this field the most dramatic examples of change and economic dynamics can be found. The series aims to contribute to the understanding of specific major economic changes as well as to advance the theory of economic development. The implications of economic policy will be a major point of focus.

Titles include:

Lucian Cernat
EUROPEANIZATION, VARIETIES OF CAPITALISM AND ECONOMIC
PERFORMANCE IN CENTRAL AND EASTERN EUROPE

Irwin Collier, Herwig Roggemann, Oliver Scholz and Horst Tomann (*editors*)
WELFARE STATES IN TRANSITION
East and West

Hella Engerer
PRIVATIZATION AND ITS LIMITS IN CENTRAL AND EASTERN EUROPE
Property Rights in Transition

Hubert Gabrisch and Rüdiger Phol (*editors*)
EU ENLARGEMENT AND ITS MACROECONOMIC EFFECTS IN
EASTERN EUROPE
Currencies, Prices, Investment and Competitiveness

Oleh Havrylyshyn
DIVERGENT PATHS IN POST-COMMUNIST TRANSFORMATION
Capitalism for All or Capitalism for the Few?

Jens Hölscher (*editor*)
FINANCIAL TURBULENCE AND CAPITAL MARKETS IN TRANSITION
COUNTRIES

Jens Hölscher and Anja Hochberg (*editors*)
EAST GERMANY'S ECONOMIC DEVELOPMENT SINCE UNIFICATION
Domestic and Global Aspects

Mihaela Kelemen and Monika Kostera (*editors*)
CRITICAL MANAGEMENT RESEARCH IN EASTERN EUROPE
Managing the Transition

Emil J. Kirchner (*editor*)
DECENTRALIZATION AND TRANSITION IN THE VISEGRAD
Poland, Hungary, the Czech Republic and Slovakia

Tomasz Mickiewicz
ECONOMIC TRANSITION IN CENTRAL EUROPE AND THE COMMONWEALTH
OF INDEPENDENT STATES

Julie Pellegrin
THE POLITICAL ECONOMY OF COMPETITIVENESS IN AN ENLARGED EUROPE

Stanislav Poloucek (*editor*)
REFORMING THE FINANCIAL SECTOR IN CENTRAL EUROPEAN COUNTRIES

Gregg S. Robins
BANKING IN TRANSITION
East Germany after Unification

Johannes Stephan
ECONOMIC TRANSITION IN HUNGARY AND EAST GERMANY
Gradualism and Shock Therapy in Catch-up Development

Johannes Stephan (*editor*)
TECHNOLOGY TRANSFER VIA FOREIGN DIRECT INVESTMENT IN CENTRAL
AND EASTERN EUROPE

Hans van Zon
THE POLITICAL ECONOMY OF INDEPENDENT UKRAINE

Adalbert Winkler (*editor*)
BANKING AND MONETARY POLICY IN EASTERN EUROPE
The First Ten Years

Studies in Economic Transition
Series Standing Oder ISBN 0–333–73353–3
(*outside North America only*)

You can receive future titles in this series as they are published by placing a standing
order. Please contact your bookseller or, in case of difficulty, write to us at the address
below with your name and address, the title of the series and the ISBN quoted above.

Customer Services Department, Macmillan Distribution Ltd, Houndmills, Basingtoke,
Hampshire RG21 6XS, England

Europeanization, Varieties of Capitalism and Economic Performance in Central and Eastern Europe

Lucian Cernat

First published 2006 by
PALGRAVE MACMILLAN
Houndmills, Basingstoke, Hampshire RG21 6XS and
175 Fifth Avenue, New York, N.Y. 10010
Companies and representatives throughout the world.

PALGRAVE MACMILLAN is the global academic imprint of the Palgrave Macmillan division of St. Martin's Press, LLC and of Palgrave Macmillan Ltd. Macmillan® is a registered trademark in the United States, United Kingdom and other countries. Palgrave is a registered trademark in the European Union and other countries.

ISBN-13: 978–1–4039–4797–0
ISBN-10: 1–4039–4797–X

This book is printed on paper suitable for recycling and made from fully managed and sustained forest sources.

A catalogue record for this book is available from the British Library.

Library of Congress Cataloging-in-Publication Data
Cernat, Lucian.
    Europeanization, varieties of capitalism, and economic performance in Central and Eastern Europe / by Lucian Cernat.
        p. cm.
    Includes bibliographical references and index.
    ISBN 1–4039–4797–X (cloth)
    1. Europe, Eastern – Economic conditions – 1989– 2. Europe, Central – Economic conditions – 1989- 3. Capitalism – Europe, Eastern.
    4. Capitalism – Europe, Central. I. Title.
HC244.C395 2006
330.947′0009′049—dc22   2005051476

10 9 8 7 6 5 4 3 2 1
15 14 13 12 11 10 09 08 07 06

Printed and bound in Great Britain by
Antony Rowe Ltd, Chippenham and Eastbourne

For Irina, Emma, and my parents: with love

Contents

List of Figures

List of Tables

Preface

This book analyses the institutional adjustment in the Central and East European countries (CEECs) in the post-1989 period, in their quest for market-led prosperity. Throughout the transition period, CEECs needed to make a choice between the existing models of capitalism in developed market economies (market-oriented Anglo-Saxon, Continental European, and developmental capitalism). Such a choice was, however, conditioned by a complex interplay between domestic and external factors. The book argues that the poor economic performance of several CEECs during the first decade of transition can be attributed to a large extent to inconsistent institutional choices.

The book makes a major contribution to the understanding of institution-building in Central and Eastern Europe by adopting, and when necessary adapting, theories developed for the study of Western political and economic systems. The theoretical framework that guided the overall research was a cross-fertilization of key concepts: Europeanization, globalization models of capitalism, policy transfer and interest-intermediation. Thus, the transition process is reconceptualized as a case of 'policy transfer' from various levels (global, European, sub-regional) using different mechanisms, each having various degrees of effectiveness. By showing that CEECs did not adopt a uniform model of capitalism, the book further clarifies the debate surrounding the issue of institutional convergence and globalization and argues that, in the case of CEECs, varieties of capitalism persist. In addition, the findings of the book contribute to the literature on growth and institutions, providing for the first time an evaluation of the growth effects of each major variety of capitalism for the specific case of Central and Eastern Europe. Finally, by assessing the effects of major external factors such as the Bretton Woods institutions and the newly constructed index of Europeanization on economic performance in CEECs, the thesis seeks to fill a gap in the literature on transition economies.

From a methodological perspective, the book consists of several distinct parts. Chapter 1 offers a good theoretical coverage of all the concepts used in the empirical section. Chapters 2 and 4 contain cross-country quantitative chapters, written for those interested in the economic aspects of European enlargement. Chapters 3 and 5 are qualitative in nature and are devoted to the political economy of Romania, in an effort to better understand the impact of domestic and external institutional factors on economic performance and the complex dynamics of EU enlargement. Therefore, given its methodological richness and its cross-country focus, the book addresses several groups of readers. First, the book has the potential to become a major reference for the increasing number of students enrolled in academic programmes related to European integration. Furthermore, the book will be appealing for practitioners and government officials involved in the EU accession process, as well as for researchers, consultants and journalists, and other scholars interested in the applicability of concepts and theories developed in the context of Western Europe to Central and Eastern Europe. In crossing disciplinary boundaries, the book has developed distinct features, in particular the Europeanization index that has the potential to become a major analytical tool for subsequent analyses of the Europeanization process as it relates to new EU members.

Writing a book needs considerable help and therefore during the last few years I have become obliged to a number of people, only a few of whom I can mention here. All of them deserve my sincere gratitude. This book would not have come into being without the support and encouragement of Peter Humphreys and Yoram Gorlizki, my two PhD supervisors at the University of Manchester. They relentlessly read and commented with a critical but sympathetic eye every aspect of the successive drafts. The PhD thesis, from which this book was distilled, was read carefully by Martin Rhodes and Mick Moran, my two PhD examiners, who each provided me with detailed, extremely helpful comments.

I am also grateful to Jeremy Richardson, Anne Deighton and Anand Menon for intellectual stimulation and sustained support during my studies at the University of Oxford, Nuffield College. At the United Nations Economic Commission for Europe I had the good fortune to encounter Radu Vranceanu, from whom I learned a great deal, thanks to his astonishing erudition and generous nature. The book also benefited from comments made by Simon Bulmer and Phil Cerny, as well as other researchers and colleagues at the University of Manchester. Daniel Daianu, Phil Keefer, James Caporaso, Henry Farrell, and several conference participants at the University of Toronto and University of Amsterdam, as well as anonymous referees, have given a number of the chapters critical but sympathetic readings.

I would also like to acknowledge the financial support from the European Union's PHARE ACE Programme, which made it possible for me to complete the research for this book.

Lastly, but certainly not least, I am especially indebted to my wife, who has been wonderfully supportive, for all the dedication, patience and wit she showed throughout the finishing of this book.

Geneva   LUCIAN CERNAT

List of Abbreviations

AP	Accession Partnership
APAPS	Authority for Privatization and Administration of State Ownership
BCR	Banca Comerciala Romana
BNS	the National Trade Unions Bloc
CAS	Country Assistance Strategy
CDF	Comprehensive Development Framework
CEECs	Central and East European countries
CES	Economic and Social Council (Romania)
CMEA	Council for Mutual Economic Assistance
CNSLR-Fratia	National Confederation of Free Trade Unions of Romania
CSDR	Democratic Trade Union Confederation of Romania
DCG	Government's Control Department
DTUR	Department for Trade Union Relations
EBRD	European Bank for Reconstruction and Development
EPAS	Enhanced Pre-Accession Strategy
ESC	Economic and Social Council
ETUC	European Trade Union Confederation
EU	European Union
EWC	European Works Council
FDI	Foreign Direct Investment
FESAL	Financial and Enterprise Sector Adjustment Loan
GDP	gross domestic product
GLS	Generalized Least Squares
IEAs	inter-enterprise arrears
IFIs	international financial institutions
ILO	International Labour Organization
IMF	International Monetary Fund
LCCs	Local Consultative Committees
MEBO	management–employee buy-out
MIT	Ministry of Industry and Trade
MNCs	multinational corporations
MPP	mass privatization process
NAD	National Agency for Programme Development and Implementation for the Reconstruction of the Mining Regions

NBR	National Bank of Romania
NCS	National Commission for Statistics
NPAA	National Programme for the Adoption of the *Acquis*
PDSR	Social Democratic Party of Romania
PHARE	Poland and Hungary Action for the Restructuring of the Economy
POF	Private Ownership Fund
PPP	Purchasing Power Parity
PSAL	Private Structural Adjustment Loan
PSIBL	Private Sector Institutional Building Loan
RASDAQ	Romanian Securities Market
RICOP	Industrial Restructuring and Professional Re-Conversion Programme
SALs	structural adjustment loans
SOEs	state-owned enterprises
SOF	State Ownership Fund

Disclaimer

This research was undertaken with support from the European Union's PHARE ACE Programme 1997 and 1998. The content of the publication is the sole responsibility of the author and it in no way represents the views of the European Commission. The views expressed herein are those of the author and do not reflect the views of the United Nations or its member states.

Introduction

In 2004, after 15 years of transition, Europe triumphed over the old division between East and West when eight former communist countries joined not only Europe's institutional architecture but also the club of liberal democracies. However, Bulgaria and Romania have missed out on the first wave of eastern enlargement. The entry of Bulgaria and Romania, pending ratification by the national parliaments of EU states, will complete in 2007 an enlargement cycle that started with the revolutions of 1989. The signature of the accession treaty, so long sought by the two countries, on 25 April 2005 has created increased enthusiasm and relief in the two acceding countries. After signing the Accession Treaty, the Romanian Prime Minister, Calin Popescu Tariceanu, said: 'we [have] ceased being a second-rank country ... On 1 January 2007 we will be EU members.' Similar euphoric statements were made by political leaders in Bulgaria and, one year earlier, by other newly-acceding states when signing or joining the European Union. EU political leaders also welcomed the accession of 10 new members as a historic moment.

However, moving from 25 to 27 EU members seems a less awaited moment by old European countries. The euphoria generated by the first wave of eastward enlargement is gradually being displaced by 'enlargement fatigue'. The evidence of such fatigue is pervasive. Political leaders and public opinion in across old European states are openly questioning the timeframe and the ability of new countries to comply with membership requirements. Anecdotal evidence and more serious doubts about the ability of the remaining two countries to fully comply in the agreed timeframe with all the accession requirements continue to surface. Doubts are also being raised about the ways in which new members will comply with specific European rules and regulations.

These mixed signals regarding the widening of Europe and the lack of widespread support for the deepening of the Union cast some uncertainty over the immediate future of Europe; but figuring out the mechanisms of EU politics and predicting their outcome was never an easy task. This is even more true of the current EU enlargement process, the EU's biggest enlargement ever in terms of scope, diversity and the number of issues involved. Therefore a book dealing with the Europeanization of the former communist countries who have joined (and, in particular, the reasons for the protracted accession process of Romania) could not be more timely.

Although Romania has tried in the last decade to adopt a market economy, from an economic point of view the results of this transition process have been disappointing, in sharp contrast with other Central and East European countries (CEECs). Why has Romania encountered so many difficulties in the accession process? What sets it apart from other CEECs?

The book offers rigorous answers to such and other complex questions regarding the CEECs using the latest theoretical developments of a long-standing intellectual tradition concerned with understanding the relationship of politics and economics. However, this book is not just about EU accession. It is about a lengthy and much more complex process that is going to take much longer: the Europeanization of CEECs. More precisely, the book tries to clarify the impact of Europeanization on the fundamental transformations that have taken place in CEECs at institutional and economic level. The central argument underlying the analysis carried out in this book is that in the context of the East-Central European transition, the choice of appropriate social, political and economic institutions is influenced by two determining factors: key domestic political actors and interest groups on the one hand, and external policy transfer processes, in particular Europeanization and globalization, on the other. The choice of institutions significantly influences the ability of a nation to engage in a sustained economic growth trajectory. In turn, both institutional and economic factors are major determinants of the enlargement process. Hence, in a period of dramatic societal transformation, such as the transition from communism to a market economy and a democratic society, it becomes crucially important to establish which institutions will ensure the efficient running of the new economic system.

The analysis undertaken in the book advances the idea that CEECs which are searching for their place in a new globalized and regionalized world are in the midst of radical structural and institutional change.

Furthermore, it is argued that the institutional choices involved in the transition towards capitalism will affect the economic performance of these countries for years to come. On the one hand, this process is influenced by the preferences of domestic actors that are involved in policy making. On the other, the emerging institutions are significantly affected by Europeanization forces which increase competition among different types of capitalist systems and the adaptation pressures on national varieties of capitalism as a result of globalization.

Recognizing the importance of these factors in explaining the differences in economic performance, the present book attempts to demonstrate that a capitalist system based on an inefficient mixture of disparate institutional arrangements largely explains why some CEECs have performed so poorly in economic terms. The book brings convincing evidence that in some CEECs, and in particular in Romania, the transition process was based on incomplete institutional frameworks borrowed from several existing models of capitalism, and that the emerging 'cocktail capitalism' did not prove to be efficient in promoting a robust, fast-growing market economy. The explanation for this inefficient combination lies in the frictions between institutional choices favoured by domestic forces and those advocated by external factors, such as the European Union and Bretton Woods institutions. The evidence provided in the book suggests that such an incongruent institutional choice has negatively affected the economic performance of CEECs in the last decade.

After developing a general quantitative analysis aimed at testing some propositions across different transition economies, the book focuses on a more in-depth analysis of the formation of new patterns of organization and governance in selected CEECs. Particular attention will be paid to Romania, in order to shed light on those factors that delayed the Europeanization of institutional and political transformation and hampered the economic process.

This hybrid methodological path using cross-country quantitative analyses and country-based cases studies will be followed in the rest of the book. As shown throughout this book, certain transition economies, and in particular Romania and Bulgaria, have not been able to overcome the inherent initial problems associated with such a systemic change, and their economic performance has so far been rather disappointing. In order to understand why some transition economies have been less successful than others, an appropriate research method is to engage in a detailed case study analysis. The use of case studies is an ideal method when in-depth investigation is needed (Feagin, Orum and Sjoberg

1991).[1] The choice of Romania as a case study was justified not necessarily by its uniqueness and by the research interest in the case itself, but also by the ability to generate new evidence and test existing theories that are applicable, to a greater or lesser extent, to most transition economies. A further rationale for choosing Romania, rather than other CEECs, is the relative knowledge gap concerning this acceding country compared to other CEECs such as Hungary, Poland or the Czech Republic. Using a case study approach enables the researcher to use multiple sources of evidence, such as surveys, interviews and a variety of primary and secondary documents. As in all research, consideration must be given to the validity and reliability of the conclusions drawn from the case study analysis. Using multiple sources of evidence is a good way to ensure construct validity, while external validity can be achieved by maintaining solid relationships between the case study evidence and the relevant theories.

As the evidence presented in the book shows, from an economic point of view the results of this transition process have been very uneven. Since 1989, CEECs have been engaged in a major systemic transformation, from communism towards market economies. After the demise of communism and the overthrow of brutal dictatorships, most analysts expected a rapid improvement in the economic and political situation in the region. While democracy has been established fairly rapidly, the economic evolution has been far below expectations. Empirically, the various experiences in Eastern Europe with the post-communist transition, both in terms of emerging types of capitalism and diverging economic performances, justify the research question of whether capitalist institutions (markets, hierarchies, networks, state and private actors) can be related to the evolution of economic outcomes. As economics itself finds it increasingly difficult to account for cross-national variations in economic performances, a more encompassing approach based on institutional political economy theories may hold the key to our understanding of post-communist transition in Eastern Europe.

The book reviews the different streams of literature that are directly relevant to the impact of institutions on economic performance. The nature of the research topic required a survey of several bodies of literature. A number of key concepts are found in the literature on *varieties of capitalism*. Another related approach with direct relevance to the literature on varieties of capitalism is the *interest-group intermediation approach*. Perhaps the most obvious motive for studying interest groups in their own right is that they are a conspicuous and important aspect of any political economy. Market economies differ markedly in terms of the role that interest groups, as actors, play during the policy-making or policy implementation process; therefore, identifying the types of interest-group intermediation at work in CEECs will be very useful for understanding the impact of institutions on their economic performance. All these insights will be used in conjunction with several important theories that explain the *impact of external factors* on domestic, institutional and political transformations: globalization, Europeanization and policy transfer.

A first stage in the empirical analysis was to investigate quantitatively how the different key characteristics of capitalism models influence economic performance across countries and time in Central and Eastern Europe. To complement this quantitative analysis, these empirical findings will be augmented by detailed, qualitative analyses of specific state, societal and institutional variables. These case studies will deal with the types of government–industry relations and the difficulties encountered in building a well-functioning, coherent model of capitalism. The main examples discussed are the mass privatization process (illustrating the failure of an incomplete Anglo-Saxon model), the problems associated with the Management–employee buy-out (MEBO) privatization that led to a distorted Continental capitalist model, the role of financial intermediaries, and the failure to pursue a developmental strategy through strategic privatization.

Using insights from the literature on varieties of capitalism, Chapter 3 will also look at the role played by other actors influencing government–industry interactions (powerful but clientelistic trade unions and the interaction between various elite groups) as an illustration of the negative effects of different interest-intermediation mechanisms.

In Chapters 4 and 5, attention will shift towards the impact that external factors have on the evolving nature of the capitalist institutions in CEECs. Chapter 4 builds a theoretical model reconceptualizing the influence of major external forces on the economic performance of transition economies, making a distinction between Europeanization (the role of the EU and the accession process) and 'institutionalized globalization' (the role of other inter-governmental organizations such as the International Monetary Fund (IMF) and World Bank, and the current international regimes). Based on these findings, the book clarifies the influence of the external factors on the emerging capitalist system in CEECs. In Chapter 5, various case studies illustrate the extent and direction of change, induced by IMF conditionality and policy advice, as well as World Bank and EU activities, on the institutional deficiencies identified in previous parts of the book.

Finally, one feature worth mentioning is the methodological diversity of the book. Each methodology uses specific sources of data and information. For the quantitative analysis, the necessary data came mainly from primary official documents and statistics. In the qualitative parts, the statistical information was supplemented with unstructured interviews conducted with former and current officials from various state institutions, employers' associations and trade union confederations, as well as business sector representatives. Several interviews proved a very useful source of information and they are cited explicitly in the text, while others have been primarily used to ensure the accuracy of information gathered from other sources. In addition to these sources of information, a significant amount of information was gathered from a systematic survey of independent newspapers. Finally, for the assessment of the various policy transfer mechanisms in Chapters 4 and 5, important sources of information were official EU documents. In particular, these documents were used for the construction of the Europeanization index, which involved reading more than 10,000 pages of such documents and reports.

1
Theoretical Considerations

In the years since the collapse of communism, issues of post-communist transformation have been the subject of intense scrutiny by a variety of scholars employing various approaches from political culture, 'transitology', nationalism and institutionalism to political economy, neoclassical economics and rational choice.[1] Given the complex reality of the radical transformation which the transition economies have undergone, this variety in approaches comes as little surprise. Despite their differences in methods and choice of perspectives, a large number of these studies assign an important role to institutions in the transition process. Institutionalists and political economists, in particular, are strong proponents of the idea that institutions matter (Williamson 1975; North 1990). Many political scientists and economists have argued that the patterns of state–societal interactions play a major role in explaining the differences in economic performance among nations (Olson 1982; Lange and Garret 1985; Hart 1992; Knack and Keefer 1995; Hicks and Kenworthy 1998).[2] Although other studies (Gray and Lowery 1988; Wallis and Oates 1988) revealed significant differences in growth performance without major changes in state–societal arrangements, the attempt to explain macroeconomic aggregates and economic growth through societal-independent variables remains a valid research pathway to the understanding of differences in economic performances among otherwise similar countries.

There have been numerous attempts to explain the variance in economic performance of CEECs during the last decade. Some theories emphasized the importance of macroeconomic policies implemented and the determination to speed up the necessary transformation of socialist economies into market economies (big-bang versus gradualism). Others have underlined more specifically the impact of openness and economic integration through trade and foreign direct investment (FDI) on growth (Cernat and Vranceanu 2001). Another significant body of comparative political economy literature has been concerned with the question of whether political and institutional factors have a determinant impact on economic growth. Particularly influential among descriptive growth studies was North (1990), who underlined the importance of institutional settings in creating an environment conducive to economic growth. Some studies looked at the importance of democracy, social capital and political rights, in particular in developing countries, on economic performance (Helliwell 1994, 1996). Others have tried to evaluate the role of bureaucratic efficiency and corruption (Mauro 1995) or the role of informal institutions such as interpersonal trust and civic norms (Knack and Keefer 1997).

Another factor that has been singled out by Poirot (1996) and Calvo and Coricelli (1992) is the institutional architecture governing the credit market. They consider that the financial and banking system is one of the key underdeveloped institutions in Eastern European economies. In their view, economic growth may be adversely affected by underdeveloped credit markets. This is clearly the case for CEECs and other transition economies.

Furthermore, several studies have established a direct link between output collapse after the implementation of the recent economic transformation programmes in East-Central Europe and the role played by the credit market (Calvo and Coricelli 1992; Poirot 1996). Other explanations for this output collapse, which was greater than expected, argued that a large proportion of the fall in gross domestic product (GDP) could be explained by trade shocks, lack of market institutions, and other distortions generally associated with such systemic transformations.

Essentially, all these analyses point to the fact that the types of state–societal relations in post-communist CEECs are major determinants of economic performance. Therefore, to understand the economic evolution of CEECs, one needs to examine the social, political and institutional underpinnings of transition. For that, it is necessary to review the existing theoretical variants with regard to the interaction between state and society in a political system and adapt these theoretical constructs (which were originally designed for Western economic systems) to the case of Eastern Europe.

The remainder of this chapter will review each of these major literature topics, starting with a brief discussion of interest groups intermediation, followed by a description of the literature on varieties of capitalism. Lastly, to understand the impact of various external factors on post-communist transition, a number of theories from international political economy (globalization, Europeanization, and policy transfer) will be cross-fertilized to create the necessary conceptual tools for the understanding of state–societal transformations and economic performance in CEECs. As will be seen, the various state–society theories, varieties of capitalism and international political economy concepts are closely connected.

State–society interaction and interest group intermediation

The first attempt to describe at theoretical level how state and society interact during the policy-making process was formulated by the *pluralist view*. Pluralist theories, dominant in the 1950s and 1960s, originated from pre-war discourses developed in the USA.[3] These theories see the state as the decision-making mechanism that pursues the national interest (Laumann and Knocke 1987). Pluralist theories are based on the assumption that all relevant social interests have organizational capabilities and thus are able to compete for political influence during the policy-making process (Dahl 1956). The concerns of various interest groups are taken over by the political parties and introduced in the political interactions affecting the rules governing the economy. In addition, the interest groups have the possibility of lobbying both parliamentarians and state officials to give them clear inputs on specific economic issues.[4]

The pluralist theories have been criticized for placing too much focus on the ability of politics (understood as the process of settling conflicting societal interests and consensus building) to allocate resources according to the preferences of all atomized interest groups. The plurarist theories also paid less attention to the institutional framework and the policy aspects of the political system, which are considered by pluralists to be determined by various interest groups and their political parties (Steinmo 1989, pp. 500–4). Another important assumption of many pluralists' theories is that corporations with different economic interests and market orientations are incapable of collective political strategy and actions, while class theorists argue that corporations have sufficient class interests to evolve a collective political class strategy.[5]

During the 1970s, the pluralist view on policy making was challenged by the emerging literature on *(neo)corporatism*. At a conceptual level, corporatism has been defined in several ways.[6] The debate was initially shaped by Schmitter (1974, 1981), Streeck and Schmitter (1985) and Lehmbruch (1977, 1979), among others, who argued that countries in which leading labour unions and business associations were deeply involved in the formulation and implementation of economic policies had better prospects for economic and political stability and even for sustained economic growth (Streeck 1992; Henley and Tsakalotos 1993; Lange and Garrett 1985). In contrast, pluralist countries where business and labour organizations were only able to articulate their own narrow interests and exert pressure on the political system ranked lower in terms of the above-mentioned criteria. Various terms – societal corporatism (Schmitter), liberal corporatism (Lehmbruch), democratic corporatism (Katzenstein) and neocorporatism – were employed to convey the conceptual distinction from earlier, authoritarian manifestations of corporatism, identified by Schmitter as state corporatism.[7]

Schmitter defines corporatism as:

> a system of interest representation in which the constituent units are organised into a limited number of singular, compulsory, non-competitive, hierarchically ordered and functionally differentiated categories, recognised or licensed (if not created) by the state and granted a deliberate representational monopoly within their respective categories in exchange for observing certain controls on their selection of leaders and articulation of demands and supports. (Schmitter 1974, pp. 85–131)

This is more or less the opposite of his definition of pluralism, which is:

> [a] system of interest representation in which the constituent units are organised into an unspecified number of multiple, voluntary, competitive, nonhierarchically ordered and self-determined (as to type or scope of interest) categories which are not specifically licensed, recognised, subsidised, created or otherwise controlled in leadership selection or interest articulation by the state and which do not exercise a monopoly of representational activity whithin their respective categories. (Schmitter 1979, p. 15)

Schmitter's definition of corporatism provides an ideal type of institutional arrangement which could in reality manifest itself in many forms, not least (as mentioned) authoritarian and democratic variants. Schmitter's distinction between state and societal corporatism is an important one and will be seen to have particular relevance for this book, as the empirical evidence will show. Essentially state and societal corporatism are 'the products of very different political, social and economic processes, as the vehicles for different power and influence relations' (Schmitter 1979, p. 22). State corporatism is imposed 'from above' by the state, whereas societal corporatism emerges voluntarily 'from below' (Williamson 1989, p. 11). As will be seen, East European style corporatism usually lacks the elements of voluntary cooperation and has more similarities with the state-orchestrated variant of corporatism.

Most theorists of corporatism stress the elements of 'social partnership' (cooperation) and the 'incorporation' of the social partners in the processes of both policy formulation and implementation. Most accounts focus on the tripartite relation between state, capital and labour (though other bilateral combinations of interests are also possible). Most authors would agree that corporatism involves the two key elements of interest intermediation and policy concertation. A number of studies make the useful distinction between macro-, mezzo-, and micro-corporatism, respectively at the level of the economy, sector or firm. Mezzo- and micro-corporatist arrangements may be part of a broader corporatist structure at the macro-level or, alternatively, they may feature as corporatist enclaves in a larger pluralist interest intermediation structure.[8]

For the neocorporatist advocates, this form of interest intermediation and policy making makes good sense, particularly for coordinating economic policies and pursuing a developmental objective commonly perceived to be in the national interest. The strength of the neocorporatist argument has been enhanced by the Keynesian economic policies pursued throughout Western Europe in an effort to restore the economic prosperity affected by the Second World War.[9] As mentioned, most empirical neocorporatist studies centred on the tripartite patterns of bargaining between organized labour, business associations and the state in setting the main national macroeconomic objectives (Schmitter 1977, 1981; Streeck 1992). The main advantage of neocorporatist arrangements was that they represented a very good implementation mechanism, involving the key interested actors in both policy formulation and policy implementation (Offe 1993). In return for a voice in policy formulation, societal actors were made responsible for delivering the policies agreed. The neocorporatist policy mechanism, by its very nature, also managed to minimize the classical principal-agent problems arising between regulators and the regulated. In this way, the regulatory capacity of the state was extended in those areas where direct state activities were unacceptable in market economies (savings and consumption incentives) or very costly to implement independently (industrial safety, environmental standards, etc.). Moreover, corporatism was a good way to deal with the increased complexity of managing the economy.

In many analyses, both theoretical and empirical, concerning the relationship between corporatism and economic performance, the role of government itself is kept rather implicit.[10] Nonetheless, governments' ability to deliver the 'social wage' in return for wage restraint arising from a corporatist 'deal' is one important feature for the functioning of the neocorporatist mechanism. A number of studies have revealed that corporatist countries are not only characterized by a centralized coordination of wage bargaining but also by relatively high government expenditure, a higher ratio of active to passive labour market policies and higher average unemployment benefits (Corvers and van Veen 1995). Moreover, the state has a role in facilitating the bargaining process between social partners. Thus, some authors have argued that the success of neocorporatist arrangements depends on the centralization capacity of the state (Katzenstein 1978, p. 134; Atkinson and Coleman 1985). This echoes Schmitter's definition, which suggests that the key interest groups are 'expressly granted monopoly over representation in the sectors for which they are responsible' (Schmitter 1974, pp. 94–5).

In recent years, however, the literature on state–society interactions has moved beyond corporatism versus pluralism. The term 'network' seems to have become 'the new paradigm for the architecture of complexity' (Kenis and Schneider 1991, p. 25). Although the literature on policy networks has produced a range of usages of the term – e.g. 'issue-networks' (Heclo 1978) and 'policy communitites' (Heclo and Wildavsky 1981) – there is a common denominator.[11] The policy networks literature distances itself from both pluralist and neocorporatist theories by arguing that state–society relations are best described as non-hierarchical and based on interdependent links (resource dependencies) between a variety of actors that are brought together in cooperative behaviour by their common interest to maximize a policy outcome in a certain sector (Börzel 1998, p. 254).[12]

The network theory addresses some perceived weaknesses of neocorporatist theories. Thus Heclo (1978) criticizes the neocorporatist literature for narrowing down the debate to the level of 'iron triangles' (state, business and organized labour). As opposed to closed 'iron triangles' based on formalized relationships, Heclo argues that in a variety of policy fields, there are a large number of actors (scientists, citizen initiative groups, journalists) that have a shaping influence, albeit in an indirect manner, on the final policy outcome. These 'issue networks' are characterized by informal, open, unstable webs of relationships between a large number of actors who are 'stakeholders' in that particular policy field. Laumann and Knocke (1987) also point to the growing number of actors involved in the state–society interactions referred to by Heclo. They further argue that this overcrowded policy space tends to blur the distinction between the state (as an autonomous governing actor) and society.[13]

Varieties of capitalism

After the collapse of socialism in Eastern Europe, the debate about different types of capitalism has been extended to cover the emerging capitalist systems in Eastern Europe. Several models of capitalism have been considered as important points of reference in history since the end of the Second World War. Among the varieties of capitalism, Michel Albert's typology captured attention for many years during the debate about types of capitalism (Albert 1993). However, one important argument against his 'Anglo-Saxon', 'Rhineland' and 'étatist' models was that the functioning of the economy became increasingly globalized and many authors argued that globalization would only spare the species most suited to capitalism, both in terms of business–state relations and corporate governance (Cerny 1997). Corporate governance represents not only a crucial difference between varieties of capitalism, but is also a major factor in determining their economic performance.

Rhodes and van Apeldoorn (1997) offer one of the best descriptions of various forms of Western capitalism. Starting from Albert's distinction between Atlantic and Rhenish capitalism, Rhodes and van Apeldoorn (1997) took further steps towards the operationalization of these concepts. They produced a three-fold classification of market-oriented Anglo-Saxon and network-oriented Germanic (i.e., Rhineland) and Latin types of capitalism. The two main dimensions along which various national capitalist systems are placed are those of corporate governance and macroeconomic institutional environment (see Table 1.1). For the purposes of this book the two network-oriented forms of West European capitalism – Germanic and Latin – are handled together under the heading of 'Continental' (European) capitalism. As Rhodes and Apeldoorn explain, there are some important distinctions between Germanic and Latin capitalism (e.g., the regulatory state and strong centralized unions in Germanic capitalism *vis-à-vis* an interventionist state and weak unions in Latin capitalism). However, it is argued here that the similarities, particularly relating to the role of networks, are strong enough to subsume the variety of West European capitalist models in a continental type, as distinct from the Anglo-Saxon type.[14] De Jong (1995) and Moerland (1995) also prefer to refer to an all-inclusive, network-oriented

Table 1.1 Varieties of capitalism: the main characteristics

	Anglo-Saxon	Continental	Developmental
Macroeconomic factors			
Role of the state	Minimal state	Regulatory state	Embedded autonomy; pro-developmental interventionism
Cooperation between social partners	Conflictual or minimal contact	Extensive at national level	Formal and informal state–business networks
Labour organizations	Fragmented and weak	Strong, centralized unions	Fragmented
Labour market flexibility	Poor internal flexibility; high external flexibility	High internal flexibility; lower external flexibility	Internal flexibility; lower external flexibility
Microeconomic factors			
Shareholder sovereignty	Widely dispersed ownership; dividends prioritized	Banks and other corporations are major shareholders; dividends less prioritized	The role of individuals, banks and inter-corporate shareholders are somewhere in between
Employee influence	Limited	Extensive through works councils and co-determination	Strong shop-floor participation
Market for corporate control	Hostile takeovers are the 'correction mechanism' for management failure	Takeovers restricted	Takeovers permitted but limited by the extensive system of corporate cross-ownership
Role of stock exchange	Strong role in corporate finance	Reduced	Intermediate
Role of banks	Banks play a minimal role in corporate ownership	Important both in corporate finance and control	Intermediate

Source: Adapted from Rhodes and van Apeldoorn (1997, pp. 174–5). In addition to the factors mentioned above, their original analysis addressed the role of education and training and the national innovation system.

continental capitalism, while acknowledging Germanic and Latin variants of it. Moreover, as the detailed discussion that follows shows, the Latin type shares some features with the third type employed herein, namely the developmental state type (e.g., state interventionism). The macroeconomic factors along which national capitalisms differ relate to the main state–societal interactions. First, there is the role played by the state in shaping the economic environment and its interaction with societal actors. Next, the organizational features of the main social partners, business and labour, as well as the nature of the interaction between them, must be addressed. The main microeconomic factors (corporate governance in Rhodes and van Apeldoorn's analysis) refer to various aspects of corporate control, management and financing.

In the following sections, each model of capitalism is described at length, with an emphasis on the key institutional interactions between state and societal actors, as well as the major consequences that these institutional settings have for the functioning of each capitalist system.

Anglo-Saxon capitalism

It is apparent that capitalism is not a homogeneous social and economic entity; rather, it exists in a variety of forms. One of these variants of capitalism is what Albert (1993) has called 'Atlantic' capitalism, referred to as the 'Anglo-Saxon' model of capitalism by other authors. Generically, this model is based on several fundamental institutional characteristics. The main characteristics relate to the three main actors involved in the state–societal interactions at the core of a capitalist system: the state, capital and labour. Several dimensions are important in characterizing the role of the state: the policy objectives of the state, the policy instruments, and the features of state bureaucracy.[15] Domestically, in the Anglo-Saxon model, states confine themselves to a minimalist economic role (with several exceptions during certain short historical periods). As a general rule, the main role of the state was to maintain a stable environment where markets could operate free from any political or social interference. The main policy instruments are in accordance with neoclassical economics and political liberalism. Therefore, in the Anglo-Saxon model the main actions that the state is willing to take are those enforcing the rule of law and macroeconomic stabilization policies with regard to inflation, unemployment, exchange rates and public deficits (Albert 1993).

With regard to the role played by labour in shaping policy making in the Anglo-Saxon system, most authors agree that the influence of trade unions is much smaller than in the Continental model.[16] Organized labour in the USA, for instance, is characterized by a relatively high level of heterogeneity and fragmentation at a national level. The Anglo-Saxon system also has a low and declining rate of unionization (Pryor 1996). In contrast to Continental and developmental capitalism, the labour market within Anglo-Saxon capitalism has poor internal flexibility due to a fragmented training system and poor skills (Rhodes and van Apeldoorn 1997, p. 174). These negative features are partially balanced by a higher mobility (both across professional groups and geographically) and by more flexible wages than those characterizing the Continental model.

The most prominent actor in Anglo-Saxon capitalism is business. Based on the concept of market capitalism, the Anglo-Saxon system is founded on the belief that self-interest and decentralized markets can function in a self-regulating, equilibrated manner. It comes as little surprise that these institutional settings are based upon, and reinforce, profit-oriented behaviour and a struggle for material success by individual entrepreneurs and managers. This short-term profit-oriented behaviour and individualism are coupled with a set of appropriate institutions to enhance their effectiveness in the Anglo-Saxon model. The structure of corporate ownership is probably the most distinguishing feature. In the USA, the principal exponent of the Anglo-Saxon capitalist model, individual shareholders account for a majority of total outstanding shares. This differs markedly from the other two exponents of Continental and developmental capitalism, Germany and Japan, where individual shareholders own a small fraction of the existing shares traded on stock markets. The same sharp differences in ownership structure are present with respect to the other two major non-financial shareholders: banks and enterprises. In the USA, banks have historically played a negligible role in the ownership structure of their clients. This principle has received legal clout in the Glass–Steagall Act of 1933. Consequently, because of this ownership structure, the Anglo-Saxon corporate governance system is one where share ownership is more widely dispersed and shareholder influence on management is weaker than in Continental or developmental capitalism. In this system, a well-functioning stock market is vital so that unsatisfied shareholders can sell their shares. In addition, the individual shareholder is protected by strict regulations on information disclosure, and against insider trading.

The Continental model of capitalism

In sharp contrast to the Anglo-Saxon capitalist system, which is based on a minimalist state, weak labour and a short-term profit-oriented business approach, the Continental model is characterized by close coordination between the state, trade unions and industry associations. While the role of the state varies from more *dirigiste*, centralized states (in the case of France) to non-*dirigiste* regulatory states, such as Germany, it is certainly the case that West European states have played a more proactive role in governing the economy than their Anglo-Saxon counterparts, both in terms of policy objectives and instruments.

Continental capitalism is generally associated with a neocorporatist pattern of interest intermediation, featuring a strong voice for organized labour in policy making (see Table 1.1). This is more clearly associated with strongly unionized 'Germanic', northern Europe than weakly unionized 'Latin' southern Europe. None the less, since the 1980s, Italy, Spain and Portugal have seen social pacts. In Lane and Ersson's view, 'corporatist patterns of policy-making loom large in the Italian political system' (Lane and Ersson 1991, p. 264). France, on the other hand, has been a rather 'awkward customer' for the corporatist literature.[17] A French version of the notion of corporatism has been applied by Jobert and Muller (1987) and Mény (1989), who have pointed to the existence of the tripartite system, particularly with regard to the public sector (Cole 1998, p. 203).[18]

In the Continental model it is generally the case that collective bargaining determines wages at the sectoral level and a minimum national wage level, thanks to high trade union membership rates (with the exception of France and Italy) and strong peak organizations. The role of labour is important not only at the macro-level but also at firm level through works councils and the principle of co-determination, although the latter is not found throughout Europe as a whole. There are well established and institutionalized business–labour forms of cooperation and information exchange, whether in supervisory boards or at a more decentralized level in works councils.

The same logic of interest intermediation also applies to business interest groups. Peak business associations in Germany have close working relationships with both land and federal governments. These leading associations are key players in public policy formulation, and are sometimes even spelled out, as in the German Constitution.[19] Other important, distinctive features of the Continental model of capitalism are to be found in its corporate governance structures. Unlike the Anglo-Saxon system, and resembling the developmental capitalist model, Continental capitalism is based on the prominent role of banks in corporate finance and control (see Table 1.1). It is quite common for banks in this model to own significant proportions of shares in their portfolios as a means of controlling the economic activities of their major clients (Dittus and Prowse 1996, p. 24). Bank representatives are also often found on the boards of directors of the companies to whom they offered large loans. These organizational features, and the close interaction between banking and enterprise, create a more secure economic environment that allows firms to seek higher profits in the long run, as opposed to the short-term view imposed on Anglo-Saxon companies by stock markets (Smyser 1992; Albert 1993). Furthermore, German banks are allowed to conduct business in all branches of banking (universal banking), while Anglo-Saxon countries strictly separate certain banking activities (Albert 1993).[20] Both features make European banks more attractive than stock markets for companies wishing to raise capital for new investment (Davidson 1998).

In addition to the banks, other shareholders and interested parties have a direct or indirect influence on corporate management. This feature is best described by the label *stakeholder capitalism*, which is often associated with the Continental model of capitalism.[21] Since the number of freely traded shares is limited and dividends are less prioritized than in the Anglo-Saxon system, shareholders do not face the classical Hirschmanian choice of 'voice or exit' (Hirschman 1970). Less fluid stock markets in Continental Europe make exit more costly, and therefore shareholders have a strong incentive to gain a powerful 'voice' in the management of the firm by acquiring a sufficiently large amount of stock to enable them to monitor the managers and reduce the relative costs of this operation.[22] The same resistance towards stock markets makes takeovers (especially hostile takeovers) highly unlikely within Continental capitalism.

Developmental capitalism

Another perspective from which the role of political institutions in economic performance has been analysed focuses on the role of the state in promoting national economic development and industrialization, in particular (Weiss 1998). After the collapse of the communist regimes, and the lessons derived from the miraculous economic success of the neomercantilist states of East Asia in the last decades, it seems appropriate to re-examine the theory of the 'developmental state' as an institutional alternative for CEECs.

At the core of this body of literature lies an attempt to characterize different types of states according to their 'strength'. The main argument advanced by this stream of research is that 'strong' states represent a crucial element of any developmental success story (Weiss 1998, pp. 5–7). Relying on the state – the major political institution – as the explanatory variable, many studies written from this perspective have sought to explain patterns of national economic development. Such studies have explained, for instance, the emergence of various Western European countries as economic powers in past centuries (e.g., Germany in the nineteenth century or France in the twentieth century) and the developmental experiences of Latin American or East Asian countries in the post-war period.[23] The developmental state perspective centres on the key role played by the state in the process of national development. Early institutionalist accounts have explained how states can provide a suitable environment for capital accumulation (Gerschenkron 1962) and have analysed the states' capabilities to organize financial markets (Hirschman 1958).

In general, interactions between state and society can be said to range from autonomy to embeddedness. At one extreme, an autonomous state comes close to an authoritarian strong state in that it largely ignores any societal input in policy making and therefore falls short on the implementation of any developmental blueprint. At the other extreme, an embedded state is a weak state 'captured' by a handful of private interests and prone to corruption, again with a detrimental impact on national economic development.[24] In constrast, developmental states can be characterized as cases of *embedded autonomy*,[25] whereby state and business collaborate positively to fulfil a common vision of economic transformation (Evans 1997).

The capacity of various states to become developmental states depends upon two main factors: the quality of the state bureaucracy and the type of state–society interactions in place (Evans 1995, p. 50). Evans (1992, 1995) argues that the replacement of a patronage system for state officials by a professional state bureaucracy is a necessary (though not a sufficient) condition for a state to be 'developmental'. The key institutional characteristics of what he calls 'Weberian' bureaucracy include meritocratic recruitment and the promotion of competent bureaucrats at higher levels of bureaucracy, instead of political or clientelist appointments. The recipe for a successful developmental state thus requires a well-trained bureaucracy, a good flow of information between state and business, and a set of economic policies (fiscal, trade, monetary and industrial) that guides entrepreneurial activities towards the most strategic industrial sectors. Numerous empirical studies have confirmed the crucial role played by capable bureaucracies and strong business associations. They show that it is not markets or states *per se* that best explain economic performance, but rather the character of relations between business and government. Economic development depends on the positive quality of, and constructive relations between, bureaucrats and capitalists. In developmental states a very close relationship links state and markets producing strong economic performance, in defiance of neoclassical expectations that such close relations lead ineluctably to rent-seeking, corruption and collusion.[26]

Several detailed cross-sectoral or cross-national studies have shown how targeted developmental state actions, in particular in East Asia, have led to the creation of new productive capacities in technologically complex sectors that eventually become or remain competitive in a global economy.[27] Japanese business, for instance, has taken on the task of national development and has formed industrial hierarchical networks (*keiretsu*: see Johnson 1982, 1995). *Keiretsu* companies are inter-firm forms of affiliation based on minority cross-ownership. These industrial conglomerates thus become directly interested in their mutual development.[28] This extensive system of corporate cross-ownership would not be possible in the Anglo-Saxon system, where such practices would be perceived as a clear infringement of the market mechanisms. None the less, this type of 'organized capitalism' has proved over time to be highly effective in promoting the economic prosperity and international competitiveness of Japan and Korea, the two countries that have made extensive use of it.[29]

While pluralist theories offer the foundation for the Anglo-Saxon model of capitalism and neocorporatism is seen as a major ingredient of Continental capitalism, network theories bring the debate closer to that on the developmental state. As theories of competitiveness at both national and company level have argued, the diffusion of information and knowledge (chief ingredients of economic, technical and societal development) is heavily dependent upon the types of societal arrangements promoting or inhibiting this process (Hart 1992; Arrow 1994). Although they put a different emphasis on this point, both developmental and network policy theorists acknowledge the importance of state–societal networks in passing on various pieces of crucial information for the subsequent functioning of the economy. As Kenis and Schneider put it:

> policy networks are the mechanisms of political resource mobilisation in situations where the capacity for decision-making, program formulation and implementation is widely distributed or dispersed among private and public actors … In situations where policy resources are dispersed and context dependent, a network is the only mechanism to mobilise and pool resources [i.e., information].
>
> (Kenis and Schneider 1991, p. 41)

Consequently, the success of network-based capitalist systems is based on the potential to produce better policy outcomes that promote national economic development (the key focus of developmental theorists). Based on their above-mentioned features, networks offer clear possibilities for better economic governance.

During the past five years, there have been a few other attempts to apply the insights from this literature to the different styles of market reforms implemented in the formerly planned economies in Eastern Europe and the former Soviet Union. However, so far the literature is quite limited in scope. Sachs (1996), for instance, analyses the applicability of the developmental state in Eastern Europe and the former Soviet Union, putting forward three related propositions. Sachs argues that the rapid growth of East Asia, compared with economic contraction in former socialist countries, reflects differences in the economic structure and initial conditions, rather than differences in economic policy making. Second, he argues that the East Asian gradualism involved in the developmental state project could not, and did not, work in Eastern Europe because Eastern Europe has chosen democratization before marketization. Third, Eastern European countries continue to face serious problems due to an overextended welfare state inherited from the socialist period. Based on these remarks, he concludes that, unlike the case of East Asia, developmental policies in Eastern Europe are doomed to fail (Sachs 1996, pp. 32–54).

While Sachs may be right in all three respects, this nevertheless does not constitute a sufficiently persuasive argument against the idea of an Eastern European developmental state. In the following chapters, it will be argued (and several examples will be given) that developmental policies should not be ruled out a priori as inapplicable.[30] It will also be shown that in the case of CEECs, the success or failure of various developmental policies depends rather on the fulfilment of several pre-conditions, as described by the authors of the developmental state model: a strong state, embedded autonomy, competent bureaucracy and strategic policy making.

Another interesting attempt to compare the divergent transformative strategies adopted in Eastern Europe, using a network perspective, was made by Stark and Bruszt (1998). Their analysis traces the differences in political and economic conditions at the beginning of the transition across East-Central Europe as a framework for understanding subsequent political and economic developments. After describing the different policy choices adopted in Hungary, the Czech Republic and East Germany with regard to privatization and economic restructuring in general, their main argument is that a transformation strategy that builds on existing networks is better suited than a free-market oriented or statist approach. This approach, according to Stark and Bruszt (1998), is followed more coherently in the

Czech Republic than in Hungary, and even more so when compared to East Germany. The cross-ownership of various enterprises and banks or other investment companies found in the Czech Republic resembles the Japanese *keiretsu* or the Korean *chaebol* (Stark and Bruszt 1998, p. 163).

The authors' main argument is that an emerging institutional framework that builds on the pre-1989 networks may prove better suited to advancing the economic reforms efficiently than a market-based strategy. Specifically, Stark and Bruszt try to demonstrate that, unlike the common view of the predatory character found in many instances, post-socialist networks may have a developmental character, such as those found in Asia, where businesses 'recombine' their assets and form efficient *keiretsu* companies ready to face global competition.[31] While this may be the case in certain countries (such as the Czech Republic in Stark and Bruszt's analysis), the remainder of this analysis will show that in the case of other CEECs, with few notable exceptions, most networks inherited from the past or introduced during the last decade are just mechanisms for rent-seeking, asset-stripping, looting, and reallocation of state resources to 'connected' individuals.[32]

Others, such as Lane (2000), have tried more explicitly to apply the literature on models of capitalism to the transition process taking place in East-Central Europe. Taking the case of Russia, Lane argues that due to the lack of consensus among ruling elites and between domestic and external factors about the blueprint of the emerging type of society, the Russian economy resembles a perverse and chaotic type of capitalism.[33] As will be argued in greater detail in the other chapters, external factors exert a crucial influence on the institutional and economic transition to capitalism in CEECs.

Despite certain methodological difficulties, the question of growth prospects in transition economies (and the factors affecting it) remains crucial. Given the complexity of the matter, the usefulness of a single theoretical approach proves limited in this endeavour. A necessary preliminary task is therefore to construct a coherent research framework from a variety of existing sources in the literature. The next section reviews the existing evidence with regard to the impact of globalization on capitalist diversity. In a similar vein, subsequent sections will investigate the effect of Europeanization, and will reconceptualize the process of enlargement as a case of policy transfer.

Theoretical cross-fertilization: globalization, Europeanization and policy transfer

Post-socialist transition to market-oriented economies in CEECs is taking place at a time of fast-growing globalization and increased integration at international level between national economies. Hence the opening and integration of CEECs with the world economy was an indispensable part of the whole endeavour. At the same time, transition economies are engaged in an encompassing process of European integration. The extent of domestic transformation, combined with economic integration at both global and regional level, requires adequate theoretical tools. Therefore, to tackle this complexity, a certain amount of theory-building through cross-fertilization between theories on state–societal interactions and theories that deal with globalization and European integration is necessary.[34] The primary objective of this section is to bring together the most relevant theories and cross-fertilize their conceptual frameworks. Thus the methodological approach used in the book will be centred around three main concepts that try to explain the impact of external factors on domestic institutional and political transformations: globalization, Europeanization and policy transfer. Both globalization and Europeanization are used as independent variables to explain various other processes at the domestic level. Policy transfer is a concept that refers to several processes and as such can serve two purposes. First, due to the complexity and multidimensionality of both the globalization and Europeanization literatures, insights from the policy transfer approach help to narrow the scope of the analysis to a manageable level. Second, referring to a process common to both globalization and Europeanization, policy transfer acts as a bridge between these two strands of literature and offers an encompassing research framework.

Before turning to the main theoretical assertions found in the various bodies of literature surveyed, it is useful to start the analysis with a few conceptual clarifications. First, perhaps due to its innate multidisciplinary nature, the literature on globalization, Europeanization and policy transfer is fraught with a certain degree of conceptual and definitional imprecision.[35] The most commonly agreed definition of globalization refers to the growth, or more precisely the accelerated growth, of economic activity across national and regional political boundaries. It finds expression in the increased movement of tangible and intangible goods and services, including ownership rights, via trade and investment, and often of people, via migration. It can be (and often is) facilitated by a lowering of government impediments to that movement, and by technological progress, notably in transportation and communications. The actions of individual economic actors, firms, banks and people drive it, usually in the pursuit of profit, often spurred by the pressures of competition.

Apart from the widely agreed conclusion that globalization has brought increased trade and capital flows, along with a convergence of ideas, the impact of globalization on national institutions and policies is still subject to debate. At least three ideal types of reaction can be identified in the literature with regard to the impact of globalization on the national diversity of capitalism. The first is the 'strong thesis' of globalization which holds that nation-states are currently undergoing a period of convergence towards a neoliberal globalization, in which both the scope for state intervention in the economy and for national networks of social interaction to shape economic policies are severely undermined (Strange 1996; Friedman 1999). Given such constraints, nation-states can only adapt to the new neoliberal agenda and try to become competition states (Cerny 1997). This view is divided between those who welcome such departure from 'embedded liberalism' and those who lament such change. The second position is an outright rejection of the convergence hypothesis, based primarily on historical empirical analyses of similar globalization tendencies at work during the 50 years prior to the First World War (Hirst and Thompson 1996; Weiss 1998). A more nuanced view acknowledges that globalization poses serious adaptational challenges to national political economies, but argues that national varieties of capitalism need not converge towards an Anglo-Saxon model (Hall and Soskice 2001; Schmidt 2002).

'Europeanization' refers to the impact of the EU integration process and EU institutions on national politics and policy making.[36] This process is viewed as a one-way influence from the supranational to the national level (Ladrech 1994), or as a two-way interaction between the two levels in which member states assimilate the influence of the EU and in turn 'project' their interests at the EU level (Bulmer and Burch 2000, pp. 2–3). The literature on Europeanization is not unanimous on the extent to which there is convergence towards a common European institutional model.[37]

Others have offered a more open definition of Europeanization based on the deregulation–regulation, or re-regulation, dimension, as Majone (1990) puts it. This conceptualization praises Europeanization for bringing depoliticization, removal of planning and public ownership, together with regulatory powers entrusted to experts, commissions and independent agencies. In the same vein, although critical, Scharpf (1996) refers to the influence of the EU as negative integration, arguing that the EU institutions have largely promoted a neoliberal form of economic integration, with few matching efforts in building a system of interest representation at the supranational level. These features fuel the claims that Europeanization is 'globalization by another name' or 'globalization with a human face'.

Concerns as to the relationship between globalization, Europeanization and European integration on the one hand, and the impact of such processes upon models of capitalism, currently animate both academic and practitioner debates across Europe.[38] Globalization is a hotly contested concept within academic circles and broader policy communities. While there is general agreement that globalization will be crucial in shaping the European political economy in the twenty-first century, a wide range of views exists about what globalization is and what its implications are. Although several angles are used in disentangling these relationships, based on various dependent variables, perhaps the main debate revolves around the extent to which globalization is leading to policy convergence and institutional isomorphism (Radaelli 2000). Other, more focused directions of research investigate the extent to which globalization and Europeanization have led to a rapid transition from the era of welfare states to that of the 'competition state' (Cerny 1997). In this context, it is often suggested that either the political economy of globalization or the political economy of European integration, *or* both, have served to undermine the distinctive Continental model of capitalism in favour of an Anglo-Saxon type of deregulated capitalism, characterized by labour market flexibility and low taxation, a process lubricated by escalating financial flows. Others have argued that, contrary to this belief, differences across national models of capitalism persist, despite high levels of exposure to both globalizing economic forces and the processes of European economic and political integration.[39]

Policy transfer is a concept that is stimulating growing interest from a variety of disciplines. While different sub-types of policy transfer have been identified and separately defined, policy transfer more generally refers to 'a process in which knowledge about policies, administrative arrangements, institutions ... in one time and or place is used in the development of policies, administrative arrangements and institutions in another time and or place' (Dolowitz and Marsh 1996, p. 344). Thus defined, policy transfer can occur through either or both Europeanization and globalization. As Dolowitz and Marsh (1996, 2000) argue, policy transfer can be situated on a continuum, from 'voluntary' *lesson drawing* to 'obligated' *policy transfer*. In voluntary lesson-drawing only the recipient country plays an active role (Rose 1991, 1993). Accordingly, this book examines in Chapter 4 the extent to which the front-runner CEECs in the EU accession process (Hungary, the Czech Republic, Poland, Slovenia) have served as models for those CEECs, such as Romania and Bulgaria, that are in the second wave of enlargement. Policy transfer involving a degree or kind of coercion clearly implies external agency. In this connection, Chapter 4 examines the effects of the conditionality attached to programmes of global or European international organizations. In particular it explores the hypothesis that the higher the degree of 'obligation' (conditionality), the greater the positive impact on performance of transition economies.[40]

Despite the innovative approach of the policy transfer literature, aimed at incorporating a vast domain of policy-making activities by classifying all types of policy transfer (voluntary, coercive, temporal, spatial, etc.), as Evans and Davies (1999) have rightly argued, policy transfer literature is at best a heuristic model without full theory status and explanatory power. By applying the policy transfer research framework to the case of CEECs in transition to capitalism, Chapter 4 seeks to fill this gap by developing an analytical model, based upon a series of hypotheses about the relationship between policy transfer and economic performance. These hypotheses are tested against empirical evidence. The quantitative findings suggest that certain features of policy transfer mechanisms are more growth-conducive than others. As in this chapter, these findings are supported and further elucidated through qualitative analysis.

The following sections discuss the impact of globalization and Europeanization on domestic institutions in general. Then the discussion moves on to the particular case of CEECs. Following this, the enlargement process is redefined in this wider conceptual framework of policy transfer. Based on these definitions, Chapter 4 will examine the relative impact of globalization and Europeanization on the institutional transformation in CEECs.

The impact of globalization on models of capitalism

Given the pressures from globalization towards a model of deregulated neoliberal capitalism, starting in the early 1990s, a large number of studies have argued that globalization of markets is forcing corporatist arrangements and developmental states to adapt and change towards a more Anglo-Saxon, deregulated type of capitalism. The internationalization of capital is reducing the ability of governments and national labour confederations to engage in effective coordination, since any constraint on the now footloose capital may cause capital flights.

In contemporary debates, the models of capitalism debate has tended to be associated with two rather different, although interrelated, claims about the impact of globalization. The first claim is that, in an era of intensified foreign direct investment, high-level taxation regimes can precipitate capital flight (Scharpf 1991a). The second claim is that financial deregulation, coupled with high levels of short-term capital transfers, as well as the threat of speculative flows of capital with disastrous effects on exchange rates and macroeconomic stability, severely reduce the policy space for national economic policies (Cerny 1993).

More generally, it is argued that globalization brings about a 'hollowing out' of the national state apparatus, with old and new state capacities being reorganized territorially and functionally on sub-national, national, supranational and translocal levels. There is a continuing movement of state power upwards, downwards and sideways as attempts are made by state managers on different territorial scales to enhance their respective operational autonomies and strategic capacities.[41]

Another general assertion regarding the influence of globalization on the state is captured by the structural dependency thesis, whereby governments faced with high capital mobility engage in a 'race to the bottom' in reducing rates of corporate taxation (Scharpf 1991a; Marquand 1994).[42] The emerging complexity of the global political economy creates great uncertainty in the global economy, which in turn limits the capacity of the state to coordinate political bargaining, and to compensate interest groups. In short, while domestic stability remains a major imperative of the state, it is now achieved through a 'competition state' (Cerny 1997) able to offer credible commitment to, or compliance with, policies directed towards ensuring the confidence of international markets.

These features stand in sharp contrast to the coordination of economic management through political bargaining, the distinctive trait of economic governance in corporatist and developmental states in Western Europe and East Asia. Accordingly, it is argued that both corporatist and developmental state structures are unsustainable in an era where capital controls have been significantly dismantled (Jayasuriya 2001). Removal of capital controls, it is argued, makes it difficult to coordinate economic behaviour and outcomes that are central to the functioning of the developmental as well as the corporatist state.

The impact of Europeanization on models of capitalism

As in the case of the impact of globalization on the diversity of national capitalist models, the impact of Europeanization is ambiguous. Some argue that Europeanization is just a 'catalyst' and an amplifier of globalization, and in this capacity, Europeanization of EU policy seems to promote the core elements of an Anglo-Saxon model of capitalism, at the expense of the Continental, corporatist model (Streeck 1984, 1997; Windolf 1989). However appealing and well documented this conclusion might be, there is no consensus on this matter. Recent empirical work has begun to challenge such a view. Thus, a number of authors, inspired by the seminal work of Cameron, and Calmfors and Driffill, argue that in an era of open economies and globalization, both deregulated neoliberalism and social democratic corporatism can be optimal institutional arrangements (Cameron 1978; Calmfors and Driffill 1988; Hall and Soskice 2001). Both economy-wide studies and sectoral analyses have brought convincing evidence that Europeanization, as a force of institutional convergence, is far from achieving its goal (Crouch and Streeck 1997; Rhodes and van Apeldoorn 1997; Schmidt 2001).[43] Blaschke (2000), for instance, using multivariate regression analysis to investigate trends in union density in Western Europe in the period 1970–95, concludes that the evidence for the impact of European economic integration on organized labour is ambiguous and that national characteristics are persistent. Such analyses have shown that far from exhibiting a tendency towards a European-wide 'best-practice' neoliberalism, any convergence may in fact serve to deepen existing national specificities in new directions. European integration appears, then, to have a rather ambiguous impact on the Continental model of capitalism.

Despite this evidence of persistent national divergence, there is an increasing interest in documenting the development of a distinctive transnational European model of capitalism. The very suggestion of a transnational European social model raises a whole series of further issues, with significant consequences for future policy making in this area, which have yet to be dealt with adequately in the existing literature. Often associated with such claims is the argument that policies and institutions at the national level have been 'hollowed out', with responsibility and institutional capacity increasingly displaced, at least in the EU, to the transnational level (Jessop 1994; Rhodes 1994). At the EU level, Hooghe (1998) suggests that the struggle for the dominant model of capitalism is between two types, which echo the distinctions drawn upon above. Hooghe distinguishes between two dominant models at the European level, labelled neoliberalism and regulated capitalism (Hooghe 1998, p. 457).

At the heart of the debate is the degree to which markets should operate free from state intervention. Within the EU, neoliberals argue for a European-wide market, but with market regulation predominantly as a matter for national governments (Hooghe 1998, p. 458). While neoliberal governments have reluctantly accepted the development of EU interventionist measures aimed at redistribution, by contrast proponents of regulated capitalism place other concerns alongside market efficiency. At the EU level, 'they want to create a European liberal democracy capable of regulating markets, redistributing resources, and shaping partnerships among public and private actors' (Hooghe 1998, p. 458).

In this context, EU cohesion policy has been described as the 'flagship' of the European Commission's concept of regulated capitalism (Hooghe 1998, p. 459). As in the case of pan-European convergence, the evidence in favour of a coherent European capitalist model advocated from the supranational level is rather weak (Cernat 2001). Therefore, it becomes questionable as to just how useful it is to speak of a distinctive, coherent European capitalist model instead of a European 'cocktail capitalism'.

There is at present a lack of consensus as to whether the processes of institution building in post-socialist East-Central Europe reflect the development of a well-defined European capitalist model or contribute to the creation of a patchwork 'cocktail capitalism'. Given the impossibility of offering a definite answer to this important question regarding the impact of Europeanization on the model of capitalism adopted in CEECs, it is more feasible to attempt some preliminary considerations, whilst pointing to the limitations of the existing literature in this area.

As mentioned above, the influence of the EU on the direction of change in Central and Eastern Europe is, with few notable exceptions that are dealt with in Chapter 5, towards a neoliberal model. A cursory investigation of EU policy advocacy in the region shows a great deal of coordination between the EU, the IMF and the World Bank with regard to macroeconomic policies, thus supporting the neoliberal influence of Europeanization (World Bank 2001a).

Even in the case of social policies, an area where the EU influence is expected to be more oriented towards the Continental model, the evidence is mixed. While encouraging transition economies to establish institutions of social dialogue and consultation between policy makers and social partners in conformity with the EU *acquis*, the EU is also rather negative towards the involvement of state actors in tripartite arrangements, being more in favour of bipartism and decentralized bargaining. For instance, in the 2000 Regular Report on Estonia (EC 2000a), the European Commission praised the bipartite agreements at branch level in the agri-food and road transport sectors.

Overall, there seems to be more evidence suggesting that the EU has a neoliberal influence in Central and Eastern Europe than that suggesting an EU-induced model of capitalism along the lines of the Continental model. What this discussion highlights is the still rather paltry knowledge of the actual mechanisms affecting the institutional alternatives to neoliberalism, not only in Central and Eastern Europe but also in Western Europe and in the wider global context. Such reflections invariably raise the crucial question of the prospects for transnational lesson drawing and institutional emulation within and between capitalist models. These processes are frequently subsumed within the general category of policy transfer (Dolowitz and Marsh 1996). This notion, however, must be further unpacked. Therefore, in Chapter 4 at 5 the analysis will be refocused towards an understanding of the mechanisms and parameters of the Europeanization of CEECs. Such a reconceptualization calls for a distinctive research agenda based on theoretical cross-fertilization between globalization, Europeanization and policy transfer, when analysing the case of EU enlargement.

2
Institutions and Economic Growth in Central and Eastern Europe: A Quantitative Analysis

During the first 10 years of the transition from plan to market, Romania, along with other CEECs, implemented comprehensive reform programmes and achieved essential economic transformations. The main goal of such fundamental change was to set their economies on sustained growth paths. At the beginning of the transition process, all CEECs liberalized their prices, dismantled the state monopoly over foreign trade and gradually lifted the existing administrative barriers. Simultaneously, with the collapse of the socialist trade cooperation system (the Council for Mutual Economic Assistance, or CMEA), they experienced a loss of their most significant import and export markets. Consequently, during these first 10 years of transition, CEECs have witnessed a significant shift in their geographical export orientation towards Western Europe, a natural partner given the accession process under way. Increased openness has also resulted in a growing inflow of FDI, both as a result of large-scale privatization programmes and greenfield investment.

However, perhaps contrary to the expectations of most people in the region, the immediate impact of reforms was a severe economic contraction during the early 1990s (see Figure 2.1). As Elster, Offe and Preuss (1998) rightly argued, transforming a socialist economic system into a market-based economy is equivalent to 'rebuilding a ship at sea', and therefore the initial output collapse reflected the major institutional changes involved during the transformation from socialism to capitalism and the disorganization that followed the sudden end of central planning.[1]

In coping with this initial economic shock, some countries have been more successful than others in transforming their economy without a

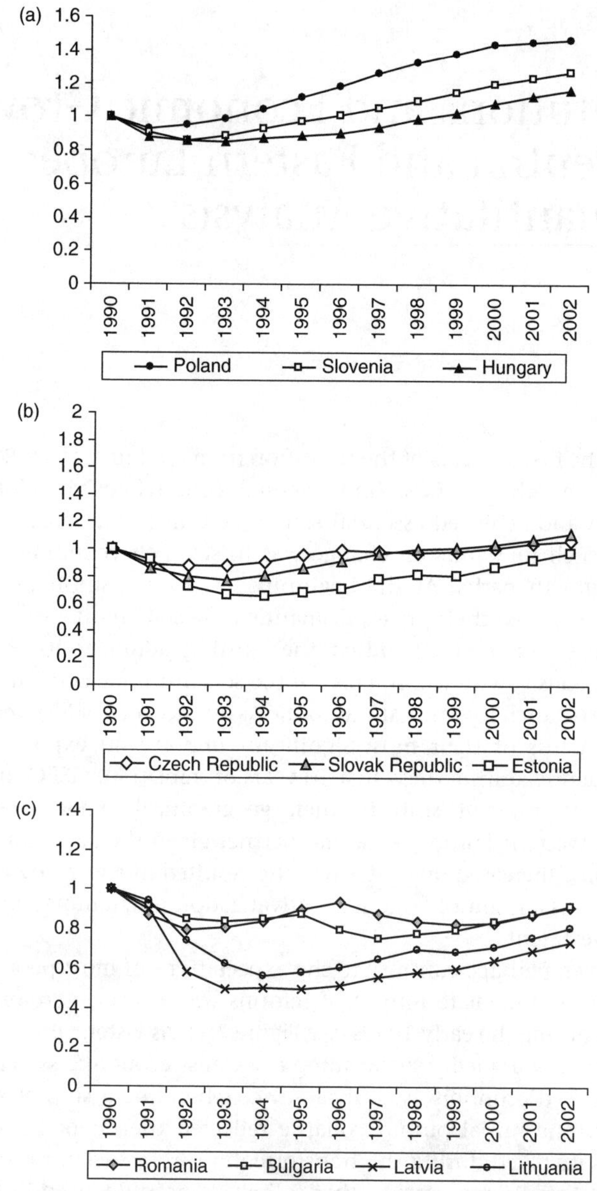

Figure 2.1 Growth in selected transition economies: real GDP index (base 1.00 in 1990)
(a) J-shaped evolution: Poland, Slovenia and Hungary
(b) U-shaped evolution: Czech Republic, Slovak Republic and Estonia
(c) L-shaped evolution: Romania, Bulgaria, Latvia, and Lithuania
Sources: Based on ECE (2000) and World Bank (2004b).

persistent decline in output. According to their growth performance, the CEECs can be grouped into three categories:

1 Countries following a J-shaped growth trend. These countries, after a short economic decline, have engaged on a steady growth path, surpassing the 1989 level of economic output (Figure 2.1a).
2 Countries following a U-shaped growth performance. These countries have been more affected by the initial economic downturn but, towards the end of the decade, they managed to fully recover and attain the level of economic output at the beginning of transition (Figure 2.1b).
3 Countries that followed an L-shaped trend. As can be seen from Figure 2.1c, for a number of countries, the initial years of transition have triggered a significant decline in economic growth, followed by a slow and only partial recovery. After 10 years of transition, most of these countries have yet to reach the 1991 GDP level.

The length and depth of the initial recession that hit most transition economies were not foreseen. As Figure 2.1 shows, growth did not, on average, turn positive until 1994 (with the exception of Poland, which has witnessed positive economic growth since 1992, after a sharp decline in 1990). Therefore, this chapter will try to establish explanations for these different economic paths. It attempts to contribute to the field of political economy of transition and institutional economics in two ways. First, using panel data on ten CEECs, it tests some of the arguments developed in Chapter 1. Second, it attempts to clarify how much of the variation in economic performance across East-Central Europe can be explained by the set of institutional variables introduced in the models of capitalism literature, in addition to a set of key macroeconomic variables.

The remainder of this chapter is organized as follows. The first section provides a broad picture of the economic situation across the region through several key economic indicators, while the second section adapts the theoretical concepts discussed in Chapter 1 to the case of transition economies. Based on these proxy variables, the third section works out a panel data regression for ten transition economies from Central and Eastern Europe and the Baltic region over the post-1989 period. This econometric model will test the influence of several economic and institutional variables on economic growth.

Diverging paths: alternative explanations

There have been numerous attempts to explain the variance in the economic performance of CEECs during the last decade. Some theories emphasized the importance of the macroeconomic policies implemented and the determination to speed up the necessary transformation of socialist economies into market economies (big-bang versus gradualism).[2] Others have underlined more specifically the positive impact of openness and economic integration through trade and FDI on growth (Cernat and Vranceanu 2001).

Against this background, a significant body of comparative political economy literature has been concerned with the question of whether political and institutional factors have a determinant impact on economic growth. Particularly influential among descriptive growth studies was the study by North (1990), who underlined the importance of institutional settings in creating an environment conducive to economic growth.[3]

Until recently, empirical studies measuring the importance of institutions for growth in CEECs have been rather scarce, mainly because of a lack of data regarding the quality of institutions. In the 1990s, major efforts have been made in this direction, both by academics and by international organizations.[4] Generally, these empirical studies shared many common features and followed some distinct lines of thought.

Whereas most of the empirical studies agree on the definition and measurement of the dependent variable, there is a wide range of approaches towards defining, selecting and measuring key institutional factors that are thought to influence economic performance. Some studies looked at the importance of democracy, social capital and political rights, particularly in developing countries, for economic performance (Helliwell 1994, 1996). Others have tried to evaluate the role of bureaucratic efficiency and corruption (Mauro 1995) or the role of informal institutions such as interpersonal trust and civic norms (Knack and Keefer 1997).

Most of these empirical investigations, however, were conducted on large samples including, most often, developing countries from different geographical regions and at different levels of development. Exceptions to this trend are Brunetti, Kisunko and Weder (1997) and particularly the work conducted by the European Bank for Reconstruction and Development (EBRD), which focused its attention solely on transition economies in Eastern Europe. These studies use subjective institutional measures constructed either from experts' opinions or surveys of private entrepreneurs in the region. Thus, EBRD *Transition Reports* from various years have produced a series of transition indicators providing evidence which indicates the importance of institutional transformation, such as that happening in Eastern Europe, for economic performance.

Based on these institutional indicators, one key conclusion of the EBRD 1999 *Transition Report* was that state–society institutional arrangements in transition economies vary quite significantly, not only in terms of quality but also in terms of their structure and forms. Furthermore, the role of the state remains central in determining the business environment in which industry, banks and other economic agents perform their activities, and consequently in understanding the differences in economic performance across the region (EBRD 1999, pp. 115–26).

Although not explicitly addressed in the EBRD report, their discussion of institutional arrangements, state–society interaction and the role of banks and industry resonates very well with another debate about Western political economies: the debate on models of capitalism. In recent years, these questions identifying national variations across macro-institutional arrangements and corporate governance and industrial relations practices have started to be addressed in the literature (Hart 1992; Sachs 1996).[5] Each of these variables was considered responsible for the international economic competitiveness of national capitalist institutional arrangements. Thus, it has been argued that varieties of capitalism represent a major factor in determining national economic performance.[6]

Models of capitalism and economic growth in Eastern Europe

Taking these elements as its starting point, this section extends the models of capitalism debate to transition economies, given the fact that these countries are in the process of building or rebuilding market economies. However, identifying the features of emerging forms of capitalism in Eastern Europe is not an easy task. The difficulty of such attempts is due not only to the dynamic nature of institutional change from socialism to market capitalism but also to the scarcity of information about specific state–society interactions. Yet, having said this, the existence of these inherent difficulties does not preclude at least some attempts to categorize the types of capitalism emerging in these countries, based on several quantifiable indicators. Such indicators capture certain key aspects of state–labour or business–labour relations, as well as the role of the banking sector in the economy.

   Table 2.1 includes several measures of such key elements identified in the models of capitalism literature. The CEECs are grouped first by the dominant type of labour bargaining. The International Labour Organization (ILO 1997b) identifies two main categories of countries: (1) countries where labour is involved in decision making mainly through enterprise-level bargaining (Czech Republic, Estonia, Hungary, Poland, Slovak Republic); (2) countries where organized labour is involved in decision making at a national level (Bulgaria, Lithuania, Latvia, Romania, Slovenia). The predominant type of wage bargaining is used as a proxy for the existence of elements specific to the Continental model of capitalism. This of course is a very rough indicator that does not capture the entire complexity of tripartite relations found in the Continental capitalism model. What can be said, however, is that the existence of centralized, national bargaining systems gives us reason to believe that such a capitalist system is closer to the Continental model than to the Anglo-Saxon model.

   The state intervention indicator in transition economies encompasses measures affecting prices, wages, employment, sales and investment

Table 2.1   Identifying emerging models of capitalism in Eastern Europe

Country	Dominant type of labour bargaining[a]	State intervention[b]	Domestic credit as a percentage of GDP (1992–98 average)[c]	Stocks traded as a percentage of GDP (1998–2003 average)[c]
Czech Republic	Company	23.4	70.5	8.9
Estonia	level	11.8	18.3	7.2
Hungary		43.9	62.7	19.7
Poland		16.4	35.5	5.5
Slovak Republic		54.2	65.7	3.6
Bulgaria	National	17.4	84.9	0.6
Lithuania	level	20.8	14.6	1.8
Latvia		n.a.	16.7	1.7
Romania		25.1	23.8	0.9
Slovenia		29.8	33.8	1.8

n.a. = not available.
Sources: [a] ILO (1997b); [b] average state intervention index, EBRD (1999); [c] World Bank (2004b).

decisions by companies surveyed by the EBRD and World Bank throughout the region. Although this is just a rough indicator of the *degree* of intervention and bears little information on the *type* of state intervention, in the absence of a more suitable indicator this variable will be used as a proxy for developmentalism.

The role of the banking sector and financial institutions is another key dimension of models of capitalism. According to these indicators, the more an economic system relies on stock markets as a finance mechanism (measured as the share of stocks traded in total GDP), the closer it is to the Anglo-Saxon model. Similarly, the more a country uses the banking system to channel capital into investment activities, the closer it moves towards a Continental model.

A higher reliance on banks for financing is, however, common to both the Continental–corporatist model and the statist–developmental model. Hence, this variable alone cannot make the distinction between the two models. Therefore, countries showing high reliance on the banking system need to be distinguished by corroborating the information on banking with the data on state–labour relations. Thus countries with strong labour movements and bank dependence will be closer to the Continental model, while countries with weaker labour movements will fall closer to the developmental model.

As shown in Chapter 1, the institutional complexity characterizing each model of capitalism can hardly be covered in a comprehensive manner by only a few aggregate indicators. However, in the absence of more precise indicators, a reasonable assumption guiding the subsequent analysis is that such broad indicators point to certain institutional features which allow us to identify the emergence of a particular model of capitalism. A succinct inspection of the data presented in Table 2.1 suggests significant differences across CEECs on each indicator but does not lend itself to a direct interpretation. Two major analytical tools can be applied in order to unpack this complexity. First, to clearly identify any tendency of the CEECs towards one capitalist model or another, a cluster analysis was used. The distribution of countries across model of capitalism clusters was then be corroborated with the economic evolution depicted in Figure 2.1.

Second, another dimension that needs to be examined is the degree of internal consistency of any emerging consistency. Given the fact that CEECs are subject to different and often conflicting external and domestic factors, apart from the three models of capitalism described at length in Chapter 1, CEECs may evolve to a model of capitalism 'à la carte'. In such a scenario, transition countries, instead of adopting a coherent transition programme that would lead them to a full working version of one of the three classical models, combine features from all three models. Although, in theory, one might argue that a 'pick and choose' strategy that combines the best features of each model would produce a better alternative than choosing an existing blueprint, the likely result of this process may well be the emergence of an inefficient 'cocktail capitalism', where key institutions necessary for the efficient functioning of the system are lacking, incomplete, or replaced by inconsistent features typical of another model.

To check this hypothesis a principal factor analysis was employed to see whether such tendencies towards one model of capitalism or another were based on a consistent pattern or rather on an 'à la carte' approach. The factor analysis technique is able to identify whether there is a unique principal component present in the sample, in which case this could be considered evidence of an institutional coherence along the lines of a particular model of capitalism. The identification of more than one principal component would be interpreted as evidence for institutional incoherence, typical of 'cocktail capitalism'.

After a standardization of the indicators included in Table 2.1, the cluster analysis technique applied to the ten CEECs has identified a clear distinction among three groups of countries, along the lines of three main models of capitalism identified in Chapter 1 (see Table 2.2).

The cluster analysis suggests that most CEECs tend to adopt state–societal institutions and policies that are closer to a Continental model of capitalism. A small number of CEECs (Czech Republic, Hungary, Slovenia) seem to have evolved more towards a developmental model of capitalism, whereas Estonia is the only country where the Anglo-Saxon model seems to prevail.

Comparing Figure 2.1 and Table 2.2 offers few clear indications on the impact of models of capitalism on economic performance during

Table 2.2 Cluster analysis results: identifying emerging models of capitalism in CEECs

Anglo-Saxon	Continental	Developmental
Estonia	Poland	Czech Republic
	Slovak Republic	Hungary
	Bulgaria	Slovenia
	Lithuania	
	Latvia	
	Romania	

Table 2.3   Institutional coherence in CEECs: principal factor analysis

Component	Total	Initial eigenvalues		Total	Extraction sums of squared loadings	
		% of variance	*Cumulative %*		*% of variance*	*Cumulative %*
1	2.1	52.9	52.9	2.1	52.9	52.9
2	1.2	29.8	82.7	1.2	29.8	82.7
3	0.6	13.9	96.6			
4	0.1	3.4	100			

transition. Among the three countries following a J-type evolution we find two countries tending towards a developmental model (Hungary and Slovenia) and one country closer to the Continental model (Poland). Countries with a U-shaped evolution (Estonia, Slovakia and the Czech Republic) feature tendencies to all three models of capitalism.

This lack of correlation between economic performance and models of capitalism can be further elucidated once the degree of institutional coherence is examined using factor analysis. As mentioned previously, the relationship between institutional choice and economic performance can be disturbed by a low degree of institutional coherence in the emerging model. The factor analysis results are presented in Table 2.3.

As seen from the significant eigenvalues, two principal components are identified, clearly suggesting that, despite some tendencies towards one model or another as identified in Table 2.2 by the cluster analysis, such tendencies are disturbed by a significant degree of institutional incoherence. Hence, the effects of the various models of capitalism on the ability of CEECs to embark on a sustained economic growth path cannot be determined based on aggregate correlations between the results of cluster analysis and broad economic indicators.

For this purpose, the next section develops an econometric model that will be better able to disentangle the influence of each institutional feature, and which possesses a control for other intervening variables. Based on a regression analysis, the next section will attempt to measure the link between these variables and the patterns of economic growth described at the beginning of this part.

The econometric model, results and implications

After the analysis of institutional tendencies in CEECs, a further step would be to disentangle the main institutional determinants and investigate more rigorously whether they can be related to various economic outcomes. Using panel data this section builds an augmented growth model for a sample of ten CEECs over the post-1989 period. This model will explore the political and economic determinants of economic growth during the last decade of transition from centrally planned economies to market-based economic systems.

Data and variables

The explanatory variables included a set of economic and institutional variables. Among the economic variables, domestic investment (and even more so foreign direct investment) is a crucial ingredient of economic growth. Given the extent to which investment is an engine for economic growth, the model includes variables that capture the importance of both domestic and foreign direct investment. To account for the variation in labour relations across the region, the regression analysis incorporated a dummy variable LAB, taking a value of 1 if national bargaining and wage formation is centralized, and 0 otherwise.

Other variables that are considered relevant in the literature on economic growth were also included in the regression. One economic indicator that is highly correlated with economic growth is the rate of unemployment, UR. According to economic theory, this variable should normally be negatively correlated with the rate of economic growth, since labour is an input factor to the growth function. Similarly, another key macroeconomic factor that was perceived in the 1990s by CEEC policy makers and international organizations (the IMF and the World Bank) as having a negative effect on the prospects for growth was inflation, INF. Since some economists criticized as exaggerated the focus on macroeconomic stabilization and the reduction of inflation, this variable was also tested.

Two financial variables were included to account for both the level of financial development and the resemblance to one model of capitalism or another. CREDIT refers to domestic credit (as a percentage of GDP) provided by the banking sector and includes total credit granted to various agents, including the public sector (central and local governments) and state-owned enterprises. Higher values for this indicator signal a tendency towards a Continental or developmental model.

The variable STOCK refers to the ratio of traded stocks as percentage of GDP. It is a general indicator of the size of the stock market relative to the size of the economy and is used as an overall measure of Anglo-Saxon capitalism. To somehow capture the extent of state intervention in the economy (without, however, distinguishing between development-oriented and inefficient intervention), another variable included was STATE, the index of state intervention reported in Table 2.1.

The variables tested also included the initial level of economic development. Some authors, using a path-dependent approach, underlined the fact that one important factor in determining the path and success of economic transition in Eastern Europe is the initial departure point. Therefore, to test this argument about the initial level of development, one of the explanatory variables included in the regression was the GDP per capita (average of 1987–8 levels), considered as the best available measure of initial level of economic development at the beginning of the transition period.

The data used in this analysis came from a variety of sources. Data for GDP, output growth, investment, FDI and inflation were taken from the United Nations Economic Commission for Europe databases. Data for all the other variables came from the ILO, EBRD and World Bank (see Table 2.1). All the other data and some missing values in the above-mentioned time series have been obtained from national statistics year-books.

To increase the number of observations, the data were pooled across time and countries. The regression model used was linear in parameters and all variables are measured so that all effects in the model are contemporaneous, with no lagged variable being introduced, due to the limited number of time-series observations.

With these specifications, the unrestricted theoretical model to be estimated becomes:

$$\text{GROWTH}_{t,k} = C_k + a_0\text{INVSH}_{t,k} + a_1\text{FDI}_{t,k} + a_2\text{INF}_{t,k}$$
$$+ a_3\text{UR}_{t,k} + a_4\text{CREDIT}_{t,k} + a_5\text{STOCK}_{t,k} + a_6\text{STATE}_{t,k}$$
$$+ a_6\text{LAB}_{t,k} + a_6\text{LOG(GDPPC87–88)}_{t,k} \qquad (2.1)$$

where GROWTH is the annual growth rate;
t denotes years and k is countries included in the sample;
INVSH is the share of domestic investment in GDP;
FDI is the share of FDI in GDP;
INF is the real inflation rate;
UR is the unemployment rate;
CREDIT is the share of total domestic credit provided by banks to both private and public agents;

STOCK is the ratio of stock traded to GDP;
STATE is the overall EBRD state intervention index;
LAB is the dummy variable, with a value of 1 if centralized bargaining is the dominant type of interaction between organized labour and business, and 0 otherwise;
GDPPC87–88 is the average GDP per capita in 1987–88, as a proxy for initial conditions.

The results

Table 2.4 contains the estimated coefficients and related statistics for the preliminary model, as described in equation (2.1). A number of other specifications were obtained by applying a data-based model simplification technique to eliminate variables that do not turn out to be statistically significant. Thus LAB and LOG(GDPPC87–88) were not considered in the analysis, as none of their coefficients in models 5, 6 and 7 were statistically significant.[7] Therefore, model 4 was chosen as the final 'best' model for further discussion. Before doing that, however, several general comments can be made about the results from all estimated equations. First, unlike Levine and Renelt (1992) who found that cross-country growth regressions were sensitive to their specifications, the results were quite robust across the estimated models. Both macroeconomic variables and model of capitalism proxies maintained their signs, magnitude and high level of statistical significance throughout all models estimated. Second, looking at the values of adjusted R^2, it can be seen that 56 per cent of the variance in the dependent variable is explained by the four macroeconomic variables. The explanatory power of the model is improved by 23 per cent when the proxies for models of capitalism are added to the macroeconomic variables.

More specifically, examining model 4, it is apparent that INVSH, FDI and INF are highly significant statistically and that all of them have the expected signs. The estimated model suggests that a 1 per cent increase in the investment share in GDP, for instance, would induce a 0.2 per cent increase in the annual growth rate, while a 1 per cent increase in the FDI share would increase the annual growth rate by 0.51 per cent. This shows the stronger effect of FDI on economic growth, compared to domestic investment.

One variable that deserves more attention is UR, capturing the effect of the unemployment rate on growth rates. In contrast to the effects predicted theoretically, the coefficient is positive, suggesting that a 1 per cent increase in the unemployment rate would bring about a 0.79 per cent increase in the annual growth rate (models 4–7). To further test this

Table 2.4   Generalized Least Squares (GLS) estimates

Sample: 1991–98 *Total panel obs: 71*	*Independent* *variables*	*1*	*2*	*3*	*4*	*5*	*6*	*7*	*8*
Macroeconomic	C	−11.70***	−9.08**	−7.74**	−10.82***	−10.79***	−17.47***	−30.14**	−13.77***
variables	INVSH	0.27**	0.28***	0.20**	0.38***	0.38***	0.38***	0.44***	0.37***
	FDI	0.50**	0.65**	0.51**	0.55**	0.55**	0.48*	0.58**	0.50**
	INF	−0.02***	−0.02***	−0.02***	−0.02***	−0.02***	−0.02***	−0.02***	−0.017***
	UR	0.57***	0.62***	0.65***	0.79***	0.78***	0.78***	0.79***	1.54***
Models of	CREDIT		−0.07***	−0.08***	−0.05**	−0.05**	−0.04**	−0.04**	−0.04**
capitalism proxies	STOCK			0.20***	0.22***	0.22***	0.23***	0.26***	0.23***
	STATE				−0.15***	−0.14***	−0.13***	−0.12**	−0.12***
	LAB					0.01		2.07	
	Log(GDPPC87–88)						0.78	1.96	
	UR^2								−0.04*
	Adj. R^2	0.56	0.64	0.74	0.79	0.80	0.74	0.79	0.82
	F-test	29.68	49.92	35.37	39.37	36.11	26.04	29.75	43.48

Notes: White heteroscedasticity-consistent standard errors and covariance.
*** for 1%, or greater, level; ** for 5%; * for 10%.

hypothesis, model 8 included a quadratic term for UR. The negative sign of UR^2 suggests that once unemployment attains a certain threshold the relationship between growth and unemployment rates becomes negative, as theoretically predicted. This may be a spurious relation picking up the effect of some omitted variable, but a closer investigation (see Chapter 3) will actually illustrate that such a 'hump-shaped' relationship between growth and unemployment may be explained by the persistence of overmanned state-owned enterprises (SOEs). Under such conditions an initial increase in unemployment may actually improve the overall labour productivity and cut labour costs, both of them with positive effects on growth.

The variables that are most interesting for the purpose of this analysis are nevertheless the proxies for models of capitalism, included in the lower part of Table 2.2. Unlike LAB, which did not show statistical significance in any of the estimated models, the other three proxy variables (CREDIT, STOCK and STATE) showed robust results. Among them, only STOCK was positively linked with economic growth. This finding proves the point made in the literature on financial systems and development (i.e., that stock markets are more important in well-developed than in less developed economies). STATE and CREDIT both had a negative impact on economic growth.

The negative relationship between state intervention and economic performance suggests that the role of the state in CEECs during transition does not fit a developmental state pattern. However, the quantitative analysis cannot identify whether a developmental strategy was pursued and failed, or whether the state intervention was a legacy of the socialist past, or both. This question will be clarified through the qualitative analysis in Chapter 3. While the findings for state intervention support the claims made by neoclassical economists and free-marketeers that state intervention inhibits rather than encourages growth, the negative relationship between CREDIT and growth needs further attention. In transition economies, the banking systems are still the dominant institution for financial intermediation. Under such conditions one would expect that an increase in the share of domestic credit in GDP should translate directly to more investment and higher economic growth. The estimated negative coefficient for CREDIT is counterintuitive and runs against theoretical predictions based on the Continental model of capitalism described in Chapter 1. Based on qualitative case study analysis, Chapter 3 uses Romania as a case study and explains the reasons behind this counterintuitive result, showing why the state–banking relations lead to counterproductive use of credit.

To conclude, the panel data analysis conducted in this chapter advanced the debate about the impact of models of capitalism on economic growth by providing a quantification of the theoretical concepts developed in the literature on types of capitalism. The approach used in this book differs from the vast majority of empirical studies of economic growth in Eastern Europe, which have focused predominantly on assessing the efficiency of a 'one-size-fits-all' formal institutional model. Instead, the empirical investigations carried out in this chapter, based on a number of rough indicators of models of capitalism, seem to suggest that stock markets, as a measure of the presence of Anglo-Saxon features, had a positive impact on growth rates. Similarly, higher initial unemployment, which is often an element of an Anglo-Saxon type of transition, also had a positive effect on growth. In contrast, higher values of bank credit as a percentage of GDP, usually associated with developmental and Continental models of capitalism, were negatively associated with annual growth rates. Moreover, the analysis also pointed out some counterintuitive results.

However, the level of analysis adopted in the econometric model was based on aggregated data; the unavailability of consistent statistical data did not allow a more in-depth analysis of the institutional mechanisms at work. One way to advance our understanding of the transition process and its final destination is to supplement these quantitative findings with more qualitative assessments of policies, laws and regulations, analysing the overall functioning of these transition economies. In doing so, quantitative and qualitative research may supplement each other and reach more meaningful conclusions. The next chapter will take Romania as a case study and will further clarify the conclusions reached in this chapter about emerging models of capitalism, their institutional underpinnings and their impact on the economic performance during the last decade of post-socialist transformation.

3
Domestic Institutions and Economic Performance: 'Cocktail Capitalism'

In Chapter 2 it was shown that despite numerous national differences among models of capitalism, the diversity of national forms of capitalism can be organized into three basic types: Anglo-Saxon capitalism, Continental capitalism and developmental capitalism. Following these conceptual clarifications, the quantitative analysis examined the links between institutions and economic performance. One of the key conclusions drawn from that econometric analysis is that, despite the difficulty of measuring institutions and key aspects of models of capitalism, various combinations of institutional factors affect growth differently because they are integral to both political and economic activities essential for economic growth.

The analysis also showed that incomplete institutional frameworks borrowed from several existing models of capitalism, and that the emerging 'cocktail capitalism' did not prove to be efficient in promoting a robust, fast-growing market economy, particularly in those CEECs characterized by an L-shaped growth pattern. However, the conclusions reached based on the results of this quantitative analysis remain at a very aggregated level. Consequently, one way to advance the understanding of the transition process and its final outcome is to supplement the findings of this quantitative analysis with more qualitative assessments of policies, laws and regulations, analysing the overall functioning of specific transition economies. Thus in this chapter the emphasis will be placed on identifying how certain key aspects of different models of capitalism operate in the Romanian political economy, which is perhaps the country that encountered the most serious difficulties in its attempts to introduce the much needed institutional and economic reforms.

State–industry relations

One crucial element in determining the national characteristics of the emerging capitalist political economy in Romania is the nature of state–industry relations. The example chosen to identify these key characteristics is privatization, in particular the institutional aspects of privatization and the role of different industrial interest groups (such as managers or trade unions) in shaping the Romanian capitalist system. Privatization has been an issue of debate among economists for many years. While it is now universally acknowledged that ownership matters, the effects of privatization seem to be dependent upon the actual means of implementation. Evidence is increasing worldwide that privatization improves firms' performance. However, in some institutionally weak transition economies, ownership change has so far not delivered on its promise. Romania is just such a case where privatization has not always led to efficiency improvements (World Bank 1997). Therefore, a qualitative case study of the political economy of privatization in Romania can be expected to shed light on this rather surprising outcome.

The privatization process in Romania

One of the central institutional features described in Chapter 1, which distinguishes one model of capitalism from another, is the structure of private property in the economy.[1] The definition of new property rights, and the transition from an economy dominated by collective ownership to one where private property prevails, are major issues in the processes of transition to market economies. In economies in transition, privatization represents an enormous break with the past and is an essential component of the change in regime. However, privatization does not always lead to the same capitalist environment. One important variable of any capitalist system is the private ownership structure prevailing in the economy.

Market systems such as the USA and the UK are characterized by widely dispersed shareholding and solid and dynamic stock markets. In contrast, the Continental model of capitalism (Germany being the classic exponent) is based on insider coalitions between institutional shareholders (banks, and other financial and non-financial enterprises), with less emphasis put on the stock market (Rhodes and van Apeldoorn 1997). Given these differences and the major implications of institutional aspects of the ownership structure for the functioning of market economies, the privatization process represents a crucial indicator of the emerging type of capitalism in Romania. As acknowledged by many authors, the privatization process affects not only the share of public ownership and the role of the state in the economy, but also the private ownership structure and the performance of newly privatized companies (Streeck 1992; De Jong 1993; Moerland 1995).

A number of privatization mechanisms have been used in Romania during the last 10 years which can be classified into four categories: (1) the mass privatization process (MPP); (2) the management–employee buy-out (MEBO) programme; (3) direct negotiations, involving the state negotiating detailed contractual arrangements with chosen investors; and (4) a heterogeneous category which does not involve any of the aforementioned strategies. This last category embraces privatization occurring through SOE liquidation, public offers using the stock market, auctions and debt–equity swaps.

By its very nature, MPP represents an attempt to move speedily towards an Anglo-Saxon capitalist system in which private property is comparatively widely dispersed. Public offers through the stock market would also be an indicator of Anglo-Saxon style of capitalism but, as Figure 3.2 shows, this has been insignificant throughout the period in Romania. MEBO privatization, by closely involving both the managers and the employees as future owners of the company, builds the foundation for the Continental model of capitalism. MEBO brings managers and employees together in interactions that create a de facto Germanic co-determination process. The third category, direct negotiations, is usually employed when the state intends to negotiate specific conditions with the future buyer, regarding the functioning of the company to be sold. The state normally proposes various forms of incentives (in terms of fiscal conditions and other regulations) and may try to impose on the potential buyer conditions related to export performance, local content or value-added requirements, or any other conditions that might create positive spillovers in the national economy. Privatization by direct negotiation, when used to attract foreign investors, clearly has all the hallmarks of a developmental state approach.

The Asian tigers are a very good example: in the early phase of their successful developmental strategy, they relied almost entirely on FDI and the foreign know-how of multinational corporations (Wade 1990). The term 'developmental' refers to the role played by the Romanian state (mainly through direct negotiations conducted by the State Ownership Fund (SOF), the institution responsible for privatization) to ensure that privatization would be conducive to the transformation of the SOEs into efficient, internationally competitive, private companies integrated into the global economy. Given Romania's relative lack of indigenous capital, efficient management and know-how, and its isolation from the global economy, the share of foreign ownership allowed in the overall privatization process can be taken as a good indicator of the extent to which direct negotiations were employed to achieve these developmental objectives.

In Romania, mass privatization started in 1992 with the distribution of free vouchers (called certificates of ownership) for 30 per cent of 6,300 state-owned enterprises earmarked for the process of mass privatization (NAP 1992, p. 4). The remaining 70 per cent of state property was retained in state guardianship, through the establishment of a State Ownership Fund for future sale to Romanian and foreign investors. MEBO privatization, which largely occurred in 1993–94 and was running down in 1995 (see Figure 3.2), was actually officially ended by a law enacted in 1996. Romanian MEBO involved the selling, under a preferential regime, of company shares to associations of managers and employees. A second round of MPP occurred in 1996, basically completing the programme initiated in 1992. From 1997 onwards, the two main forms of privatization in Romania have been through the SOF, either by organizing public tenders and auctions, or by engaging in direct negotiations with chosen investors. The stock market, as a privatization mechanism, has been insignificant throughout the entire period (see Figure 3.2).

How does Romanian privatization compare with that in other CEECs? The following brief overview highlights some additional features of privatization in Romania. Both in terms of scale and timing, Romania was a late starter, comparatively little privatization occurring during the period 1990–95 under the Leftist Iliescu governments. For instance, the Czech Republic's MPP voucher programme in the early 1990s was praised as a success story not only for its speed but also for the scale of privatization. In the Czech Republic up to 97 per cent of SOEs were privatized via vouchers, while in Poland 55 per cent of SOE assets were privatized, again through MPP voucher distribution (OECD 1993a, pp. 32–4). As Table 3.1 shows, as early as 1992 in the Czech Republic, almost 60 per cent of the privatization process was completed. By contrast, although the first privatization laws were adopted in 1990 and 1991, at the end of 1992 Romania was lagging far behind all other countries in terms of privatization, with less than 0.22 per cent of the total number of SOEs.

According to the World Bank (1997, p. 9), by 1995 both Hungary and the Czech Republic had privatized more than 80 per cent of the total number of SOEs. In contrast, Romania had only privatized 20 per cent of

Table 3.1   Measures of privatization across CEECs in the early years of transition (1992–5)

| | Firms (% of total number of SOEs) | | Industrial firms (1995) | |
Country	1992	1995	% of total industrial firms	Weighted by industrial output (%)
Bulgaria	n.a.	15	8	7
Czech Republic	60	87	89	93
Hungary	27.5	82	67	65
Poland	20	55	61	60
Romania	0.22	20	15	12
Slovak Republic	43	74	79	83
Slovenia	n.a.	54	41	41

n.a. = not available.
Sources: Based on OECD (1993a; 1993b); World Bank (1997).

SOEs. Similarly, the percentage of privatized firms in Romania's manufacturing sector was lower than in all other CEECs (with the exception of Bulgaria). When weighted by output, the percentage of privatized firms is even lower, suggesting that MPP and MEBO privatization was largely confined to small- and medium-sized firms rather than larger SOEs (see Table 3.1). On both measures, the Czech Republic, Slovakia, Hungary and Poland were the front-runners, while Bulgaria and Romania lagged far behind.

To conclude, what has this brief comparative overview revealed? The comparative data show that in comparison with other CEECs (except Bulgaria) Romania's privatization was slow and small-scale, at least until the mid-1990s. By this time, a number of CEECs had privatized extensively, but Romania was a clear laggard. The Romanian MPP had projected an ambitious target, but achieved comparatively little. In any case, it only involved 30 per cent of the shares of the companies (see below). In fact, at the end of the MPP only approximately 5 per cent of state assets had yet been privatized (Earle and Telegdy 1998). In order to understand better the reasons for Romania's comparatively poor performance, we turn now to a case-by-case examination of the institutional arrangements surrounding Romanian privatization.

In the following sections, each of these three distinctive privatization strategies will be examined in turn from an institutional perspective, identifying their respective contribution towards the adoption of one capitalist system or another.

The mass privatization process as a case of failed
Anglo-Saxon capitalism

Property rights are an essential feature of any economy, not only in terms of its underlying rules and institutions but also in exerting an impact on its functioning (Riker and Sened 1991; Riker and Wiemer 1993; Daviddi 1995).[2] One of the most striking features of the privatization process in Central and Eastern Europe has been the widespread reliance on mass privatization (Nuti 1995). This cashless method based on free vouchers has been promoted as a fast way of privatizing state-owned assets in an economic environment short of capital liquidities in the hands of potential domestic investors.

By its very nature, mass privatization represents an attempt to move speedily towards an Anglo-Saxon capitalist system whereby private property is widely dispersed.[3] The concept of mass privatization is based on various distribution schemes through which the property rights for SOEs are transferred to citizens for free, through the issuance of privatization vouchers or coupons. Furthermore, it was argued that mass privatization is the best way to ensure the fairness of the process and a level playing field for all citizens. In this manner, the creation of 'large-scale capitalism' will produce, in a relatively short period of time, a nation-wide shareholder class, as found in Anglo-Saxon capitalism.

Different mass privatization schemes were implemented in most East-Central European transition economies, and transition countries relied to different degrees on this process, and different institutional structures were put in place for its implementation (OECD 1993b; Estrin and Stone 1996, pp. 8–9). Therefore, although in theory mass privatization schemes should have introduced several Anglo-Saxon capitalist features with respect to corporate governance, the outcome varied markedly across East-Central European countries.

Apart from the extent (both in number and share of enterprises to be privatized) and pace of MPP schemes, another important element in establishing the type and efficiency of the emerging capitalist system is the role played by intermediary institutions acting on behalf of the individual shareholders (Rousseau and Wachtel 1998). When looking at the investment funds and stock exchanges involved in the valuation and trading of these vouchers and their associated shares, it becomes evident that both the Czech and, to a lesser extent, the Polish MPP led to the introduction of a balanced package of Anglo-Saxon capitalist institutions: not only diffuse ownership, but also an increased role of private investment funds and a well-functioning stock market that enabled individual shareholders to exert some degree of control during the process.

In Romania in 1990, when the first Iliescu–Roman government declared that it was time for the communist slogan 'National wealth is the property of the people' to come true, the details of this significant social and economic transformation were not announced, as the government preferred to leave this open to public debate. Certain ideas were brought forward regarding the various privatization methods and the share of the economy to be privatized. After two years, as in the Czech Republic and Russia, Romania adopted a mass privatization plan, by which a large number of state-owned enterprises were earmarked for mass privatization by free vouchers. Free vouchers were distributed to all Romanian citizens over 18 years of age, allowing for 30 per cent of the SOE shares to be passed into private hands. The privatization strategy included as an intermediary step the transfer of property from the government's hands into six newly created institutions: a State Ownership Fund (SOF) in charge of 70 per cent of state assets, and five regional Private Ownership Funds (POFs) managing the remaining 30 per cent of state assets (Law 15/91). Thus the main institutions in charge of state assets were the SOF and five POFs, based on territorial divisions. The shareholding of each commercial company was divided in the ratio of 70:30 between the SOF and one of the POFs (*Monitorul Oficial*, No. 169, 1991).

The creation of these intermediary institutions was justified on several grounds. First, these funds were conceived as temporary institutions in charge of the privatization process. Second, it was argued that in Romania the shareholder culture was non-existent and therefore dispersed, so that indifferent shareholders would be unable to act as active shareholders monitoring the management of their companies. The benefits of concentrated ownership are theoretically clear: it provides the investors with both sufficient private incentive, as well as the power to monitor and control management, and to achieve profit maximization (Shleifer and Vishny 1996).

The POFs were already considered private shares because they were supposed to operate on a commercial basis on behalf of the approximately 18,000,000 adult Romanian citizens who became shareholders in these funds. However, instead of issuing real shares in specific companies, the Romanian government at that time decided to introduce the POFs as an intermediary between the shareholders and the state itself.

In the Romanian programme, the creation of the POFs, quasi-governmental investment funds established to hold a percentage of enterprise shares on behalf of Romanian citizens, was not conducive to a functioning secondary market or to the efficient representation of equity rights for their shareholders, two crucial elements for the efficient functioning of an Anglo-Saxon capitalist model. On the contrary, these institutions and the first mass privatization scheme lacked transparency towards the shareholders and leverage towards the management of the enterprises where they held shares (Earle and Telegdy 1998, 1999).

The initial popular momentum behind this privatization scheme gradually faded away as privatization-related activities became relatively centralized in the SOF and POFs.[4] These organizations started to act more as state bureaucracies than investment funds. As a result, the Romanian MPP did not to any degree produce the expected advantages of an Anglo-Saxon market-oriented system. The institutional arrangements did not place poorly performing managers under pressure from external threats of takeovers or bankruptcy, as evidenced in the literature on the advantages of the Anglo-Saxon capitalist system (Albert 1993; Moerland 1995; Kristensen 1997), and neither did the Romanian MPP produce an internal surveillance mechanism for managerial performance via shareholders. The only constraint mechanism left in place was political, identical to that regulating SOEs.

Consequently, all of these national characteristics resulted in the Romanian MPP more closely resembling the institutional architecture of 'state corporatism *cum* political clientelism'. The corporatist structure was further emphasized by the structure of POFs' portfolios. POFs were organized following a corporatist logic by region and sector. Each major geographical province was assigned to a POF. In parallel, each POF was given shares in enterprises falling primarily within its assigned sectors and industries.

To contrast the outcome of MPP in Romania with Rhodes and van Apeldoorn's ideal type characteristics of the Anglo-Saxon capitalist system, the main features of MPP are summarized in Table 3.2.

This synthetic comparison shows that on most accounts the MPP failed to emulate the main features of a functioning Anglo-Saxon capitalist model. Instead, given the strong role played by the state and its intermediaries, as well their geographical and sectoral divisions, the MPP's institutional design comes closer to a mixture of political clientelism and corporatism.[5] In Schmitter's view, contemporary corporatism is

> a system of interest representation in which the constituent units are organised into a limited number of singular, compulsory, non-competitive, hierarchically ordered and functionally differentiated categories, recognised or licensed (if not created) by the state and granted a deliberate representational monopoly within their respective categories in exchange for observing certain controls on their selection of leaders and articulation of demands and supports. (Schmitter 1974)

Table 3.2 Comparing Anglo-Saxon capitalism and MPP-induced capitalism

	Models of capitalism	
Factors	*Anglo-Saxon capitalism*	*MPP in Romania 'State corporatism cum political clientelism'*
Role of the state	Minimal state	Regulatory state
Shareholder sovereignty	Widely dispersed ownership Dividends prioritized Liquid stock markets allow an easy 'exit' option for individual shareholders	Widely dispersed ownership Dividends not prioritized Low sovereignty since financial intermediaries are not accountable
Employee influence	Limited	Extensive, when Romanian MPP was combined with MEBO
Corporate governance	General separation of equity holding and management	Managers remained political clients in the case of incomplete privatization
Management boards	One-tier board	Two-tier boards; political involvement at both levels
Managerial labour market	Strong incentives for managers (stock options)	Limited incentives for economic performance Strong incentives for asset stripping
Market for corporate control	Hostile takeovers is the 'correction mechanism' for management failure	Takeovers forbidden Foreign investors discouraged
Role of stock exchange	Strong role in corporate finance	No stock market or other market correction mechanisms
Role of banks	Banks play a minimal role in corporate ownership	State-created financial intermediaries play a key role
Availability of finance	Explosion of venture capital companies	Lack of venture capital Favourable credits easily available only for the initial purchase of the company

Private Ownership Funds are indeed institutions *created* by the state with the intention of acting as intermediaries between the state and individual shareholders' interests for an initial period of five years (Ordinance 10/07.08.92, Article 1.7, in *Monitorul Oficial*, No. 208, 1992). The five POFs were singular institutions having separate territorial bases; therefore, competition between the POFs was not introduced. All the corporatist attributes identified by Schmitter (1974) were reflected in the POFs' statutes. They were institutions with clear functions, having a representational monopoly of shareholders' interests in the administrative boards of SOEs and in all other instances. Although hierarchy is not directly applicable, several power relations were introduced from the very beginning, others being developed by de facto institutional functioning. POF membership was virtually compulsory, since it was assumed that no citizen would decline a share of the national wealth. The POF statute stipulates that every future certificate holder has to accept entirely its statute, in order to become a POF member (Article 5.1). Surprisingly, the POF statute did not give any powers to the large number of shareholders assigned to each of the five POFs. There was no shareholders' annual meeting, and no other mechanisms for providing accountability, as in the Anglo-Saxon capitalist system. Again, in this case disparate Anglo-Saxon and corporatist institutions were combined in a very ineffective way. This institutional framework, where the shareholders had virtually no control over the POFs' activity, coupled with the clientelist political culture manifested in filling the positions, led to a capture of state corporatism by private interest groups engaged in *clientela–parentela* relations (LaPalombara 1964) with key politicians.[6] POFs were not only a method of reducing the complexity of the mass privatization programme but also very efficient institutions for implementing it in the interest of the political class.

Consequently, POFs failed in their main task as state agencies acting on behalf of the new individual owners and their interests, since the individual owners had virtually no say in the process. The main task of POFs was supposedly to counteract the Olsonian 'collective action' that diffuse ownership would create (Olson 1965).[7] The selection of POF board members became a highly politicized process (Ronnås 1996) and the almost negligible possibility that the certificate holders could ever influence the decisions of the POFs is a valid argument in favour of the idea that in Romania, the emerging capitalism, at least in the early 1990s, was characterized as a state corporatism rather than a system closer to an Anglo-Saxon ideal type.

All these indicators reflect, especially during the 1990–6 period, the reluctance of the Romanian state to evolve through the MPP towards a minimal role in the running of the economy, as in the Anglo-Saxon model. However, this outcome cannot be exclusively explained by the reluctance of the Romanian state to accelerate the privatization process. As shown here, the answer lies instead in specific state–society relations governing the privatization process. As will be shown in the following sections, the financial institutions created by the state to handle the privatization process (SOF and POFs) were entirely captured by the industrial elites interested in delaying the process until the insiders were in a favourable position to take control as the new owners.

MEBO and the failure of Continental-style capitalism

The second privatization method incorporates a variety of specific measures for transferring enterprises to their own managers and employees, known variously as insider privatization, closed joint-stock companies, or management and employee buy-outs (MEBOs). In some cases, management and employees acquire a controlling interest. In others, minority shares are transferred to employees at preferential terms. Direct, large-scale transfers to 'insiders' were the most popular form of privatization in Romania.

Through MEBO programmes, most privatized firms became primarily owned by managers and employees, sometimes at highly preferential prices. Taking into account that the changes under way by the early 1990s had increased the power and autonomy of enterprise managers, it was argued that no other form of privatization was politically feasible. This method was deemed fair in that 'ownership' passed to employees already considered 'stakeholders'.

Romania's attempts at mass privatization can only be described as futile for the reasons explained so far. In fact, the only truly privatized firms up until 1995 were from MEBO schemes, accomplished by direct negotiation between the SOF and enterprise employees. In a 'pilot privatization programme' originally intended to experiment with alternative privatization techniques for a sizeable number of companies (350 according to the Privatization Law), only 22 were finally completed and, of those, 15 were exclusively and four partially privatized by MEBO (Earle and Telegdy 1999). Subsequently, at the insistence of advisers financed by the British Know-How Fund, application of the MEBO method was greatly expanded and encouraged through special credits and tax reduction throughout the period of repayment (Law 77/1994, Article 50 in *Monitorul Oficial*, No. 209, 1994).

The typical MEBO was financed as follows: employees would trade their MPP vouchers for the 30 per cent of shares in their company held by the POFs. They would then use those shares as collateral to obtain a bank loan to buy the remaining 70 per cent of shares from the SOF. MEBO privatization, by closely involving both the managers and the employees as future owners of the company, builds the foundation for the Continental model of capitalism. MEBO brings managers and employees together in interactions that create a de facto Germanic co-determination process, without the legal requirements found in Germany regarding the election of supervisory boards, or the presence of a labour director on the board of management. However, MEBO required capital and labour groups to seek peaceful solutions to conflicts at firm level, with all the benefits arising from stable corporate governance structures.

There is little question that MEBO represented an improvement over the previous situation, when the state retained 70 per cent of the shares in all companies, and the quasi-private POFs were unable to influence management, even had they been so inclined. In theory, MEBO should have involved majority privatization, and they permitted the subsequent evolution of ownership structure and depoliticized enterprise behaviour. Furthermore, as evidenced by Chaplinsky, Niehaus and Van De Gucht (1998), when excess pension funds are used in the privatization process, employee participation improves the financial situation of the newly privatized firm.

However, a number of features of the Romanian MEBO privatization method diminished, and in some cases even eliminated, any benefits expected from SOE privatization. Unlike in the Czech Republic, for instance, in Romania MEBO was combined with the MPP process.[8] As a result, many employees and managers had an incentive very early on to circumvent the MPP programme in favour of MEBO. This was also a consequence of the POFs' lack of shareholder accountability, the institutions responsible for representing the interests of individual MPP voucher holders. Therefore, MEBO had a significant impetus in 1993–5, when the MPP was badly presented and poorly understood by the population. Most obviously, in an economic system characterized by an excess supply of labour and a lack of good managers, insider ownership (be they employees or managers) is unlikely to produce drastic restructuring, particularly in ways that may disadvantage the insiders themselves. In a former socialist economy, restructuring is crucial to ensure profitability and increased efficiency.

Thus MEBO created a coalition of employees from overmanned firms and incompetent communist managers, both these groups having the most to lose from genuine restructuring, which would mean layoffs for employees and dismissals for incompetent managers. MEBO before restructuring, as was done in the early years in Romania, is a recipe for failure. Indeed, this conclusion is acknowledged even by the SOF official documents that confirmed the theoretical expectations of MEBO privatization: according to SOF estimates, between 1992 and 2000 the majority of the 18 per cent of privatized firms whose economic position deteriorated after privatization were firms privatized by management–employee buy-out methods.[9]

Compared to the importance of this privatization method there were very few studies examining the post-privatization evolution of MEBO companies in Romania. Moreover, the existing literature does not point out some of the significant deficiencies of this privatization method. One notable study, based on a survey of 447 MEBO companies regarding the main economic and financial indicators one year after privatization (Table 3.3), concluded that MEBO had resulted in a noticeable improvement of their economic performance (Munteanu 1997).

However, these definite conclusions do not clearly result from the indicators presented in Table 3.3. On the contrary, these results suggest several opposing conclusions about the impact of MEBO privatization on firm performance.[10] The financial indicators included in Table 3.3 may serve as good proxies for certain privatization features. The equity capital offers some information about the corporate investment decisions with regard to productive capacities and fixed assets. All sectors surveyed show an increase of the equity capital after privatization apart from culture. This could be a deliberate decision by the new private owners or just the effect of reinvesting some of the money received by the SOF from privatization. Also, the reduction in the number of employees shows that labour restructuring continued after privatization. With the exception of the construction and transport sectors (see the shaded figures in the fifth column of Table 3.3), firms' profitability had increased one year after privatization. As a common explanation for this effect, most authors suggest the increased incentives for both employees and managers to allocate resources more efficiently and improve firms' economic performance.

While this may be true, another explanation of these results is the asset-stripping phenomenon by insiders *before* privatization occurs. Both labour and management, as future buyers of the company, have an incentive to depreciate the value of the SOE as much as possible before privatization. One usual way to do this is to reduce the profitability of the SOE in the period prior to the privatization process.[11] This may

Table 3.3 Post-privatization financial situation of 447 companies one year after being privatized through MEBO (31 December 1993–1 October 1994)

Sector	Number of firms in the sample	Equity capital (billion lei)	Number of employees	Profit rate (%)	Degree of indebtedness (debt/total income)
Agriculture					
31.12.93	94	51.7	29,601	6.28	0.14
01.10.1994		86.9	22,408	6.44	0.22
Industry					
31.12.93	96	43.2	50,910	6.61	0.37
01.10.1994		72.9	47,484	9.05	0.56
Trade and tourism					
31.12.93	33	11.7	6,325	4.62	0.73
01.10.1994		13.4	5,921	5.59	0.20
Construction	58	11.1	27,109	8.43	0.25
31.12.93		34.3	26,613	7.23	0.31
01.10.1994					
Transport					
31.12.93	22	8.2	6,447	10.49	0.18
01.10.1994		28.1	5,991	9.36	0.26
Culture					
31.12.93	5	0.4	363	3.04	0.2
01.10.1994		0.4	314	5.12	0.29
Local companies					
31.12.93	144	21.4	23,023	4.55	0.16
01.10.1994		37.7	21,598	5.27	0.24

Source: Munteanu (1997).

explain the observed increase in profitability one year after MEBO, compared with one year before (see column 5 in Table 3.3).

In contrast, the debt/equity ratio shows, with the notable exception of trade and tourism, a general deterioration (the shaded figures in the sixth column of Table 3.3). This is a clear indicator that MEBO privatization worsens the financial situation of the enterprise, since employees and managers have to obtain a bank loan (often using enterprise fixed assets as collateral) to cover the value of the stock package acquired. Moreover, using vouchers rather than real cash flows did little to improve the viability of the SOEs included in the MEBO.[12]

Furthermore, as will be shown below, when put in a larger context, the improved performance (as shown by the two above-mentioned studies and statistics) becomes less impressive. One of the key areas of concern regarding MEBO privatizations is that the pace of economic restructuring (i.e., streamlining of activity through layoffs of surplus labour) will be undermined by the new workers–owners.

Using the reduction in the number of employees one year after the MEBO privatization as a proxy for enterprise labour restructuring, Munteanu (1997) concluded that was a clear indicator of microeconomic reform as a result of MEBO privatization in companies burdened with overemployment and bureaucracy. However, a closer look at MEBO will reveal the opposite. As Table 3.4 shows, when compared with sectoral averages, MEBO does not seem to be best at restructuring labour. While it is true that the number of employees has declined in virtually all MEBO companies and sectors surveyed, it is also true that this reduction is far less abrupt in MEBO companies than the average sectoral reduction in employment, with the exception of trade and tourism, and culture and education, where the national average change in employment was positive (see Table 3.4).

While in agriculture the difference is marginal and cannot really be interpreted as a tendency of MEBO-privatized firms towards less labour restructuring, in all of the other sectors that account for the main economic sectors and the bulk of companies surveyed (construction, local activities, transport, industry), labour restructuring was significantly lower than the national sectoral average, suggesting that MEBO firms

Table 3.4   Changes in employment level in MEBO companies as compared with sectoral averages, 1993–4

Economic sector	Average employment ('000)		% change in employment (sectoral average)	Employees in the sample ('000)		% change in employment (MEBO sample)
	1993	1994		1993	1994	
Agriculture	484	364	−24.8	29.6	22.4	−24.3
Industry	2856	2586	−9.5	51	47.5	−6.7
Trade and tourism	619	696	12.4	6.3	5.9	−6.4
Construction	515	431	−16.3	27.1	26.6	−1.8
Transport	448	398	−11.2	6.4	6	−7.1
Culture/Education	428	432	0.9	0.36	0.31	−13.5
Local activities	163	143	−12.3	23	21.5	−6.2

Source: Based on data from NIS (1998).

were less inclined to streamline labour, as compared to other companies, including SOEs.

One explanation for these results lies in the fulfilment of certain conditions determining the success of MEBO privatization. As evidenced in theory, employee ownership needs to reach a certain minimum level of concentration in order to create the employee–owner identity necessary to achieve labour restructuring. When the would-be redundant worker expects, as owner, to gain at least as much as his lost salary, he or she will be more inclined to accept the layoff (Pendleton, Wilson and Wright 1998).

This new employee–owner identity is easier to achieve in smaller firms where the reduced number of employees allows them to obtain a 'shareholder' self-perception. Based on this argument, it is possible to understand why restructuring has taken place at a higher rate in only two sectors: trade and tourism, and culture. Table 3.4 shows that these were the sectors with the smallest firms in the sample. Firms in the culture sector had, on average, 73 workers before privatization, and trade and tourism companies had, on average, 190 workers each. This contrasts sharply with 314 in agriculture, 530 in industry, and 314 in construction.

Restructuring after MEBO will fail unless real power in the firm is vested in people committed to defending the interests of capital. Most MEBO contracts also contained provisions to prevent change in the level of employment and in the main activity of the firm and to restrict the price of the shares in the case of resale (Decision, No. 85535/94). These restrictions, which usually last for several years, have made various types of restructuring difficult or, in some cases, even impossible.

One way to quantify the post-MEBO restructuring process is to look at the link between average labour productivity growth and wage increases. In the absence of trade union pressure, salary increases should largely be a function of labour productivity. Higher labour productivity should translate into higher wages. In the presence of strong trade unions, the relationship is distorted and wage increases may arise without a corresponding increase in labour productivity. Table 3.5 provides a comparative perspective on the average annual labour productivity growth in several transition economies during 1992–5, by type of ownership.

Across the sample, Romania registers the lowest increase in labour productivity in privatized companies and actually shows a decrease in labour productivity in state-owned companies. Table 3.5 shows strikingly not only the comparatively low level of labour productivity growth in Romania in the period 1992–5, but also that privatization in Romania had a negligible impact on labour productivity, in stark

Table 3.5 Average annual labour productivity growth in the manufacturing sector: 1992–5 (%)

Country	Privatized firms	State-owned firms	Private–SOE differential
Bulgaria	12.4	−1.4	13.8
Czech Republic	8.6	−2.6	11.2
Hungary	6.0	3.2	2.8
Poland	7.5	1.4	6.1
Romania	**1.0**	**−0.5**	**1.5**
Slovak Republic	7.8	−4.1	11.9
Slovenia	7.2	1.8	5.4
Average	7.2	−0.3	7.5

Source: World Bank (1997), p. 2.

contrast to all the other CEECs. One obvious explanation is related to the privatization methods in Romania. As previously explained, during this period the principal method of privatization was MEBO, which gave workers a strong position from which to oppose labour restructuring.

These conclusions are supported by Frydman *et al.* (1999), who suggest that insider privatization is not effective in enhancing the revenue and productivity performance of privatized firms. Based on a survey of 506 mid-size manufacturing firms in the Czech Republic, Hungary and Poland, the study concludes that privatization has no beneficial effect on any performance measure in the case of firms controlled by insider owners (managers or employees), and that it has a very pronounced effect on firms with outsider owners, especially foreign investors (Frydman *et al.* 1999, p. 1).

Earle and Brown (1999), examining privatization in Russia, have also found that although on average privatized firms appear to perform somewhat better than state firms, the companies that perform best appear to be those with large, concentrated outside blockholders. By its very nature, MEBO privatization was poorly equipped to add much value to the resource needs of a newly privatized company, such as fresh capital, management expertise, technology and access to markets, compared with foreign owners (Frydman *et al.* 1999, p. 16).

However, MEBO managed to discourage factory managers who were quick to spin off valuable assets into special firms under their control, leaving the state firm with hollow shells and massive debts (Dabrowski, Gomulka and Rostowski 2000, p. 15). In an SOE or a mass-privatized SOE, a manager will sell his products below the market price to his son's or his wife's private company. The latter sells it on at market value and pockets the difference. After continuing this trick for a few years, the private company attains millionaire status, and the SOE becomes bankrupt. At this stage, the private company buys the SOE very cheaply, with the money earned unlawfully from the SOE. MEBO usually preclude this outcome simply because some insiders – the employees – are also the owners, and managers cannot escape the monitoring process as easily as when the owners are thousands of dispersed outsiders.[13]

It is important to understand that the predominance of MEBO as the main method of privatization before 1996 was due less to its objective necessity or economic advantages, and more to the lack of interest in other privatization methods, especially those involving foreign investors. This in turn can be easily explained by Romanian party politics. The MEBO method was a convenient ideological compromise for a large political spectrum. PDSR – the main Socialist party in government – and other Leftist parties supported MEBO since it allowed them to please their particular political clientele: trade unions and SOE managers.

Strategic privatization and the failure of the developmental state model

From the pioneering work of Alexander Hamilton and Friedrich List to more recent work on East Asia's developmental success, theorists have argued that a central feature of the developmental state has been its interventionist role. While the extent and type of state intervention have differed from one period or region to another, state interventionist policies have always affected trade and investment.

Given the importance of investment for economic development, the role of state policies in this area become crucial, especially in today's economy when multinational corporations (MNCs) and capital flows are so globalized. Although the role of MNCs in promoting the economic development of host economies has been controversial, in the developmental state literature the state–MNC interaction has been clearly evidenced by several studies (Evans 1979; Amsden 1989; Wade 1990). Wade partly attributes the success of Korean capitalism to the different policies pursued by a developmental state towards FDI. In the first stage, the Korean state encouraged inward FDI flows. Foreign investors brought in new managerial skills, know-how and more advanced technologies. In this first stage, FDI contributed to the emergence of other domestic firms connected in production networks with the competitive MNC subsidiaries, which in the longer term contributed to the creation of 'national champions', large-scale industrial conglomerates (*chaebols*) in the 1990s operating on a global scale (Wade 1990, pp. 63–75). Once these goals had been achieved, the developmental strategy of the Korean state shifted towards a discouragement of majority foreign ownership of its major companies, promoting instead strong state–business links and strategic industrial planning. The Korean state became protectionist towards inward flows of foreign trade and capital. This new strategy was supplemented by an active policy promoting other forms of technology transfer, such as licensing and sub-contracting (Wade 1990).

In the East European context of transition, the role of state policies in facilitating the necessary investment for economic development becomes evident during the process of privatization involving MNCs. MNCs were considered by many economists to be the best solution for the problems encountered by SOEs: low profitability, lack of competent management, overemployment, obsolete technologies, poor marketing skills, etc. Most transition economies of Central and Eastern Europe state as official policy their intention to attract additional direct foreign investment, and many offer substantial incentives to encourage it (Froot 1994; Rondinelli 1994).

While these arguments have previously been forcefully advanced in the literature (Frydman and Rapaczynski 1994; Boycko, Shleifer and Vishny 1996, pp. 309–20; Hansmann 1996), in the case of Romania strategic privatization did not produce the effects to the extent predicted by general theoretical studies or empirical studies conducted in neighbouring countries. Romania in fact did the opposite to the successful Korean experience. As Figure 3.1 suggests, FDI was initially discouraged by the Leftist regime between 1990 and 1996, leaving the Romanian

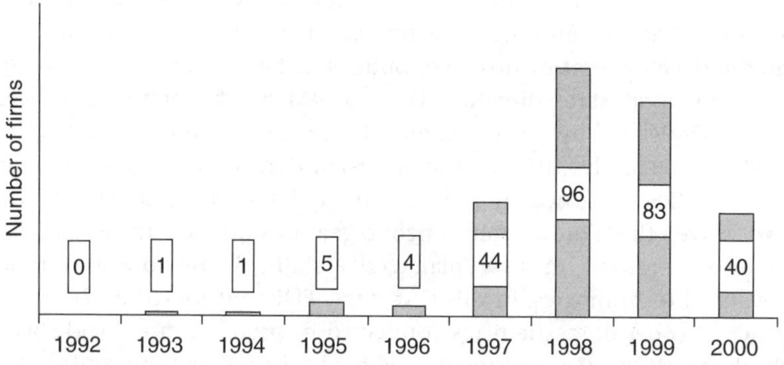

Figure 3.1   The number of privatization deals leading to foreign control
Source: SOF database.

industry at the level of the 1970s in terms of investment, technology and sectoral composition. Based on this structure, licensing and sub-contracting has been confined to textile and other low-skilled activities, with few horizontal and vertical spillovers to other domestic sectors. This naturally was an inadequate path and did not allow Romania to build a strong basis for a subsequent developmental strategy.

The reasons for this unexpected outcome have much to do with the manner in which strategic privatization was conducted. As pointed out by the developmental state theory, the role of the state in promoting strategic investment remains crucial for both FDI attraction and its endogenization.[14] That the Romanian state failed to perform its developmental tasks becomes obvious when looking at several indicators. The most obvious of these is the slow pace of privatization involving foreign investors (Figure 3.1). The difference in openness towards foreign investment between Leftist and centre-Right governments is noteworthy: during the Iliescu government (1990–6), out of 2,471 privatization contracts, the SOF concluded only 11 privatization deals leading to foreign control. The number of foreign investors attracted by the Romanian state is a telling figure, in its own right, of the failure of the Iliescu regime to pursue a developmental strategy. Instead of relying on foreign investment as an initial source of capital, new technologies, management and marketing techniques, and export markets to reinvigorate the domestic economy, the first six years were wasted on redistributing the existing state assets to the political clientele.

Moreover, a comparison of Figure 3.1 and Figure 3.2 clearly shows that even under the centre-Right governments (1996–2000) there was a marked and continuing reluctance to allow foreign control of strategically privatized SOEs. Thousands of privatization deals were concluded during the period, but only in 263 cases did foreign investors manage to take control of privatized firms during 1997–2000. Given the fact that foreign investment is less conducive to a long-term commitment and an efficient management in the absence of majority ownership, the low number of privatized deals leading to foreign control is hardly a sign of the adoption of a sustained developmental strategy, even in the post-Iliescu period.

Further evidence suggests that in many instances privatization through direct negotiation in Romania was not pursued in a developmental manner. Instead of focusing the negotiations with the private investor on ways to promote the transfer of technology and know-how or to enhance the export performance of the company, the actual policy objectives pursued during strategic privatization were aimed at avoiding labour shedding.

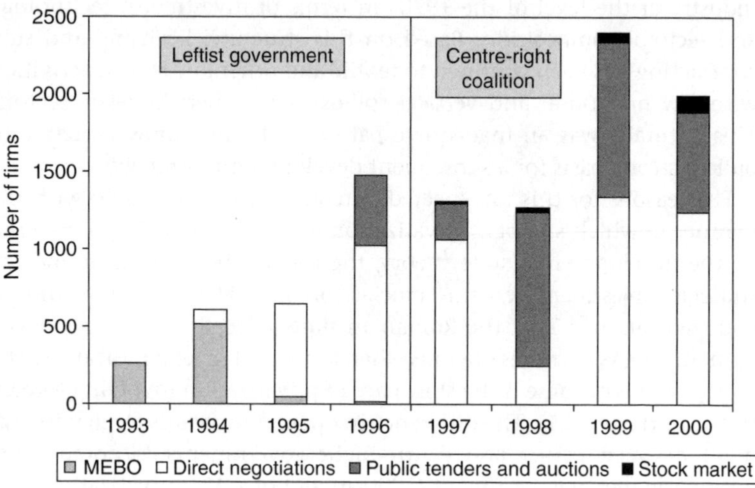

Figure 3.2   Number of privatized firms (annual figures), by method of privatization
Source: based on OECD (2002), p. 55.

Several laws passed during the last decade spelled out the types of objectives that should be pursued during strategic privatization and direct negotiations. Thus Government Ordinance 48/1997 imposed clear restrictions on the ability of future private owners to restructure the labour force. According to the Government Ordinance, it has become mandatory that any privatization contracts contain clauses regarding the conditions under which layoffs can occur. When the SOF and the private investor negotiate a restructuring programme including layoffs, the trade unions have to be informed prior to the conclusion of the privatization deal and, if such layoffs are approved, appropriate compensatory payments need to be granted.

Throughout the decade of its functioning, the SOF's failure to actively implement a development-oriented privatization strategy was a constant. The basic principle for a developmental-oriented privatization strategy is simple: an SOE needs to be made profitable by a full restructuring package affecting labour, capital, technology, management and marketing. Since the state does not have the means to do this, or does it inefficiently, privatizing the SOEs seems to be the only feasible solution. Therefore, the SOF should not spare any effort to attract potential investors in the process of privatization. However, there is vast anecdotal evidence as to how the SOF adopted anti-developmental privatization strategies.

One typical example is the issue of company debts to the state. On many occasions in the middle of the privatization process of one loss-making company, the SOF position regarding the company's debts was either unpredictable or inflexible. In the case of GEROM, a major glass manufacturer, for instance, the SOF (as well as other state agencies) threatened the company with bankruptcy just before its privatization, as a consequence of its serious indebtedness. A Turkish investor interested in acquiring GEROM offered to rescue the company through a debt–equity swap but in the end pulled away from the negotiations when the swap was refused by the SOF and the Finance Ministry. The deal was finally concluded after strong lobbying of several state agencies and officials, including the Prime Minister and President.[15] In many other instances the SOF showed very little flexibility. In the case of UPETROM, an industrial conglomerate specializing in petrochemical drilling equipment, instead of breaking up the plant into several smaller units according to their specialization, the SOF tried to privatize it as one entity, discouraging many potential investors who were interested in only a few of its activities. The same SOF lack of flexibility and determination was the main cause of the failure to privatize ARO, a car manufacturer, and TEPRO, a pharmaceutical company.[16]

Regarding the privatization process, a vital part of a successful transition from socialism to an efficient capitalist model is making sure that transferring SOEs into private hands improves the overall national economic performance. Moreover, the above analysis shows quite clearly that the method of privatization matters profoundly. It matters not only for the subsequent performance of the SOEs privatized, but also because it determines the emerging type of capitalism in various East-Central European countries engaged in transition.

SOF and POFs: state capture or state corporatism?

In addition to these general institutional characteristics of the MPP and its impact on the emerging capitalist system, further evidence of the misuse of the process by strong interest groups can also be found by examining the conflict around these institutions between various elites and interest groups and the policy style imposed by the new bureaucracy involved in the privatization process. The evidence put forward in the following pages strengthens the argument that the defining characteristics of the Romanian capitalist system have less to do with institutions per se and more to do with the *people* creating, running and responding to these institutions.

The importance of bureaucrats and private interest groups in shaping both the policy formulation and implementation raises the issue of whether the Romanian state has been 'captured' by private interests or whether it followed more a corporatist pattern, as in the case of the *Treuhand* in East Germany.[17] In all CEECs, the importance of the privatization process led to an intense process of state–societal interactions aimed at shaping the process in particular ways. However, as the subsequent pages will show, unlike the case of Germany where both political and societal interest groups interacted with the privatization agency through formal channels aimed at coordination and reaching compromises, in Romania there were no coordination mechanisms. Instead, this lack of formal state–societal coordination mechanisms and the uncertainty of outcome exacerbated the incentives for all actors (private interests, politicians, bureaucrats) to engage in state capture activities.

Among the private interests affected by privatization, the most vulnerable group was the industrial elite of SOE management. In the absence of formal mechanisms for coordinated policy making, SOE managers had to find other ways to reduce the uncertainty surrounding them. One such way was to use their political influence so that the SOF and POFs administration councils and executive management reflected their narrow interests, rather than the interests of millions of shareholders.

Through their close links with most parliamentarians representing the governing coalition, the industrial elite managed to gain representation for its conservative interests within the architecture of these new and crucial institutions in the course of the economic transition that followed in Romania.[18] The industrial elite thereby secured for itself a comfortable position from which it managed to 'capture' and divert the results of the privatization process.

In Romania state capture activities, as defined by Hellman *et al.* (2000), between industrial managers and politicians followed a paradigmatic situation, whereby high-ranking politicians are members on the management boards of SOEs engaged in the privatization process. This symbiosis ensured the stability and endurance of state capture activities that resembled a *clientela–parentela* relationship (LaPalombara 1964).

The battle around the institutions involved in the privatization process was motivated by the obtaining of a privileged position not only in the privatization process but also in the period *before* privatization. Two elements made the pre-privatization period very interesting for both managers and politicians. First, the design of the MPP process did not allow for a concentration of ownership to facilitate corporate control after privatization. Second, in the early 1990s, the negative effects of structural adjustment policies led many SOEs to become unprofitable. In these conditions, the preferred strategy for both managers and politicians was to benefit as much as possible from the pre-privatization process, rather than make a bad acquisition.

The pre-privatization process was generally defined as corporatization of the SOEs. State-owned companies had to be converted into share companies. In reality this was mainly an accounting process of revaluing the company assets at market prices, and sometimes of reorganization (Law 15/90). Instead of this rather straightforward process, the pre-privatization process became an end in itself. The main condition necessary for outsider interest groups to alter and benefit from this stage was to act on behalf of the owners at company level: the five POFs and SOF. The main condition for insiders (employee and managers) was to have loose supervision from the owners or to collude with them on asset-stripping.

The first step in this mechanism was for outsiders to become appointed to the two-tier management board of SOEs. Outsiders were either bureaucrats from POFs and the SOF or politicians acting as their representatives. The extent of this phenomenon is startling. Out of 935 employees in the SOF Headquarters, 326 persons represented SOF in 796 management boards. Despite the provisions of Law 31/90 forbidding the participation of any persons in more than three administration councils or boards of directors, many SOF employees considerably surpassed this maximum participation number. In the other SOF regional offices, 400 employees were members of 1,713 management boards (Ionascu 2000). Furthermore, despite high salaries and bonuses granted to ensure the professionalism of SOF employees, there were numerous cases of unlawful insider trading.[19] Although SOF status does not allow SOF employees to take part in the privatization process, SOF officials were actually associates of several companies that had been recently privatized.

The situation became acute in 1996 after the adoption of a law making parliamentarians ineligible to sit on management boards. The law was reportedly adopted grudgingly by the Romanian Parliament, at the express wish of President Iliescu, who did not want his image of 'poor but honest' to be stained by his party members being accused of gaining huge compensation from board membership. The law was finally adopted a few months before the 1996 presidential and parliamentary elections.

Despite its clear provisions, the Romanian legislators were the first to breach the law. Under the shelter of their parliamentarian immunity, they ignored the provisions of the new law and continued to maintain their position on the management boards. Since there was no instance in post-1989 Romanian democratic history of suspension of parliamentary immunity, there was no risk associated with breaching the law. Although all of the parliamentarians should have either withdrawn from management boards and administration councils or resigned from their legislative position, this never really happened. The political parties kept declaring publicly that their members withdrew from management boards, but at times the press published breaking news of a large number of parliamentarians still taking part in management boards and administration councils (Cotidianul 1999).

A first report by the Government's Control Department (DCG) in 2000 found that 75 parliamentarians were members of 51 boards of directors, management boards or audit commissions. In addition to parliamentarians, government officials were also among those breaching several laws (Law 31/90, HG 66/1991 and HG 755/1994). Thus, 63 high-ranking state officials were delegated by the SOF as representatives to 86 management boards. Among these officials, one could find the Minister of Agriculture and the Secretary of State for Customs. At lower levels, 3,100 civil servants from the Ministry of Finance were on audit commissions for various SOEs (DCG 2000).

Although all of these are clear cases of incompatibility between public and private positions, there were virtually no legal consequences for the politicians or bureaucrats involved in this scandal.[20] The rent-seeking and clientelistic behaviour was stronger than any law or reports of governmental control bodies. Once these revelations were made, the POFs and SOF bureaucrats found a way to maintain their onerous direct involvement in corporate management. They changed their positions in the management boards for other more obscure positions that did not attract public attention, reserving for themselves the key role of commissioners for the selection of management in companies under privatization. In other words, it was they who were deciding if one SOE manager was competent enough to be kept in place once the company was advertised for privatization.[21]

This situation actually has several implications. On the one hand, it shows a deep and constant politicization of the Romanian economy throughout the 10-year period after 1989. By taking part in management boards, top politicians and bureaucrats preserved a situation similar to the previous communist system when the ruling party was omnipresent in decision-making at enterprise level. On this issue, both the state (understood as public sector bureaucracy) and government (understood as top political leaders) were interfering deeply in the economic activity of SOEs, this time for their own profit. Therefore, in post-communist Romania, politicians are still in business!

On the other hand, although public attention in Romania has mainly been focused on the personal benefits accumulated by politicians as a result of their board membership, a more important aspect is the systemic implications of this widespread phenomenon for state–business relations and the emerging capitalist system. One can hardly think of a more favourable mechanism for *clientela–parentela* relations between state and business than board membership for politicians. The political patrons expected allegiance, financial contributions and political activism from their client enterprises. One should not forget that in many cases board membership put politicians in control of thousands of employees, or tens of thousands voters, if family members were included. There is therefore a direct relationship between membership and the electoral process.

The best example for illustrating this phenomenon is SIDEX, the huge loss-making steel plant located in the south-east of Romania. Over 36,000 people, mostly men, were employed in the company (SIDEX 1999). When families are included, this figure may reach 150,000 voters, or around 25 per cent of the total number of votes in Galati County. When a politician becomes a key member of SIDEX's board, he, as the man who funnels state subsidies and/or delays painful company restructuring, will actually secure an easy victory in parliamentary elections. Evidence for this populist state–business link in the case of SIDEX comes from the fact that a former SIDEX Chief Executive Officer is now a parliamentarian for PDSR. The PDSR parliamentarian for Galati County remained a strong political patron of the steel plant, as evidenced by the constant number of interventions in the Parliament on behalf of the company.[22]

In this victory, the industrial elite secured itself a comfortable position from which it managed to undermine the restructuring and privatization process. Djankov (1998) produces empirical evidence suggesting that SOF-led restructuring in Romania did not improve the operational or financial performance of state-owned companies included in isolation programmes. Moreover, due to clientelistic relations between managers and trade union leaders, the restructuring process did not lead to labour restructuring or to an elimination or reduction of soft loans.[23]

The primary role of SOF in its initial conception was to subordinate the industrial elite to an independent institution acting *temporarily* on behalf of the owners of SOEs. This subordination process was understood by the industrial elite to be a clear attack on its own power base. By owning 70 per cent of all state assets, the SOF emerged as one of the most influential bureaucratic institutions.[24] The SOF now performed many tasks previously dealt with through the Ministry of Industry Trade (MIT).

It has to be said, however, that the industrial elite was not, in principle, against economic reform. Its opposition was directed against any reformist measure by which its dominant economic role would have been drastically reduced, at the expense of other emerging interest groups. With regard to SOF control, the power struggle was not over when the industrial elite won the first battle. The government soon realized that the powers given by its own law to the SOF were too overarching and it tried unsuccessfully to subordinate the SOF. As is typically the case with institutional design, the new SOF bureaucracy managed very easily to play the principal-agent game in its own rapidly developing interests. Although during the next 4–6 years the interests of the industrial elite were fairly well protected, the SOF bureaucracy acquired private gains directly proportional to the power invested in their institution. As for the political actors, they managed to maintain their control over the SOF and, through this and other mechanisms presented below, to maintain control over the industrial elite.

In addition to establishing these new organizations, the Privatization Law set targets of future privatization for them to fulfil. The SOF was given the 'obligation' to privatize 10 per cent of the shares initially held (Law 58/1991, Article 28). Although the law permitted the SOF to apply a broad range of methods – public offering, auction, direct negotiation or some combination of the three – it provided no detail on how the methods should be accomplished. The SOF was somehow supposed to be helped out in this process by the POFs, which were given, in addition to the task of the maximization of the value of certificates of ownership held on behalf of the actual owners, the additional task of working together with the SOF to privatize the SOF shares of the companies in their portfolios (Law 58/1991, Article 7, 51, 60).

At least in retrospect, it seems obvious that this privatization plan was doomed to failure. Although the recentralization of authority in the SOF could have been a useful step towards privatization (as was proved in East Germany by the Treuhand[25]), avoiding the possibility that the de facto property rights in the enterprises might become diffuse and vested in branch ministries for enterprise management, the new institutions had neither the ability nor the incentive to privatize a large number of companies in case by case sales. According to the activity report of the SOF, the first transfer of ownership took place only towards the end of

1992, some 16 months after the adoption of the privatization law (SOF 1996, Appendix 1).

Conclusions

Despite two rounds of mass privatization during the first seven years of transition in Romania, only limited progress had been made by early 1997 in transferring some major areas of economic activity to the private sector. While many small enterprises had been privatized, almost all large industrial enterprises remained under state ownership. Overall, privatized enterprises accounted for less than 20 per cent of the total equity in commercial companies. Furthermore, several strategic SOEs and public utilities (representing around 20 per cent of employment in

Table 3.6   Privatization methods, economic effects and capitalist models promoted

Privatization method	Mass privatization	MEBO	Strategic Privatization
Model promoted	Anglo-Saxon capitalism	Continental capitalism	Developmental capitalism
Main features	Diffuse ownership	Workers' participation in decision making	Integrating the SOEs into the global economy
Disadvantages	Long agency chains	Resistance towards restructuring and elimination of overmanning	Hit-and-run privatization
	Inefficient monitoring		Creation of private monopolies
	Asset stripping by managers	Lack of new capital inflows	Domestically oriented investment
	Maintains the soft budgetary constraint	No transfer of technology and know-how	
Advantages	A very good strategy for gaining political capital	Short agency chains	Infusion of capital
		Insider knowledge improves monitoring	Transfer of technology and know-how
	It may contribute to the creation of a private ownership structure and the further development of financial markets	Improved incentives for workers and mangers	Efficient management
		Reduces the risks of industrial conflict	Market access and integration in production networks
		Reduces the risks of insider opposition towards other forms of privatization	

the economy) had not even been included in the privatization programme, and remained largely unrestructured.

Therefore all the attempts towards privatization created an institutional and incentive structure that emphasized the disadvantages of each method at the expense of its positive features (see Table 3.6). Moreover, from the findings presented in this part it is clear that in Romania one of the major assumptions behind the urge towards privatization did not work. Privatization was supposed to be the best mechanism for ensuring that the role of the state and politics in running the economy would be considerably diminished at the expense of free market mechanisms.

As Frydman and Rapaczynski (1994) rightly pointed out, the argument that privatization will act as an efficient instrument of depoliticization was based on the assumption that privatized firms and the state would be less inclined and less able to engage in close relationships; yet in many cases privatization (especially privatization to insiders) was a poor substitute for real restructuring and only created a perverted votes-for-jobs and subsidies equilibrium.

This is the only explanation for those cases when, even after privatization, both owners and unions lobbied governments for more subsidies. The new private owners (in most cases state-controlled POFs or the SOF) offered to keep redundant jobs in exchange for a vocal request from organized labour for subsidies. The union, benefiting from the excess labour, persuaded the government to grant a subsidy directly, or through a soft loan, tax breaks, etc. It is therefore possible that transferring control increases the amount of subsidy without decreasing the level of excess employment. This mechanism could also explain the results of a World Bank study regarding the lack of improvement in the economic performance of many privatized SOEs in Romania (World Bank 1997).

Another negative feature of the privatization process was the procrastination with which the privatization process took place. The very nature of the SOF ran counter to speeding up privatization since the end of privatization also meant the end of the SOF. Although it was repeatedly stated by senior Romanian officials, including the Prime Minister and the President, that the deadline included in the SOF statute would be met – by the end of 2000, the SOF had to finish the privatization process and then move to the stage of post-privatization surveillance agency – the SOF civil servants still took the view that the better they worked, the closer their layoff. While slow privatization has been reported in other transition economies as well (see Savov 1999, p. 19, for the Bulgarian case, or Blaszczyk 1999, p. 31 for Poland), in Romania the pace of privatization was much slower. Apart from the actual number of privatized SOEs, another good indicator for the pace of privatization was the private sector's share of GDP. In 1998, in Romania this was less than 60 per cent, while Hungary reached 80 per cent, the Czech Republic 75 per cent and the Baltic States around 70 per cent (IMF 1999a, p. 21). Very illustrative is also the fact that the carefully prepared public stock-offering campaign at national level in 1997, after a lot of time and effort, resulted in only one privatized company. One may argue that the records of public offerings in Poland, Hungary, Lithuania or Slovenia are not very impressive, but Romania is by far the laggard among them.

Of course, theoretically speaking, one could simply auction off thousands of companies without any minimum price or conditions. However, in fact this never happened, due to populist reasons. Many politicians thought that they would be 'skinned alive' if large SOEs were to be sold for the prices that resulted from public offerings, and they could no longer exercise their power. It was only through giving out contracts for consulting firms that did valuations, getting points for 'saving jobs' through requiring the new owners to keep the bloated employment levels, and making sales conditional on specific post-privatization investments that privatization bureaucrats managed to stay in business.

To conclude, privatization in Romania shares features common to all three capitalist systems, but the emerging type of capitalism in Romania falls in between. The Romanian 'cocktail capitalism' never managed to emulate the efficient mechanisms of any of the three well-established models of capitalism. The emerging capitalism in Romania is a model of partial reforms in which 'winners take all' (Hellman 1998, pp. 232–4).

Instead of creating incentives and political support for further reforms, the Romanian 'cocktail capitalism' maintained the incentives for private rent-seeking, in sharp contrast to a well-functioning Continental capitalist system or an Asian developmental model. As a result, the capitalist institutional architecture emerging from the different privatization schemes led to an inefficient capitalist model (see Figure 3.3). The three-peak graph suggests that there may be more than one efficient model of capitalism, and that 'institutional switching' from one to another involves significant costs (Freeman 2000).

The graph also shows that the Romanian transition has remained trapped in a 'valley of tears' (Dahrendorf 1990, p. 84), since all privatization methods were incompletely implemented. The idea that reforms are only partially implemented not because of opposition from net losers in transition but from net winners is convincingly advanced by

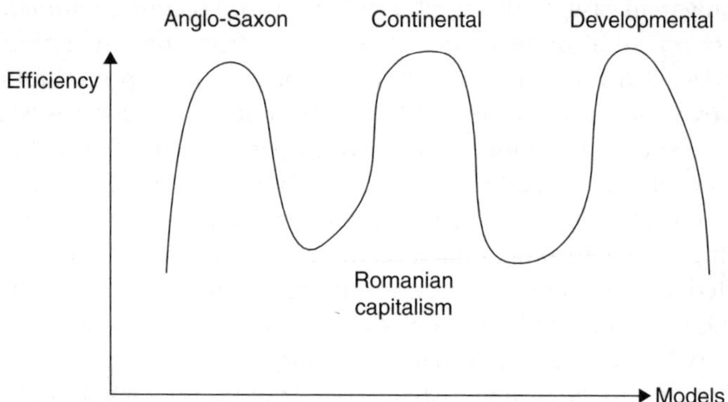

Figure 3.3   Efficiency and capitalist institutional architecture

Hellman (1998). He pointed to the problems of 'partial reform', which creates 'winners' who then prefer the preservation of the 'transition period' and its high rents rather than completing the reform process. Russia and Ukraine stand out as obvious cases of this, examples where the 'new *nomenklatura*' has fared well in the grey zone between communism and the market, and has organized itself against more sweeping reforms. This explanation is equally valid for Romania since many of the negative results of transition may be considered to result from the powerful insider elite's opposition to introducing additional reforms.

State–labour relations

After the discussion of state–industry relations, we turn our attention to the patterns of state–labour interactions in Romania. The following discussions examine some of the distinctive aspects of state–labour relations and the special challenges faced by Romania during the first decade of post-communist transition.

Before looking at the institutional aspects it is important to sketch the post-1989 economic environment in which the new state–labour institutional arrangements emerged. The demise of the CMEA and the domestic dismantling of central planning imposed severe strains on the functioning of the Romanian economy. Romania launched its economic reform and macroeconomic stabilization programme in 1991 under very unfavourable conditions resulting from both endogenous and exogenous factors. One of the internal difficulties was the continuous decline in industrial output (by about 40 per cent in the period

1989–94), which led to increased pressure on the labour market and rising unemployment. A further negative impact on employment was the inability of the state to introduce measures enhancing enterprise productivity through new technologies and improved production processes during the 1980s. As a result, many SOEs were plagued with overmanning, which reduced labour productivity.

Given this difficult starting point, the cost of necessary restructuring was initially imposed on workers, as reflected in decreasing real wage rates and increasing unemployment. Unemployment rates have soared since 1993. Simultaneously, major real wage decreases were registered. By 1993, the average real wage was 59.4 per cent of the 1990 real wage (NCS 1998). The only years with significant real wage growth throughout the entire post-1989 period were 1995 and 1996.[26]

Despite their inability to stabilize their real wages, trade union confederations have been a significant force, capable of influencing the course of every government in power during that time. Given the inability of successive governments to stop the macroeconomic decline, trade union leaders had their bargaining chips in the political game and they used them to a large extent to attain their own personal interests.

That trade union leaders have managed to successfully play a two-level game with their members and with the political parties is evidenced by their ability to maximize the political benefits for themselves, as intermediaries between the political class and the workers. By using their ability to mobilize workers for street demonstrations, and the willingness of trade union federations in key industries to strike in support of their demands, trade union leaders used demands for real wage increases as a bargaining chip in exchange for personal political careers or other forms of clientelism (see the discussion on asset-stripping below).

Thus labour was the area that carried the costs of low capital productivity, instead of capital.[27] This is not surprising when it is remembered that until 1996, SOEs represented an overwhelming majority in the manufacturing sector and hence the capital was well represented at the state level by the SOF and POFs, as well as through politically appointed managers at the firm level. Therefore, restructuring meant only cost-cutting measures, structural adjustment and privatization, all with a negative impact on the labour force.

At the same time, high inflation and declining living standards, as a result of dramatic cuts in welfare expenditure, significantly increased the potential for social convulsion. As a consequence of this deterioration in economic conditions, soon after the euphoria of the 1989 Revolution, Romania became prone to social conflict. To avoid explosive social conflicts, the political parties tried to use several strategies, both at the level of social dialogue and in terms of economic policy making. In the quasi-generalized conflictual period of 1990–92, there is little wonder that the fragile ruling coalition (and President Iliescu in particular) sought to forge certain state–labour alliances that would have allowed them a stronger social base for their coalition. As the following sections will show, the special relationship between the state and organized labour from the mining sector was used by the Iliescu regime to achieve otherwise difficult political ends.

The Romanian model of state–labour relations: between clientelism and corporatism

One essential prerequisite for successful state–labour relations and tripartism is that each party in the process should recognize and respect the other's interests and their right to pursue them. Thus, if unions refuse to recognize that the employer's role is to maximize profits and promote the competitiveness of their companies, or if employers fail to acknowledge that trade unions are, precisely, instruments for promoting higher employment levels and better working conditions and living standards, cooperative relations between them can hardly exist. Likewise, if the state does not recognize the appropriate role that social partners must play in policy making, there is little room for either a corporatist or a developmental state–labour relationship to emerge.

At the institutional level, the situation in Romania was closer to the pluralist extreme, where the relationship between state and social actors is highly competitive. In Romania, 20 trade union confederations were created after 1989. Data on union membership were uncertain but there were only four main trade union confederations recognized by the state in the National Collective Wage Bargaining Law: BNS (the National Trade Unions Bloc), CARTEL ALFA, CNSLR-Fratia (National Confederation of Free Trade Unions of Romania) and CSDR (Democratic Trade Union Confederation of Romania). The first attempt to institutionalize tripartite state–labour relations was the early Joint Government–Trade Union Commission. The initiative to form this Commission dates back to 1990 and came from both trade unions and government. However, because of the highly fragmented structure of the trade union movement and the dual role played by the state, as both owner of SOEs and mediator, the tripartite initiative never got off the drawing board. Given the slow pace of privatization and the overwhelming state ownership and control of SOE management, in the first years after 1989 employer associations were almost non-existent. In such conditions, tripartite consultation mechanisms could not be established.

In 1991, after failing to set up a functioning Joint Commission, the Prime Minister, Petre Roman, created a Department for Trade Union Relations (DTUR) directly subordinated to the Prime Minister. However, the newly established DTUR did not engage in regular, formal consultation mechanisms such as those found in the Continental model of capitalism. Instead, it preferred to adopt an ad hoc reactive strategy. In addition, trying to diffuse even minor labour conflicts at enterprise level DTUR tried to gain political capital by showing its concern about labour relations. The drawback of this institutional design was the emergence of highly politicized relations between state and labour, as the following pages will further illustrate. The department became a sort of fireman ready to extinguish open conflict using dialogue and empty promises. But by doing this, the trade unions soon realized that the special department for labour relations was powerless, even though directly attached to the Prime Minister. Increasingly they refused to speak with the intermediary and demanded that the Prime Minister himself be the interlocutor. This is how it became regular practice in Romania for the Prime Minister to go and talk to the workers directly at the shop-floor level or in Bucharest. As will be shown below, these numerous precedents, when organized labour demanded (and obtained) concessions from the Prime Minister, were behind the emergence of *Mineriadas*, and aggravated their consequences.

Despite several tense periods, however, informal state–labour relations were not always conflictual. The labour movement in Romania maintained strong informal links with political parties and state officials. Instead of a corporatist or cooperative arrangement, the boundaries between the actors become blurred. It has become a general pattern for trade union leaders to take advantage of their positions and get involved in politics. Over time, this has had a corrosive effect on the legitimacy of trade union leaders, since trade union members increasingly started to see them as political opportunists.

State–labour links are perhaps most visible during electoral campaigns. Trade unions not only publicly supported one political party or another, but they signed electoral protocols and very often trade union leaders were included on electoral lists in exchange for trade union electoral support. Many trade union leaders were thus elected to Parliament, while others have become prominent party leaders or were given key positions in various governments.

One such example is Victor Ciorbea, ex-trade union leader and Prime Minister. During his time in government (1996–7), there were two key advances towards a more formal tripartite state–labour–business interaction. The first was the setting-up of an institutionalized tripartite body at national level: the Economic and Social Council. Whether the Council emerged primarily as a result of the EU's influence or thanks to Ciorbea's own vision is not entirely clear.[28] What is certain however, is that, unlike his predecessors, he accelerated the process. The Council brought together, in a tripartite structure, a government representative, employer associations and major trade union confederations.

Apart from this consultative and mediation body at national level, the second set of innovations introduced during Ciorbea's mandate were the *Social Dialogue Consultative Commissions*, tripartite commissions at ministerial and local level. These commissions had monthly meetings and discussed the problems that had arisen from the reform programme, technological change and restructuring. In these fora, the employer associations and trade unions could discuss various issues regarding potential conflicts, social protection, labour training, education, health, and so on with ministry officials and local authorities. The ministerial commissions had a loose organization and involved bureaucrats from various line ministries and employer and trade union representatives at branch level. The local commissions brought together the local administration and social partners from each county. Even if such structures were not hierarchically linked to the national council, they required close communication and an exchange of information between these three levels. This, however did not happen, and soon local and ministerial commissions lost their momentum and were held erratically.[29]

Another interesting feature is the weakness of tripartite interactions even among interest groups belonging to the same political factions. Business associations and trade union confederations sharing the same political patron have failed to develop strong links between themselves, or to strike mezzo-level cooperative deals in a neocorporatist fashion, through the intermediation of the political patron. More importantly, business–labour relationships at sectoral or enterprise level (similar to the cooperation mechanisms found in the Japanese model) aimed at enhancing productivity continue to be absent from the Romanian political economy. Furthermore, the political cleavages described above go across economic sectors, and consequently political cleavages preclude not only the formation of peak associations at national level, but also contribute to the fragmentation of sectoral interest-group associations that have conflicting interests and have difficulties in cooperating towards a consistent and coherent sectoral industrial policy.

In this case, the state cannot act as a third party mediator between business and labour because of its symbiotic relationship with business, given the slow pace of privatization and the large proportion of SOEs in the economy. The state is in control of business in the public sector at all levels (i.e. at firm level, at sector level, and at national level). All SOE managers, sectoral federation and national confederation leaders need the formal or tacit approval of various state agencies, the two most important being the MIT and the State Ownership Fund. The first one virtually controls the largest employer association CONPIROM, which shares the same building as the MIT and is led by an ex-bureaucrat. The same bureaucratic origin is found for most sectoral federation leaders, who are not necessarily SOE managers, although they are elected by SOE managers in their sectors.

The lack of consistency characterizing state–labour relations in post-1989 Romania is easily understood when put in comparative perspective. The successful developmental and growth-oriented states, both in post-war Europe and East Asia, were those managing to compensate for the costs of transition and restructuring of the declining sectors of the economy by using the economic power of the state to steer economic development into new competitive sectors (Esping-Andersen and Friedland 1982, pp. 19–20). In contrast, the Romanian experience shows that the iron triangle of politicians, managers and trade union representatives in declining sectors led to the imposition of the costs of transition on politically weaker groups, while the state did not manage either to impede this process or to compensate for it by encouraging an economic policy reorientation towards viable sectors. A particularly distinctive example of this anti-developmental relationship between the state and entrenched labour interests is the case of Romanian coal miners, described below.

Mineriada: anti-developmental state–labour relations

Besides the factors determining the emerging type of capitalism embedded in the institutional framework of privatization mentioned in the previous section, an illustrative case-study for understanding the role of state and organized labour in Romania concerns the *Mineriadas*, the recurrent role of the coal miners' trade union from the Jiu Valley in the emerging capitalist system in Romania. *Mineriadas* represent a special case of state–organized labour relations that is both exceptional due to its magnitude and implications for the Romanian transition, and is also a typical but extreme example of the strategies employed by state actors and labour unions to influence the political process in Romania during the transition period. As will be seen below, *Mineriadas* proved to be a very useful case-study, allowing government–labour relations in Romania to be dissected and a distinction to be made between corporatism and clientelism in government–labour interactions.

Why are *Mineriadas* so important for understanding the emergent type of capitalism in Romania? What information can one draw from a violent protest movement that might shed some light on an apparently different question? The answer to these questions resides in the special interactions and links between different organized interest groups and the state, (which is a core question regarding the emerging type of capitalism).

Mineriada: still the century of proletarian dictatorship?

Before focusing on the motives and the significance of *Mineriadas* for the emerging type of capitalism in Romania, it is necessary to briefly describe the social context of the coal-mining industry in Romania. The principal coal basin is located in the Jiu Valley, in the south-east province of Oltenia. The Jiu Valley is a mono-industrial zone. Virtually all its inhabitants are dependent on this economic activity. This situation was created deliberately during the Stalinist planning period, based on a strong emphasis on heavy industries (steel, chemistry, and energy-intensive industries: see Crowther 1988). However, regardless of whether this strategy based on heavy industry and large-scale industrialization was appropriate or not during the 1950s, it certainly became increasingly difficult to sustain in the 1970s. The Romanian communist regime, as with others in the region, ignored all these signals and continued to expand coal production, for both steel and energy production, according to the slogan 'For our country, as much coal as feasible!' (PCR 1972, p. iv). Simultaneously, in propaganda material, coal miners were characterized as the 'leading group for the proletariat' (PCR 1975, p. 16). All these factors (the development of economic sectors dependent on coal production, the incentives given to miners) created a high level of expectation among miners, leading them to believe that their activity and their role were crucial for the national economy.

However, despite the official rhetoric, the economic competitiveness of Jiu Valley coal mining deteriorated. Due to intensive exploitation of the coal basin, the quality of the coal declined (Shafir 1985). In addition, the benefits for miners were diminished as a result of the drastic cuts in domestic consumption and investment required by the debt repayment plan. In the 1970s this led to a series of local labour conflicts that were unusual for communist Romania and could have set a dangerous precedent for the Ceauşescu regime (Deletant 1996). To avoid this, wages and other benefits were increased, but miners were put under surveillance by the Securitate. During the late 1970s and early 1980s, when the economic situation deteriorated, Securitate agents were infiltrated among the miners to prevent similar conflicts arising in the future.[30] As will be shown, these events had a long-lasting impact on the post-1990 economic and political transition in Romania.

The post-1990 evolution has radically changed not only the domestic situation but also the regional economic environment. The dismantling of the CMEA in 1990 severely reduced the export capabilities of several Romanian sectors, including those that used coal as one of their inputs. This led to a significant decrease in demand for coal and consequently a crisis of excess supply. When this new pressure was added to the existing low productivity as a result of obsolete technology, insufficient investment and the poor coal content of the Jiu Valley basin, a radical restructuring of the coal-mining sector became necessary for the Iliescu–Roman government in 1990–2.

This combination of a sensitive economic sector facing a prolonged decline, and political control after the ex-Securitate agents had infiltrated the miners, produced an unexpected outcome: coal miners became a powerful weapon for political pressure.[31] Immediately after the 1989 revolution, coal miners from the Jiu Valley took part in several riots, which culminated in their arrival in Bucharest to try to influence political life towards 'the right way'. These disturbances were called *Mineriadas*.[32]

During the *Mineriadas*, large numbers of coal miners, under the command of their trade union leaders, came to Bucharest and embarked on different violent activities aimed at annihilating or discouraging 'undesirable' political parties, movements or activities. Notorious results of *Mineriadas* have included the violent dispersion of a stubborn student strike, the forced resignation of the Prime Minister and his government, and the destruction of an opposition party headquarters. All of these events have made the headlines in the Western press, thus negatively impacting on Romania's image for many years (Gheorghe and Huminic 2000).

The first *Mineriada* started in late January to mid-February 1990, when opposition groups conducted political demonstrations against the governing National Salvation Front. Opponents of the regime mounted non-stop protests against it, in University Square in central Bucharest. President Iliescu declared them fascists and hooligans seeking to overthrow the government with violence, and called upon the Romanian workers to come to Bucharest to defend it (*Romania Libera* 1990, p. 1). Thousands of coal miners from the Jiu Valley promptly descended on the capital, where, together with workers from some local factories, they roamed the streets for two days attacking students, intellectuals, opposition party leaders and newspaper offices. The precise extent of collaboration between President Iliescu and the miners' leaders has always been vague, but he publicly praised and thanked them in a speech given in the midst of their rampage (BBC 1990).

In September 1991, angry at what they saw as broken promises to increase their pay and benefits in return for their services in the June 1990 *Mineriada*, the miners began a strike at their workplace, asking for the Prime Minister to come to the Jiu Valley and meet their demands. When the Prime Minister refused to do so, thousands of miners descended on the capital and four days of rioting ensued, in which the miners, joined by thousands of Bucharest residents, attacked government buildings with fire bombs, held mass rallies and generally took the city and government hostage. Faced with this chaos, Prime Minister Roman and his cabinet submitted their mandate to President Iliescu, who promptly accepted their resignation and appointed a new coalition government, headed by Theodor Stolojan, a respected economist.

Why were the miners able to provoke such major political turmoil in Romania? After all, other countries had larger coal-mining sectors, within similar political and economic contexts.

The reasons for this outcome are to be found in the political cleavages within the ruling party, and between it and opposition forces. During the 1990–1 period, President Iliescu's position was threatened both by opposition forces organizing anti-presidential demonstrations in Bucharest, and from within by Prime Minister Roman, who was seen as a reformist compared with the old-style, 'neo-communist' Iliescu. Confronted with such an uncertain political environment, Iliescu decided to take advantage of the political force represented by coal miners (*Romania Libera* 1990). As President, Iliescu was in charge of the army and other security forces, and the fact that both institutions (as well as the police force) turned a blind eye to the *Mineriadas* cannot be a coincidence.

Thus, the Jiu Valley coal miners were bestowed with powers that went beyond self-regulation and miners became a tool of political repression turned against uncomfortable political forces and their leaders. *Mineriadas* followed a distinct pattern of state–labour relations and showed how a powerful interest group can shape the outcome of political and economic transition for many years, when the state lends it extensive authoritarian powers that are generally the monopoly of the state. While *Mineriadas* resemble to a certain extent a state corporatist pattern (as defined by Schmitter 1977 and 1981), *Mineriadas* do not represent a case of neocorporatist state–society interaction, as found in the

Continental model of capitalism. While it is true that the attribution of public status to interest groups by the state is a distinguishing corporatist feature (Pryor 1988; Offe 1993, p. 123), this public status and delegation of state attributes to interest groups and trade unions is clearly circumscribed by interest-group self-regulation. However, in Romania the pattern of state–trade union interactions in the case of *Mineriadas* was far from the usual pattern of interactions common in the Continental style of capitalism at work in Germany and the Nordic countries. For that reason, the *Mineriadas* from the 1990–6 period more closely resemble the populist alliance between trade unions and charismatic politicians, such as Argentinean Peronism.[33] Iliescu's attempts to control and shape the post-1989 Romanian political system for the following years are comparable to the process of creation and utilization of authoritarian mechanisms for the generation of political consent and mass mobilization during the Peronist regime in Argentina. Like Peron in Argentina, Iliescu tried to generate political consensus in the context of a highly divided society, through the creation of a system of populist slogans and the mobilization of certain social sectors – such as the coal miners – that had seen their group status threatened by the new economic and political conditions. Just as with Peron, Iliescu's strategy even included repressive measures taken against those who refused to participate in Iliescu's consensual politics. These policies, however, not only failed to create consensus, but also further alienated the middle class and the intelligentsia.

Mineriada: 9 years after

Things changed, however, when the opposition coalition came into power. Some of the former victims of previous *Mineriadas* were now ministers. Being fully committed to democracy and the rule of law, and taking into account the above-mentioned incidents, unsurprisingly the new government tried to put an end to the special relations between the state and the miners. Moreover, the post-1996 governments have not developed such special relations in order to insulate themselves from social inputs, either in favour of or more likely against, painful reformist measures.

This change has actually been the first sign that the way in which the political system worked would also change, at least at the upper level. However, as will be shown, many institutions and bureaucratic practices remained unchanged, showing either an unwillingness or the inability of the new political elite to significantly alter the pre-1996 pattern of state–society relations.

That *Mineriadas* were not just a minor element in the political transition from communism to democratic capitalism in Romania is demonstrated by the return of the phenomenon 9 years later, against the same political actors now in power. It shows in fact the disadvantages of a political system characterized by a weak state and strong labour in promoting economic restructuring and necessary reform measures that are against the short-term interests of sectoral groups, as predicted by many authors (Katzenstein 1978, pp. 311–16; Dyson and Wilks 1983; Evans 1995).

The true clientelistic pattern of *Mineriadas* became clearer in January 1999 when a new *Mineriada* took place. Yet, unlike the pre-1996 *Mineriadas*, the 1999 incident was directed not against vocal opposition groups but against core state institutions (the presidency, executive and Parliament). As in the early 1990s, the same trade union leaders responded only to directives received more or less directly from populist party leaders.

This time the miners' strike started in protest against government plans to close some of the mines, as they had remained economically non-viable for years.[34] Encouraged by their charismatic leader, Miron Cozma, the coal miners once again set out on a *Mineriada* to Bucharest, intending to force the government to change its policy. On 20 January 1999, some 10,000 coal miners began a slow advance on the capital, battling police, smashing roadblocks and plunging the country into chaos (Cook 1999a).

The Interior Minister resigned after police failed to halt the miners' caravan in a bloody, tear-gas choked encounter west of Bucharest (AFP 1999a). Faced with the prospect of the capital in ruins, on 22 January Prime Minister Vasile reversed his refusal to negotiate personally with the miners and met Cozma at a monastery west of Bucharest where he agreed to Cozma's demands, said to include a 30 per cent pay rise, the reopening of two mines previously closed, the freezing of layoffs and the spending of hundreds of millions of dollars of EU development funds on projects in the Jiu Valley (Cook 1999d).

The agreement averted a declaration of a national emergency by President Constantinescu and a virtually certain deadly clash with the army, which awaited the miners on the road to Bucharest. The labour dispute had threatened to ignite a social crisis of immense proportions. It was widely feared that disaffected workers in other industries, who were also facing the elimination of their jobs, might revolt as well. Even darker allegations were made: that the miners' action was intended to spark a *coup d'état* and that some ultra-nationalist politicians, namely the leader of the Greater Romania Party (Romania Mare), Corneliu Vadim Tudor, were allied with Cozma (Cook 1999b). Cozma, who was expelled from Romania Mare, denied these allegations and, to date, no such conspiracy has been proven (Rompress 1999).

Cozma returned to the Jiu Valley a hero, but within a month he was in prison. This dramatic turn of events came as a result of a Romanian Supreme Court decision. The court sentenced Cozma to 18 years in prison for 'undermining state power' during the 1991 *Mineriada* (Cook 1999c). Cozma's arrest and imprisonment appear to mark the end of a violent Romanian transition to capitalism and democracy (Porte 1999b). Due to the previous state–society relations promoted during 1990–6, and embodied by Iliescu's party and Miron Cozma's miners, the reverberations of this labour conflict went beyond the restructuring of the mining industry (Patapievici 1999a). Coal-mining restructuring also happened in other East-Central European transition economies and yet the event did not lead to incidents such as those that threatened the existence of democracy in Romania. *Mineriadas* were so significant that they led some political commentators in Romania to compare the 1999 events with the fragility of the Weimar Republic (Patapievici 1999b; Tanase 2000).[35]

This example of public status attribution to an interest group by the state may look at first sight to be a perverse case of corporatism. In a normal pattern of corporatist intermediation (such as that described by Offe 1993 in the German case), interest groups in 'organized capitalism' may be requested to assume an active role in legislation, policy planning or implementation concerning the governance of their sectoral economic activity. However, two elements make *Mineriadas* a case of clientelism or a case of perverted corporatism rather than the classical Continental-style societal corporatism. The *Mineriadas* show sufficient evidence to render them a case of state corporatism based upon an extreme type of licensing public responsibilities to a particular group. Rarely is it found in quasi-democratic regimes that the state 'franchises' what remains at the core of Weber's definition of the state: the legitimate use of violence. First, in the case of *Mineriadas*, coal miners were vested with a far-reaching task, well beyond the role played by trade unions in the Continental capitalist model: to impose 'consensus' through violence, reducing to silence other societal interest groups. Second, although the miners seemed to be generally anti-government, Miron Cozma's miners represented more than a case of 'private-interest government' (Streeck and Schmitter 1985, pp. 1–29), serving the political purposes of various political forces.

Tripartite clientelism: asset-stripping and the parasite firm

Tripartite clientelism affected not only the institutional architecture of state-labour relations; it also affected the microeconomic conditions of many SOEs. An important feature of state–labour relations in Romania is the fusion between state, business and labour interests in the public sector. The key players making the tripartite link are SOE managers, who are under double political control. The most obvious political control mechanism of SOE managers is through the State Ownership Fund, which is the major shareholder directly representing the state. The less obvious one is through the company boards, which are populated by a large number of parliamentarians and high-ranking bureaucrats. Therefore SOE managers are in a very close relationship with individual politicians who develop a direct interest in all the firms for which they act as board directors.

The politicization of company boards is a very plausible explanation for the creation of iron triangles between SOE managers, politicians and trade union leaders. The same relationship explains the perpetuation for 10 years of soft loans to loss-making SOEs that almost bankrupted certain state-owned banks, the widespread tax evasion and the lack of enforcement of bankruptcy laws.

SOE managers also have much to gain from being on good terms with the unions. Trade union autonomy and power at enterprise level were constantly eroded by managers who were ready to offer several personal advantages to trade union leaders in exchange for a non-aggression pact. One common concession offered to trade union leaders was to coopt them (along with politicians) into the asset-stripping process of their own state-owned enterprise. This mechanism will be explained in detail using the case of SIDEX, the largest steel plant in Romania.[36]

This pattern of interaction shows quite clearly that trade union leaders and managers and state officials are neither in opposite camps, as in Anglo-Saxon capitalism, nor in institutionalized tripartism, as in Continental capitalism, but have rather become business associates. This 'perverted tripartism' is clear in the special case of a 'parasite' firm. In the classical situation, SOE managers use the SOE assets to shift profits to their own 'letter-box companies'. In this tripartite parasite firm, state officials, trade unions and SOE managers create their own company in a sector that is usually characterized by high market-entry barriers. These monopolistic or oligopolistic rents are then captured 'legally' through the market mechanism by actors who are usually involved in other types of contacts: clientelism, bribery, lobbying in the case of state–capital relations, or conflict and bargaining in the case of state–labour and business–labour relations. Unlike the SOF case, this time not only did the state become captured by private interests, but so too did the trade unions.

The same mechanism was applied to other cases where state–business–labour triangles were formed with the sole purpose of asset-stripping. Trade union leaders exploited their insider information on clientelistic relations between managers and political patrons and they offered their complicity for a share of the illegal benefits. Unlike enterprise directors in countries such as Czechoslovakia and Poland, where SOE reform laws enabled the Communist Party to remove underperforming managers as early as 1989, Romania had no such opportunity. Here, enterprise insiders – managers and employee – had both the incentive and the power to defend themselves against any attempts to reallocate property rights through rapid privatization. Workers, due to the absence of flexible labour markets and the direct provision of housing and other social services by enterprises, were extremely vulnerable and could not constitute a distinctive group with interests opposed to management. Consequently, workers and managers together constituted a strong pressure group, which aimed at ensuring that they, as enterprise insiders, received the numerous privileges that made their way into the MPP. Even in firms that were not included in the programme, workers' representatives and managers were frequently united either in asset-stripping or in their common struggle to bargain for more subsidies and other forms of state support.

Stripping assets at SIDEX

To illustrate this mechanism, it is useful to consider, for instance, the case of SIDEX. This example clearly shows the *asset stripping networks* that exist in some sectors of the Romanian economy, not only between state and capital but also including organized labour. SIDEX Galati is one of the largest steel-making companies in Central and Eastern Europe and obviously one of the largest SOEs in Romania, based on its workforce and its activities. At the same time, SIDEX is the second largest loss-making SOE in Romania. This combination of factors rendered SIDEX one of the most difficult restructuring cases for all post-1989 Romanian governments.[37] This situation certainly has many economic causes, but one factor that should not be neglected is the anti-developmental pattern of state–business–labour relations that eroded the profitability of this SOE. The key to understanding this tripartite relationship is the functioning of a typical SOE.[38]

State-owned companies inherited from the socialist system a corporate structure that was poorly adapted to a market economy. The main activity of an industrial SOE was limited to production. Since in the socialist system production was planned and distributed in a centralized manner by line ministries, management and marketing departments in individual enterprises were disproportionately small in their productive capacities. This situation persisted in the first years after 1989. To correct the situation, instead of upgrading the SOE marketing departments, the method that prevailed was to outsource the marketing to private companies, thus creating a distribution network. This is the economic basis for the most widespread form of clientelist relations in Romania.

SIDEX followed this strategy very soon after 1989, but obtaining a licence as an authorized SIDEX distributor was not easy and was not solely based on economic criteria. Many local politicians and parliamentarians managed to obtain lucrative contracts for their own companies as official SIDEX distributors.[39] However, these private companies were often just letter-box companies, which did not have the necessary storage and transportation facilities required for the handling of bulky steel products. However, based on their political connections, these letter-box companies received storage and transportation facilities from SIDEX. Thanks to this fruitful cooperation, the SIDEX manager who initiated the process became a senator for PDSR soon afterwards. The clientelist relations were further required to obtain an export licence since the export of Romanian steel products to the EU market was restricted by quotas. The same politicians were therefore in charge of obtaining an export licence from the MIT and Trade. This method of asset-stripping functioned very well until 1996, during the period of Leftist coalition government. SIDEX was thus stripped of its profits by intermediary companies who bought the steel cheaply in Romania and sold it for good money on the protected EU market. Although the SIDEX workers were not directly involved in this asset-stripping, they received generous salaries and state subsidies, as a reward for their acquiescence in this process.

After 1996, the same clientelistic mechanism continued with centre-Right local politicians and parliamentarians, who were aware of the profitability of getting involved in the steel business but were not allowed do so by their political opponents. Consequently, after 1996 the asset-stripping process continued with other political actors. However, the 1996 elections brought to power a centre-Right wing government with an ambitious restructuring programme. One of the first measures of the new government was an attempt to reduce the budget deficit and the inflationary pressure of inefficient wage increases and state subsidies.

This new macroeconomic environment added some strain to the asset-stripping process. First, the production flow was hampered by the difficulties that SIDEX had in paying its suppliers, including the state-owned electricity company, RENEL. Second, the workers started to complain and protest against what they considered to be incompetent managers and mistaken economic policies. The first problem was soon surpassed by the asset-stripping clientelist structures, since SIDEX was allowed to accumulate massive debts: SIDEX did not pay its utilities bills or other contributions to the state budget (pension contributions for its workers, unemployment contributions). Thus the direct state subsidies were replaced by hidden state subsidies.

The problems created by workers had to be dealt with in a different manner. Salaries were more visible than the hidden subsidies and a wage increase at SIDEX would generate a chain movement for a wage increase in other SOEs. The solution found was very ingenious: official SIDEX distributors started to pay SIDEX for the steel products using in-kind payments. Barter trade was concluded at lower prices in both senses: steel products were bought cheaper and in-kind payments were also sold cheaper. These cheaper products, in the form of food and electronic goods, were then given to the employees as part of their salaries. Workers were happy to see that, using this barter trade, their purchasing power increased, even though often they had to receive more than one television set or refrigerator. These products were then resold at an intermediary price on the open market.

In this state–business–workers triangle the only losses were registered by SIDEX, which became unprofitable, and by the state budget, which did not receive taxes from SIDEX. After 1990, the asset-stripping process was the only profitable part of SIDEX. Nobody tried to upgrade the technology or open new avenues to ensure the survival of this huge SOE. No efforts were made to streamline the production structure or to improve labour productivity by laying off inefficient workers. The result is a company that, today, despite a high percentage of exports from total production, is a major loss-making SOE in Romania.

Conclusions

The Romanian labour movement has represented a paradoxical mixture of strengths and weaknesses. Given their degree of fragmentation, underfunding, uncertain membership and ideological cleavages, the Romanian labour movement hardly fits into a government–industry corporatist framework. However, to conclude that government–trade unions relations in Romania can be characterized as pluralist or statist (because of trade union organizational weaknesses) would be too simplistic, because this conclusion would overlook some central features related to state weaknesses and privileged clientelistic relationships cultivated between political actors and organized labour. Indeed, both the Romanian trade unions and state actors had weaknesses that did not allow them to reap the benefits of normal corporatist interaction.

With the exception of *Mineriadas*, state–labour relations in Romania are far from being corporatist, regardless of what prefix is attached: 'state', 'neo', 'liberal', 'democratic' or 'social'. This is because neither the system of interest representation (as understood by Schmitter 1979, p. 13) nor the pattern of policy-formation (in the sense of Lehmbruch 1979, p. 150, Pryor 1988, p. 317, or Woldendorp 1997, pp. 49–50) are corporatist. None of the main ingredients identified by the corporatist literature really characterize state–labour relations in Romania.

The existing trade unions do not take a coordinated approach in their relations with the state and government and are highly divided along political lines. There is virtually no institutionalized input of business and labour in the government policy process, including the drawing-up of the budget. In fact, the state only nominally recognizes business and labour as being joint 'social partners' (Katzenstein 1985, pp. 87–8) since in reality their views are not incorporated in the policy-making process. In these conditions, trade unions react as having neither formal rights nor responsibilities, as opposed to a strong social consensual policy style. Therefore, despite the long-term political role of the Communist Party and a subsequent Social Democratic Party that produced a Leftist political infrastructure, Romania is far from being a corporatist polity.

In turn, during 1990–2 *Mineriadas* were an extreme strategy to use a well organized interest group for broader, undemocratic purposes. This 'perverted' corporatist arrangement resembled the Peronist period in Argentina. The *Mineriadas* of the early 1990s can be seen as a case of state corporatism, whereby coal miners were allowed and encouraged by the state to impose 'consensus' through violence. The second wave of *Mineriadas* during 1999 showed that the same political allegiance involved in the earlier state corporatist arrangement led the coal miners to engage in what many commentators have called a *coup d' etat*.

State–labour relations in Romania are not developmental either since the lack of a strong performance-based work ethic for trade unions and the non-existence of an export-oriented strategy for the state hampered any effort to promote economic development. There is little attempt by the state or interest groups to identify and promote strategic industrial sectors that need special industrial policy measures, and to curtail sectors and enterprises that are not viable. The state is over involved in bargaining with labour at enterprise level such that we cannot consider Romanian state–labour interaction to follow an Anglo-Saxon pattern. The trade unions are more powerful and organized than in a typical Anglo-Saxon capitalist economy and social democratic values are stronger.

What really characterizes state–labour relations in Romania is political clientelism, short-termism and a rent-seeking behaviour manifested in a 'subsidy/wage increase for silence' equilibrium between state and labour. In conclusion, the inherent tendency towards fragmentation and the lack of representation (in the case of business associations) have precluded these interest-group associations from becoming effective regulatory and enforcing agencies in their fields, one of the defining conditions of 'liberal corporatist' state–societal arrangements. In short, Romanian state–societal arrangements may be characterized as clientelist, power-sharing and as an ineffective form of societal bargaining.

State–finance relations

As shown previously, differences in the financial system are key elements that distinguish between the Anglo-Saxon model on one hand, and the Continental and developmental model on the other. It goes almost without saying that the financial and banking sectors represent crucial elements in the functioning of an economy, for its performance and development prospects. Most influential and durable theories of economic growth have emphasized the role of capital formation in ensuring a good economic performance.

The starting point of transition is typically a financial sector dominated by banks that were owned directly by the state. These banks provided resources, in the form of credits, mainly to state-owned enterprises, enjoying the explicit or implicit guarantee of the state. They had little or no risk-management skills and produced accounts under an accounting system designed to facilitate production planning, as opposed to illuminating their financial condition. As a result, the socialist banks, although closely controlled politically, were subject to little or no regulatory supervision. Their role in the economy was to provide funding, as directed, for the central economic plan. This starting point is also characterized by an absence of legal infrastructure, including collateral and bankruptcy legislation defining debtors' and creditors' rights, and little or no securities market activity.

The final objective of transition was to create a financial system that would be familiar to a European or an American banker. It is mainly characterized by private banks, offering a wide range of sophisticated financial products, supported by strong collateral, bankruptcy and other laws, publishing accounts on a sophisticated basis acceptable under international standards. These banks are subject to prudential standards enforced by an effective regulatory system administered with some seriousness, normally by a modernized central bank. The terminal point also involves relatively deep and well-regulated securities markets, dealing in government paper and private debt and equity issues, as well as some significant level of specialized finance, private insurance and pension activity.

Although this sounds good in theory, the practical experience of transition thus far suggests, however, that the journey from socialist banking to capitalist banking is not simple. Post-communist countries' credit markets were still in their early stages of development. External channels of financing were limited and, in the early years of transition, close to non-existent in many post-communist countries, so governments were forced to maintain a certain level of intervention in credit markets. Thus the continuation of hierarchically organized government intervention in the form of low interest rates and state-backed credit was justified by the belief that it would result in a smoother and less painful transition. Governments may also intervene to target strategic sectors important for national development or industrial goals.[40]

However, state intervention is not always beneficial. Although governments may intervene in targeted ways to further development, their actions could also have the same consequences as rent-seeking behaviour: namely, inefficient allocation of resources and financing decisions that are not based on sound market principles. Worse still, in clientelistic regimes politicians may intervene in financial markets and maintain ownership of banks in order to enhance electoral prospects and reward political supporters.[41]

While these patterns of state–bank relations are found in all transition economies, the transition process has certain unique circumstances in each of the CEECs. The content, sources and uses of banking regulations are all very different, as are the observed behaviour patterns of bankers, industry and bank regulators. The remainder of this chapter will focus on the case of state–banking relations in Romania. The next section describes the introduction in Romania of a market-based banking system and its main characteristics. Then, in the following sections attention is focused on the features of the emerging Romanian banking

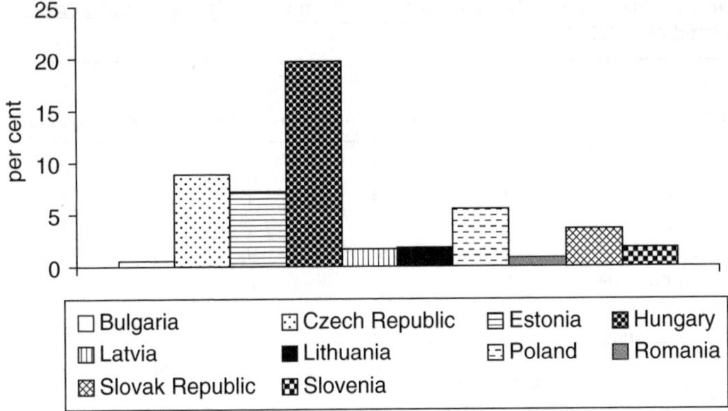

Figure 3.4   Stock market capitalization in CEECs, 1998–2003
Source: World Bank (2004b).

system, its failures and their determinants. The analysis will address
issues such as the establishment of business relationships between
bankers and politicians, and the role played by political influences in
the application of sanctions by banking regulators.

In search of a model: the Romanian case

In shaping its post-communist banking system, Romania had a choice
between two broad financial models: a credit-based or a stock-market
oriented system. In fact, the choice of a financial system, together with
privatization, dominated the debate regarding the appropriate model of
capitalism.

Given the starting point of transition, the natural choice between
these two models of financial systems was the credit-based model.[42]
While the banking system was underdeveloped and state-run, stock
markets were non-existent in communist countries. However, unlike
other CEECs that used their stock markets extensively as part of their
overall privatization process (Hungary, the Czech Republic, Estonia), in
Romania the stock market remained marginal (Figure 3.4). Even after
1998, when the stock market was introduced as one of the privatization
methods, the ratio of stocks traded to GDP (a common measure of
equity market development) remained below 1 per cent of GDP.[43] This
indicator in itself is a proxy measure of the models of capitalism that are
emerging across CEECs. Some countries tend to evolve towards a more
stock-market oriented capitalist system, while others (such as Romania
and Bulgaria) are clearly bank-oriented.

Table 3.7   Structure of the banking system in the early transition period, 1989–2 (selected countries)

Number of state-owned:	Romania	Czechoslovakia	Hungary	Poland	Bulgaria	Russia
Commercial banks	4	2	3	9	59	5
Foreign trade banks	1	3	1	3	1	1
Savings banks	1	2	1	1	1	1
Specialized banks	1	1	10	3	8	3
Number of private banks	9	43	32	72	7	2,200
With foreign stakes	5	18	18	7	3	n.a.
Total number of banks	16	51	47	88	76	2,210
Percentage of state banks' assets in total bank assets	80	43	75	89	n.a.	n.a.
Bank concentration[a]	0.80	0.77/0.88[b]	0.70	0.50	0.80	0.49

n.a. = not available.

[a] *Concentration* is measured as the ratio of the three largest banks' assets to total banking sector assets. A highly concentrated commercial banking sector might result in a lack of competitive pressure to attract savings and channel them efficiently to investors. A highly fragmented market might be evidence for undercapitalized banks. The data are averaged for the available years in the period 1990–97.

[b] The first figure is for the Czech Republic, the second for Slovakia.

Sources: Bloomestein and Spencer (1994); Caprio (1995); Beck, Demirgüç-Kunt and Levine (1999).

As the subsequent discussion will show, in Romania the choice of a predominantly bank-oriented financial system found support in the patterns of interest intermediation between major political and economic actors. Since in Romania the stock market was introduced only in 1997 and remained a marginal element in the Romanian financial system thereafter, the analysis is aimed at providing a detailed description of the functioning of Romania's banking sector (the main source of capital) and, more importantly, aimed at the understanding of Romania's economic problems through an extensive account of the malfunctioning encountered in the banking sector.

As shown in Table 3.7, Romania has maintained a highly concentrated banking system in the early years of transition, having the smallest number of banks across the region. The number of private banks was equally low compared to other transition economies, as was their share in total bank assets. The Romanian market continued to remain oligopolistic, banking being concentrated in the hands of the three biggest state-owned banks, who owned 80 per cent of total bank assets. Not surprisingly, given the general reluctance of the government to encourage foreign investment in general, foreign participation in the banking sector remained limited and confined to foreign bank subsidiaries. The importance of foreign penetration in the banking sector is well evidenced in Demirgüç-Kunt, Levine and Min (1998), who show that higher foreign-bank penetration enhances economic growth by boosting domestic banking efficiency. However, state-owned banks in Romania were not included in the privatization programme until the late 1990s, and therefore the benefits of foreign bank penetration were not attained.

The number of banks in Romania remained relatively low compared to the number in Russia, for instance, or even that in Poland or Bulgaria, and not only in the early stages of transition but also up to 10 years after. Thus, in 2001, there were 54 banks operating in Romania, out of which 23 were domestic private banks, seven were state-owned and 24 were subsidiaries or branches of foreign parent banks. The new domestic private banks continued to remain small and fragile, as evidenced by the high incidence of licences withdrawn and bankruptcies among them, compared to state-owned banks or foreign subsidiaries (although state-owned banks also had asset illiquidity problems due to their inheritance of loans to increasingly troubled state-owned firms in the pre-liberalizing period). However, although banks were permitted to function as German-style universal banks, they generally avoided investment in enterprise equity and usually preferred to be bailed out by the government in one way or another. One reason for this lack of German-style cross-ownership stems largely from the reluctance of banks to own large stakes in SOEs whose future situation and economic performance were highly uncertain. Therefore, despite the fact that Romania moved slowly towards liberalizing its banking sector, the transformation from rigid state control to a free market system has been far from smooth and is far from complete. As shown below, central to the unsuccessful transformation was the emergence of a weak, unstable, poorly regulated banking system in which bank credit was still largely allocated based not on creditworthiness but on political interference.

The main problems

The banking system that emerged in Romania in the early years of transition was, as in many other cases in Eastern Europe, an extreme example of government-controlled banking. Gradually, however, and at different paces across the regions, the break-up of the mono- or state bank system resulted in the creation of a commercial banking system blended with a hint of investment banking. In the emerging transition, financial and banking systems faced several difficulties, as a result of two types of problem. The first type of problem occurred as a result of either too many (as a bank owner) or too few (as regulator) state interventions. The most pervasive problems that hampered the ability of the financial and banking sector to act as a catalyst for economic growth were the political economy of elite interaction, the soft budget constraints and financial repression. The second type of problem is related to the weak regulatory capacity and can generally be described as bank fraud.

Financial repression.   A systemic characteristic that may arise in state-controlled banking systems such as that in Romania is financial repression. On the one hand, financial repression is a reference to a specific set of policies involving a variety of controls on the activities of the main financial institutions in an economy. In simple terms, financial repression means heavy regulatory pressure to deal with issues that could be left to market forces. On the other hand, as will become evident from the subsequent discussion, financial repression does not ensure the minimum regulatory framework, such as contract enforcement, clear property rights, efficient banking supervision, transparent accounting, and so on. Policies of low administered interest rates have often been labelled 'financial repression', the suppression of market-based supply/demand mechanisms for credit and finance.[44] The theoretical motivation of free-market oriented financial reforms aimed at curtailing government

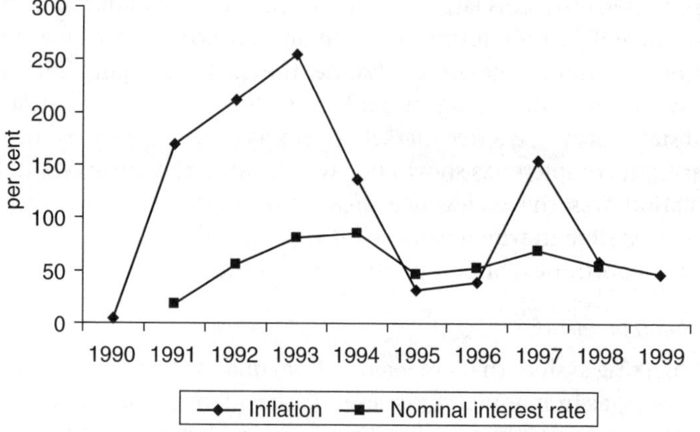

Figure 3.5   Financial repression in Romania: negative real interest rates
Source: National Bank of Romania (various Annual Statistical Reports).

intervention has its roots in the literature on financial repression (McKinnon 1973; Fry 1988). This theory holds that, in state-controlled credit markets, interest rates are artificially low (and even negative in an inflationary environment). This in turn discourages savings both by individuals and by companies.

Figure 3.5 illustrates one major aspect of financial repression: low administered interest rates. As can be seen, with the exception of 1995 and 1996 where nominal interest rates were above the inflation rate (positive real interest rate), throughout the rest of the 1991–8 period (where data are available for bank nominal interest rates), real interest rates were negative, favouring debtors and decapitalizing banks and depositors. Although several factors might contribute to this situation, one can reasonably assume that state-owned banks were 'forced' to grant loans to SOEs at lower interest rates than a free-market based banking system would sustain.[45]As saving is depressed, investment is constrained by an insufficient supply of credit. In such circumstances, since repressed financial regimes are characterized by direct government control of credit, it is quite likely that resources are allocated on the basis of political rather than efficiency considerations. The financial repression argument concludes that growth is retarded because of both the low quantity and low quality of investment.

Certain legacies of the socialist financial system suggest this possibility. First, the banking sector remained among the more state-controlled parts of these economies, with few governments having taken steps towards their full privatization. Thus the line between 'public' and 'private' finance often remains unclear, with governments prompting banks to act as quasi-fiscal agents of the state through interest-rate controls or, more directly, through directed credit programmes. In the post-communist transition economies, moreover, financial repression may be used less as a source of cheap money for public deficits, and more as a means of maintaining a soft banking system that essentially absorbs enterprise losses in the short run.

Although the theoretical foundation of financial repression is quite strong, the empirical analysis of such policies does not easily lend itself to systematic study. A manifest example of this interplay and balance of financial and political interests is where government policies are in favour of development and try to maintain artificially low interest rates (rates below market equilibrium) for strategic industrial sectors. Low interest rates raise the demand for capital, when the government is able to influence its allocation by rule and administration. The question is whether such low interest rates inherently dampen the supply of capital and distort its allocation by politically motivated loans, or whether they create 'opportunities' that induce economically efficient actions which private markets would not undertake because of a divergence between private and social returns (Hellman, Murdock and Stiglitz 1995).

Based on this distinction, Hellman, Murdock and Stiglitz (1995) differentiate between two types of preferential credit schemes. One, discussed above, is 'financial repression', with its *transfers* to government or political supporters. They distinguish that from 'financial restraint', which generates profit opportunities for banks and businesses. In financial repression, government actors extract rents from the private sector and re-allocate them to themselves or their supporters. In contrast, financial *restraint* can generate wealth-creating opportunities that drive real growth.[46] Thus, it is possible to refer to 'wealth-creating' rents, and differentiate them from 'transfer rents'. Hellman, Murdock and Stiglitz (1995) argue, however, that what is important is not simply the policy of administratively lowered interest rates, but also whether the rents are wealth-creating or simply transfers.

Yet, as the following section clearly shows, financial repression in Romania did little by way of wealth creation, and much more in terms of transfers to politically-connected private pockets.

The soft budget constraints. Stemming partly from the existence of financial repression, a related problem affecting the establishment of an efficient banking system capable of promoting sustainable economic growth is the persistence of soft budget constraints.[47]

Several recent studies (including Borish, Ding and Noël 1996; Anderson and Kegels 1998) have stressed that the state continues to dominate the banking sector of CEECs, both in terms of ownership and

Table 3.8   Non-performing loans across CEECs (as % of total loans)

Country	1994	1995	1996	1997
Bulgaria	7	13	15	13
Croatia	12	13	11	10
Czech Republic	34	33	30	29
Hungary	18	10	7	4
Poland	29	21	13	10
Romania	19	38	48	57
Slovakia	30	41	32	33
Slovenia	22	13	14	12

Source: EBRD (1998), p. 133.

macroeconomic influence but also at a microeconomic level in credit decisions. This situation becomes obvious when looking at the proportion of non-performing loans. Table 3.8 shows the evolution of non-performing loans, in terms of total loans (i.e., as a share of total loans) over a 4-year period (1994–7), in selected Eastern European countries.

As shown in Table 3.8, with the exception of Romania, all the other countries in the sample have more or less constant or declining values of non-performing loans. Romania remains an atypical case not only because the share of non-performing loans has steadily increased over time, but also because the values are relatively higher than those of most other countries throughout the period examined (with the exception of the beginning of the period).

As noted previously, one characteristic of socialist banking was the irrelevance of credit risk assessment by banks for the simple reason that central planning managed to compensate one way or another through state intervention. Assuming that, even during transition, most non-performing loans are granted as a result of state intervention in the banking system, data on non-performing loans are a good indicator of distortions introduced by political interference in banking operations.

The disparity between Romania and other countries was accentuated in 1996–7, with the share of non-performing loans in Romania as high as ten times that in Hungary.[48] Although there may be other causes for this high share of non-performing loans, these data provide information on the state–industry–finance relationships and suggest a highly interventionist government modifying the incentives of the two sides of the credit market (banks and SOEs), and reducing their risk aversion. While this may be beneficial in certain exceptional situations when business confidence needs to be established, in the case of Romania, the experience of state intervention in the credit market and the associated number of non-performing loans in the last decade has shown that the problem was not one of temporary exceptional measures. Instead, these causes were systemic and had to do with the state acting as a guarantor for these non-performing loans to loss-making SOEs. This situation became so endemic that Romania witnessed several spectacular crashes of banks and other financial institutions.[49] Faced with the possibility that many other banks would collapse, the government had to bail the banks out. The financial effort involved in this process was considerable: in 1999, for instance, the losses at Banca Agricola that had to be covered by the government amounted to around 10 per cent of the state budget.

This is a crucial element in understanding the link between institution, policies and economic outcome. Institutional links similar to those in the Asian 'developmental capitalist' system, based on heavy state intervention, produced the very detrimental outcome in Romania. The best explanation for this is probably that offered by Amsden (1989), when she argues that what matters is not the degree of state intervention but rather the type of the interventionist policy. Unlike a developmental strategy based on state intervention in favour of 'national champions', by offering subsidized credit to enterprises conditional upon strong economic performance in Romania, political pressure was exercised to give loans either to loss-making SOEs or to politically connected individuals. In any case there was no conditionality attached to the loan, and no monitoring activity on enterprise creditworthiness. Therefore, under such conditions, state interventionism had little to do with Asian developmentalism. Instead, it was purely predatory and rent-seeking behaviour.

How was this situation possible? Why did the central bank, which is the key institution in charge of monitoring the efficient functioning of the banking system, allow such a disastrous situation to become widespread across the state-owned banking sector? Are all the answers to be found in the irresponsible and predatory behaviour of the political class? In fact, the greed of politicians and their bad judgements offer only half of the answer; the other half lies in the greed of bank managers. Close state–banking relations created a mutual interdependence between bankers and politicians that gave bank managers full immunity from any legal or audit control. Consequently, bank managers had room for all sorts of illegal financial operations.

Conclusions

All the case studies described above suggest that the economic decline in Romania is determined by growth-inhibiting factors, such as predatory politicians and clientelistic ties between SOEs, the political classes and the banking system. One last figure should show the extent to which this practice has become rampant in the last few years in Romania. In 1999, two major state-owned banks have been brought to near-bankruptcy, declaring default on their payments. The government had the choice between declaring the banks bankrupt, or bailing them out. The government chose the latter and paid around US $3 billion to cover these 'black holes' (Serbanescu 1999).

How much do these losses mean for Romania? It is enough to say that the entire state budget in 1999 was around US $7 billion, and covering these losses probably meant a drastic reduction in budget allocation for many crucial elements of a developmental strategy. Diverting around 40 per cent from the state budget to cover these losses surely meant an increase in what was already a hyper-inflationary situation in the following period, with damaging effects on the entire economy. Furthermore, this decision probably meant a drastic reduction in the budgetary allocation for other sectors: education, infrastructure, research and development.

All too often, bank crises such as those described below were attributed to fraud and mismanagement on the part of bank directors, but the problem was not that the managers did not know or suspect the problems they were about to face; on the contrary, the problems were clear for many people in decision-making positions. What hampered any precautionary measure taken, once these early warning signals appeared, was that those heading the bank into a crisis were too well-placed politically or too well connected. Therefore, supervisors were not able to take a determinate course of action against a negative outcome.

This regulatory weakness occurred because basic conditions of a functioning bank-based system, as found in the Continental model of capitalism, were not in place. Retrospectively, both the initial conditions and the subsequent evolution of the Romanian financial system do not suggest that a stock-based financial system would have been a better choice for Romania. Even though direct political interference would be less feasible in a stock-based financial system, the regulatory challenges are much more daunting, as the recent US corporate governance crisis has demonstrated.

Financial restructuring, privatization and deregulation are not always, as the case of Romania has proved, unequivocal solutions to the transition problems. Instead of increasing efficiency in the sector, deregulation created rent-seeking opportunities due to unstable rules and codes in credit and foreign exchange markets. The financial sector became a source of wealth accumulation for the politically connected elite who used their position in the political spectrum to get a head start in the licensing of new banks, to create monopolies, and to conduct illicit financial dealings. As rent-seeking took precedence over productive financial intermediation, the financial system became more exposed to financial fragility. Financial liberalization, which was expected to help pull the country out of economic stagnation, eventually accentuated the economic crisis and further weakened the financial and banking sector.

Despite the special developmental role that an efficient bank-based financial system could play, the reality after a decade of transition showed that Romanian banks are not the source of dynamic corporate governance reform that some had hoped to see. Unlike the Continental or developmental models of capitalism, in Romania signs of inspiring leadership by the financial sector in reforming SOEs were few.

This section has presented evidence that the impact of political factors on banking has been far more significant in Romania than in mature financial systems. In particular, it has been shown that state-owned enterprises remained a highly significant category of borrowers for banks until privatization, and their creditworthiness had little significance in credit allocation decisions. Furthermore, political influences on credit allocation inhibit the growth of essential credit analysis and risk assessment skills in general. Instead, they encourage the continuous nurturing of closer bank relationships with the politicians and bureaucrats who control the fate of these enterprises and determine the risk of default. In practical terms, bankers rely heavily on these political relationships, rather than developing the necessary technical credit monitoring and other information processing skills.[50]

Indeed, such skills are likely to be regarded as an unnecessary luxury. Political influences on the application of sanctions by banking regulators also place a premium on the establishment of cosy and lucrative relationships between bankers and politicians. The reluctance of politicians to apply sanctions against banks that are in trouble until the last possible moment is thereby intensified and, in its turn, this encourages excessive risk-taking when banks first encounter financial difficulties, and asset-stripping when the insiders realize that a bank's continued viability is in jeopardy.

All of these examples have shown quite clearly that successive Romanian governments intervened in the banking sector to provide transfers to its evident supporters, regardless of the economic consequences of such policies. Unlike a developmental-oriented government, the Romanian state did not seek to generate the possibilities of wealth creation for a larger set of firms or for strategic sectors. The result was that financial repression dampened growth without creating marketplace winners and driving development. Thus, the creation of the coalitions to support growth, and the character of the market dynamics, were the missing ingredients in Romanian 'cocktail capitalism'.

In sum, the analysis undertaken so far has shown that this negative outcome was a direct consequence of the incomplete policy choices. Moreover, as will be show later, these policy options are constrained by the frictions between the policy preferences of international institutions and domestic elites. Whereas the former are exerting their influence in order to accelerate the integration of Romania into the world economy and stimulate the adoption of neoliberal policies, the latter are more concerned with stabilizing their own position and resisting change.

4
External Policy Transfer and Economic Growth: Reconceptualizing External Influences

The previous chapters looked in detail at the domestic institutional factors determining the emerging type of capitalism – the relationships between state, labour and capital – and their impact on economic performance in CEECs throughout the past decade. Moreover, the empirical analysis on Romania carried out in the previous chapter showed that, although sharing features common to all three major capitalist systems, the emerging type of capitalism in Romania never managed to emulate the efficient mechanisms of the main models of capitalism at work in developed economies. The emerging Romanian system of 'cocktail capitalism' was a model of partial reforms and mal-functioning institutions. Instead of creating incentives and political support for further reforms and the emergence of growth-oriented elites, it maintained the mechanisms for private rent-seeking and clientelistic reallocation of assets.

Yet, as mentioned in the Introduction, in addition to these domestic factors, the economic transformation and institutional adaptation taking place in transition economies, together with the shape of the emerging capitalist systems across Central and Eastern Europe, are also influenced by external factors. Models of capitalism adopted in CEECs are determined not only by the domestic conditions prevalent in each transition economy, but also by the interaction between these domestic and international forces, such as globalization and Europeanization.

So far, this theoretical debate has been conducted to a large extent as if CEECs, in their systemic transformation, were somehow marginally involved in the international arena. Apart from acknowledging that the demise of the Cold War and the collapse of the communist system gave way to the reintegration of this region into a globalized world, these analyses fall short of integrating CEECs into the main academic debates about the impact of (and linkages between) globalization and Europeanization on domestic institutions, policies and policy making. Moreover, the insights from conceptual research on the impact of 'Europeanization' on domestic change in the member states (Knill and Lehmkuhl 1999; Börzel and Risse 2000) have not yet been applied to the CEECs.[1] As the applicants prepare to take on the obligations of EU membership, the domestic effects of transferring policies and institutions to them are, in principle, comparable to the effects of the EU on its current member states.

The analysis undertaken here is an attempt to fill this relative gap in research. Ladrech's definition of Europeanization could well be applied to the case of enlargement, without danger of stretching the concept too for (Radaelli 2000).[2] The conceptual frameworks employed in the 'Europeanization' literature will nevertheless need to be adapted to take account of the distinct case of the CEECs. This chapter has two main objectives: (1) to reconceptualize and apply a range of relevant strands of literature on external influences and institutional transformation to the case of CEECs, and (2) to examine the impact of Europeanization and globalization on the economic performance of CEECs during the enlargement process.

Institutionalized globalization and policy transfer: carrot and stick policies

The main objective of this section is to cross-fertilize several theories about the impact of global factors, such as the World Bank, IMF and multinational companies, on the institutional transformation in CEECs. The section will briefly review the main arguments related to the role played by the IMF and World Bank in institutional transformation and their relevance for CEECs.

Over the last decade, institutional reform in transition countries has become a core objective for international financial institutions (IFIs). The main strategy used to contribute to, and often shape, the institutional reform taking place in transition economies, for instance, was to use various combinations of 'carrot and stick' policies as part of their aid and conditionality for a broad range of institutional areas, including monetary and fiscal institutions, corporate governance, financial and asset market supervision, labour-market practices, business–government relations, corruption, transparency and social safety nets.

This increased role of international organizations such as the IMF and World Bank *vis-à-vis* sovereign states has been fuelling a debate on the one hand about the rationale of conditionality, and on the other about its effectiveness. In their activities, international organizations have intensified their efforts to strengthen cooperation and coordination in their policies. The notorious 'Washington consensus' (J. Williamson 1990) was based not only on shared views on the right policies for development by the two organizations but also on formal arrangements between the IMF and the World Bank.[3]

Such coordination was particularly visible in the context of cross-conditionality.[4] However, neither conditionality nor cross-conditionality were part of the original mandate of Bretton Woods institutions (Guitian 1981). Yet, since the 1960s, the perceived importance of domestic reform for the successful implementation of financial assistance programmes suggested that the extent of policy transfer from the IFIs to a recipient country is not only a function of the funds made available but also of the conditionality attached to the programme. Such a relationship is based on the assumption that beneficiary countries are often reluctant to implement the policies advocated by the Bretton Woods institutions voluntarily, either for ideological reasons (as in the case of communist countries) or for their short-term negative impact. Moreover, non-compliance with strict conditionality would lead to a poor credit history, which in turn would decrease the chances of a country receiving financial assistance from IFIs in the future.

However, the empirical evidence contradicts this last assumption. As Thacker (1999) argued, poor credit history and new IMF lending are positively correlated. In other words, having had an IMF loan cancelled increases the likelihood of receiving another loan in the future. This evidence runs counter to the argument that IMF conditionality promotes greater policy transfer towards recipient countries.

One reason behind this mixed implementation record was the perception among beneficiary countries that the IFIs cannot overcome their bias towards a particular Anglo-Saxon model of capitalism. Such an approach that presumes or advocates the superiority of a particular model of a capitalist economy would significantly restrict the range of institutional variation that CEECs could adopt, and would lead to convergence towards a specific model of capitalism. However, some convergence towards more efficient institutions can be useful. For instance, technical issues covered by the IMF and the World Bank in their programmes, such as the introduction of international accounting standards or improved prudential supervision of financial intermediaries, can be adopted without restricting institutional choices at macro level.

In addition to the role played by global financial institutions such as the IMF and World Bank, another 'agentless' policy transfer (Rose 1991, 1993) phenomenon is the impact of 'carrot and stick' strategies used by market and societal forces (MNCs, non-governmental organizations, etc.) to influence policy and institutional choices in CEECs. Given the importance of foreign direct investment worldwide, multinational corporations are probably the most visible vehicles for the globalization of the world economic system. Hence, the importance of multinational corporations has focused attention on their impact on domestic politics and economics. For instance, the expansion of managerial coordination and control across national boundaries in multinational firms is viewed as changing both the nature of those firms and, by extension, that of the business system that they developed within, as well as the characteristics of the host economies in which they invest.[5]

MNCs are able to induce policy diffusion not only because of their size and economic strength but also because of free movement of capital. Due to the scarcity of capital in developing and transition economies, footloose MNCs can effectively play the 'voice or exit' game with national governments, which, in the end, forces the latter to engage in a 'race to the bottom' to attract and maintain MNCs within their boundaries.[6]

Apart from the impact on domestic institutions, MNCs also have very often a sizeable impact on their host country's growth prospects. The value of multinational investment lies not only in the capital it provides, but also in a number of potential benefits, including employment creation, technology transfer, technical and managerial skills and access to world markets. Hence its impact on growth is expected to be manifold and to vary a great deal between technologically advanced and transition countries.

However, MNCs are not the only factor behind policy diffusion. As Dolowitz and Marsh (1996, 2000) rightly argued, policy diffusion may emerge as a result of large networks of university scholars, professional consultants, aid administrators, and other 'epistemic communities' from both donor and recipient countries who conceive and eventually popularize new ways of thinking about various policy issues. This diverse group may, over time, influence policy and institutional choices in recipient countries.

The Europeanization of Central and East European Countries: main policy transfer elements

Despite the relevance of the theory of globalization and EU integration on the one hand, and the models of capitalism debate on the other, these theories largely remained poorly adapted to tackling the special case of post-socialist transformation, both for the economic and institutional transformation taking place in CEECs.[7] As shown in Chapter 1, while the debate about the impact of globalization and Europeanization on existing models of capitalism in Western Europe is fairly advanced, this is not the case in the context of transition economies. International political economy, a major contributor to the debate around globalization, paid relatively little attention to the link between globalization, capitalist institutions and economic performance in Eastern Europe. For example, some excellent contributions by Keohane, Nye and Hoffmann (1993) systematically tested the relative importance of institutions, state strategies and domestic politics on different aspects of the evolving relationship between the EU and the CEECs. Unfortunately, however, there have been no comparable analyses since then.[8]

Likewise, European integration theory, despite the subsequent waves of EU enlargement, remained concentrated on EU 'deepening'. Furthermore, when the question of enlargement is addressed within this debate, the focus is on whether the decision-making power on certain enlargement-related policies (financial assistance, conditions for accession) lies with the supranational institutions or member states. Neither have more recent studies of European integration, based on a 'multilevel governance' approach, paid more attention to the question of 'widening' (Friis and Murphy 1999, p. 213). On the other hand, analyses of enlargement issues are in abundant supply but a large majority of them are policy-oriented and remain descriptive or prescriptive. Current research on the EU's impact on the CEECs consists mainly of in-depth studies, which are often technical and descriptive, and rarely comparative across sectors or countries (for certain exceptions, see, e.g., Inotai 1999).

Therefore it appears that there is no 'enlargement theory' as such (Friis 1998; Wallace 2000), and that in the case of CEECs there is not much theoretical cross-fertilization between globalization, Europeanization and models of capitalism debates. At this juncture, it is important to establish why such an approach is important or useful to the present analysis. What are the reasons that suggest that these theories are better adapted to enhance the understanding of EU enlargement, compared to the theoretical research undertaken so far? Why is such a cross-fertilization necessary in the first place?

The answer to these questions is that, in order to comprehend the nature of EU enlargement, this needs to be examined from a wider political economy perspective, capable of going beyond the detailed technical analyses of the enlargement process. In order to have such a wider perspective, reconceptualizing transition, globalization and EU enlargement as a case of policy transfer offers a coherent theoretical framework for understanding not only the impact of globalization and Europeanization simultaneously, but also their interaction with domestic factors.

Overall, the EU influence is mediated through a range of factors, both domestic and international, and embedded in much wider processes of change. In ways that are familiar to students of Europeanization in existing member states, initial domestic conditions, institutions and structures, bureaucratic and party politics and issues of sequencing and learning are shaping the impact of the EU in the CEECs, sometimes reinforcing existing features as much as changing them.

Three main types of Europeanization factors will be addressed in some detail below:

(a) legal harmonization through the adoption of the *acquis communautaire*;
(b) EU financial assistance, in particular the Poland and Hungary Action for the Restructuring of the Economy (PHARE) programme;
(c) the process of twinning.

Each Europeanization factor will be briefly described and reconceptualized in terms of policy transfer literature.

Such theoretical cross-fertilization helps to explain the diversity of outcomes among the candidate states, and the evolution of EU policies towards stricter conditionality.

The adoption of the *acquis communautaire*

Over time, enlargement moved from a largely voluntary policy transfer towards a conditional process subject to detailed scrutiny from the European Commission. 'Carrot and stick' strategies could also be the name of the policies gradually adopted by the EU *vis-à-vis* acceding countries. Owing to the nature of the accession process designed for the CEECs, the EU has a particularly strong influence over candidate states. Just as the prospect of enlargement is by now suffusing all aspects of the

EU (Wallace 2000), so the prospect of EU accession has influenced virtually every aspect of post-communist change in the candidate countries (Iankova 2000). However, the nature of EU conditionality for the CEECs has rendered EU influence across a range of fields and processes more significant than that enjoyed over existing EU members (Grabbe 1999, 2003).

The Commission regularly presented applicant states with a variety of documents assessing their progress on the road to accession. First, a highly important document was undoubtedly the White Paper of 1995, which defined the scope of the legal harmonization required to include the CEECs into the EU internal market (EC 1995). This document provided the CEECs with clear guidelines and reduced their degree of freedom in deciding the scope of the process. The EU has also made such membership conditional upon the CEECs' immediate adoption of certain fixed and 'core' EU democratic, constitutional and economic principles, as well as, and vitally so, their adoption of the *acquis communautaire*; their creation of the legal and institutional machinery necessary for the effective adoption of the EU's evolving, but common, objectives and policies, as well as its existing legislation and regulatory system.

The coercive nature increased in 1997 when the Commission issued its opinions on membership applications. The *Avis* for each candidate country identified the progress achieved so far and the necessary steps to be taken in order to fulfil the membership criteria. Since 1998, the regular annual reports and Accession Partnerships have created a pre-accession strategy for applicant countries. The degree of EU influence in the process led some authors to conclude that CEECs are 'governed by accession' (Iankova 2001).

The key element and the driving force of the EU accession process is for EU candidate countries to demonstrate that they are able to comply with the EU's *acquis communautaire*. The *acquis communautaire* is, in the first instance, a legal concept. Candidate countries have to adopt and implement 31 chapters of the *acquis*, comprising thousands of pages of legislation.[9] However, notwithstanding the importance of this existing body of settled laws, the *acquis* is also a far wider notion. A major insight guiding the analysis undertaken in this part comes from the neo-institutionalist contributions to the analysis of EU law. In developing a dynamic approach to the relationship between law and public action, authors such as Bulmer (1994) have shown that EU law is not only about legal decisions but also modifies the 'institutional capacity' of the actors involved.

Consequently, the implementation of the *acquis* serves very particular goals and requires specific accession-oriented policies as well as very particular legal and administrative structures to be established within acceding countries. The *acquis* encompasses – in the Commission's own words – 'an impressive set of principles and obligations' (EC 2000b, p. 44) going far beyond the internal market and including areas such as agriculture, the environment, energy and transport. The Commission has identified the main elements within the *acquis* that CEECs must transpose and implement in the pre-accession *acquis* phase. According to Agenda 2000, of primary importance are the obligations stemming from the Europe Agreement, particularly those relating to the rights of establishment, national treatment, free circulation of goods, intellectual property and public procurement. Equally important are the priorities highlighted in the White Paper, in areas such as taxation and banking. Lastly, significant and far-reaching adaptations will be needed in the fields of environment, energy, agriculture, industry, telecommunications, transport and justice and home affairs (EC 2000b, p. 45). Thus, the adoption of the *acquis communautaire* is not only a formal condition for accession but also an encompassing measure and a key indicator of the extent of Europeanization in CEECs.

EU financial assistance

Apart from the adoption of the *acquis*, another key element designed to enhance the capacity of CEECs to adapt to EU standards has been financial assistance. Over the last decade the EU has put in place a vast array of technical assistance programmes earmarked for CEECs. As part of this strategy, the PHARE financial assistance has been a major instrument in helping candidate countries to adopt the *acquis* as it helps with institution building and investments designed to improve the regulatory framework, thereby facilitating the adoption of the *acquis*.

EU financial assistance further extended the terms of conditionality, making financial assistance under the PHARE programme dependent upon progress towards membership. Thus the EU linked the availability of PHARE financial assistance to the fulfilment of the conditions mentioned for each individual candidate country in their Accession Partnerships. Although the conditions laid down in the Accession Partnership are not legally binding, nonetheless tying the 'carrots' of the accession process – the generous aid under PHARE – to the 'sticks' of stalled negotiations and blocked aid provides enough reasons to consider the adoption of the *acquis* and its PHARE financial counterpart as a coercive policy transfer.

Twinning

Twinning was officially launched by the Commission in May 1998 with the aim of assisting the accession applicants to apply the *acquis communautaire* to the same standards as the current member states. Twinning was therefore the implementing companion of legal harmonization. The EU initiated a process of transfer of expertise, encouraging and formalizing the transfer of national experts and civil servants from EU member states to CEECs. Twinning has been designed to overcome the problem of a lack of personnel within the Commission who possess the necessary technical and expert knowledge to aid the CEECs in their efforts to adapt to the *acquis*. The rationale behind the project was that the best placed institutions to assist national administrations and policy makers to adapt to the EU requirements are the EU members themselves. Because of these characteristics (*acquis* implementation, EU member states experts), twinning acted more as a 'horizontal policy transfer' from EU member states of 'best practices' in coping with EU requirements rather that a vertical, coercive, Europeanization process.

Another notable feature of the twinning programmes is that they are based on a principle of free choice on the part of the candidate country. Candidate countries are responsible for the initiation of a twinning project, its specific content and partners. As a result of this, twinning acts as a lesson-drawing mechanism from EU member states to acceding countries.

Empirical testing

The theoretical linkages described above and the impact of different external forces on domestic transformation in transition economies can be operationalized from a policy transfer perspective. The analytical framework offered by the policy transfer literature allows us to map the main external influence that could affect the institutional choices made by CEECs during the transition process and offers the basis for the subsequent analysis of policy transfer and economic performance (Figure 4.1). The impact of Europeanization can be operationalized as a direct effect (the EU influence) and indirect effect (the interactions among various acceding countries). As described in the previous section, EU enlargement may be reframed as an 'obligated', coercive policy transfer.

As mentioned previously, twinning is an indirect force of Europeanization. For instance, Howell (2004) calls 'Europeanization by stealth' or 'cross-loading' the horizontal policy transfer through

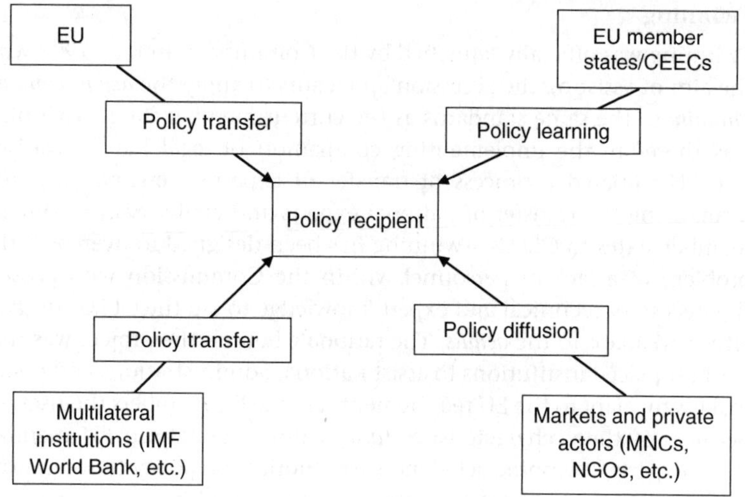

Figure 4.1 Theorizing external influences on systemic transformation in CEECs

twinning occurring between EU member states and acceding countries. Apart from EU member states, a process of lesson drawing is possible among CEECs themselves. The impact of other CEECs may be significant, given the numerous channels of interactions between them allowing for best practice policies and institutions that are successfully adapted in one country to be emulated by others. As with twinning, the impact of other CEECs is not coercive and relies mainly on the willingness of the recipient country to 'learn' from its peers. Therefore, instead of coercive policy transfer mechanisms, this interaction is best understood as 'policy learning'.

The impact of globalization is, similarly, two-fold. First, the impact of global governance, as developed by international organizations, is typified as a case of policy transfer. For the most part coercive, given the lending conditionality in the case of the IMF and World Bank, both institutions rely on policy transfer linked to financial assistance. The various elements are tied in through conditionality, the degree of coerciveness and effectiveness of which varies.[10]

In the case of market and private forces, as in the case of 'policy learning', the level of coercion is minimal or non-existent. Moreover, unlike the transfer of 'best practices' and institutions, the linkages between measures adopted by recipient countries and specific external forces are more elusive, since the structure of the external force (MNCs, non-governmental organizations, etc.) is more diffuse. Therefore, this influence of market and private forces falls closer to what is called 'policy diffusion' in the policy transfer literature.

Based on this conceptual framework, the impact of various external factors on the economic performance of CEECs may be quantitatively assessed and examined empirically in a cross-section and time-series analysis. Thus far econometric modelling has not been applied to the policy transfer literature and therefore this sets up an explanatory framework through which other types of policy transfer processes could be analysed.

As described in Figure 4.1, the impact of external factors on growth in CEECs is modelled as a function of two main factors: on the one hand, the influence of the EU through the various policy instruments targeted to assist CEECs in this process and, on the other, other globalization forces. In its most general form, the equation underlying the policy transfer model can be written as a function of two main types of institutional influences:

$$\text{growth} = f(\text{external pressure, domestic conditions}) \tag{4.1}$$

The various elements of the model are fully explained below.

Data and variables

The sample of countries under investigation is restricted to the ten candidate countries that have been involved in a systematic evaluation in the EU documents: Bulgaria, the Czech Republic, Estonia, Hungary, Latvia, Lithuania, Poland, Romania, the Slovak Republic and Slovenia. The time span for which data were available covered most of the transition period, from 1990 until 2002. As in Chapter 2, the dependent variable capturing the impact of institutional factors on economic performance is the growth rate of GDP in ten transition economies. Tables 4.1 and 4.2 below contain a list of independent variables and their sources.

Europeanization

The two main elements of the Europeanization process mentioned above (the *acquis communautaire* and financial assistance) are proxied by an index measuring the annual progress made by CEECs in the adoption of the *acquis* (EUR) and annual PHARE contributions as a percentage of GDP (FIN) respectively.

Several reasons justified the choice of these variables. According to the EU criteria, the ability of CEECs to implement the *acquis* will be central to their capacity to function successfully within the Union and therefore to the accession process.[11] Second, the adoption of the *acquis* also fits nicely with the definitions of Europeanization (Ladrech 1994) and policy transfer adopted in this study (Dolowitz and Marsh 2000). The arguments of Ladrech (1994) are particularly relevant for the choice of annual progress as a dependent variable. Ladrech (1994, p. 69) defines Europeanization as 'an *incremental process* [emphasis added] reorienting the direction and shape of politics to the degree that EC political and economic dynamics become part of the organizational logic of national politics and policy-making'. Third, the assessment of the process, as recorded in various EU documents, particularly the EU annual progress reports, offers an invaluable source of consistent information that allows the quantification of an otherwise elusive concept such as policy transfer. [12]

For the Europeanization variable (i.e., progress in adopting the 31 chapters of the *acquis communautaire*), the analysis relied on a textual analysis of primary policy documentation. The construction of the *acquis* adoption index entailed a large-scale systematic coding of more than 10,000 pages of EU documents pertaining to enlargement. The information was corroborated with assessments made in other EU documents, such as EU composite papers and Accession Partnerships. The index components corresponding to each of the 31 chapters of the *acquis* take values between 0 (no progress), 1 (little or unsatisfactory progress), 2 (satisfactory progress), and 3 (significant progress).[13] The overall values of the Europeanization index is the simple average of chapter-specific scores for each country and year from 1990 to 2002, the last year when the European Commission assessed progress towards accession using a common methodology across all ten countries. The index was normalized to range between 0 and 1. Since 1998 was the first year for which such information was available, prior to this there was no systematic evaluation and monitoring exercise on the adoption of the *acquis* required by the EU agreements. Therefore, between 1990 and 1998, the values for the Europeanization index are estimates, with the index set to zero at the beginning of the transition process.[14]

The 1998–2002 average Europeanization index for each of the CEECs is depicted in Figure 4.2. The figure shows significant differences both across countries and time, with a pronounced acceleration of the Europeanization process, as measured by the adoption of the *acquis*, in recent years and in particular in 2002. For instance, Lithuania and

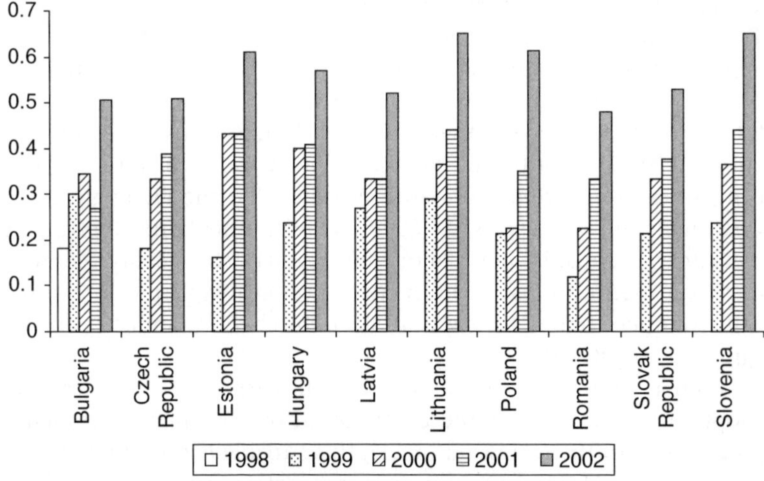

Figure 4.2   The Europeanization index, 1998–2002

Sources: Author's calculations, based on various EU accession documents (Progress Reports, Accession Partnerships, Composite Papers, Strategy Papers, etc.).

Slovenia have shown a vigorous acceleration of Europeanization in 2001, despite very low figures for the first years. In contrast, Romania has the lowest average Europeanization index among the candidate countries, giving support to the EU decision to include it in the second wave of enlargement.

However, throughout the entire period no country scored more than 0.7 on the Europeanization index, reflecting the fact that even newly acceding countries met the *acquis*-related commitments and requirements only partially, as acknowledged by various EU reports monitoring the progress achieved at the end of the negotiation process.

In terms of its impact on economic performance, the comprehensive implementation of the *acquis* within the CEECs is a double-edged sword and the impact of the Europeanization variable on growth is a matter of empirical investigation. On the one hand, full implementation is essential for preserving the homogeneity and credibility of existing Union policies in new members. The *acquis* is also a crucial element for ensuring that CEECs will be in a position to compete fairly within the Single Market. This transposition requires CEECs to impose EU standards on enterprises and large SOEs. This is primarily the case in areas such as the environment, working conditions, transport, nuclear safety, energy, marketing of food products and the control of production processes, sound commercial practices and large state-owned industrial plants. Those sectors and companies that are export-oriented, and largely dependent on the EU market, are already adapted to these EU conditions or, if not, would welcome such changes if they reduced the regulatory burden on their export activities. A sound market environment, with enforced EU standards and commercial practices, will insulate these companies from various non-tariff measures that the EU might otherwise impose on the exports of CEECs.[15] On the other hand, applying EU regulatory standards (environmental regulations, quality controls, technical specifications, etc.) can create non-negligible pressure in several economic sectors, such as coal, steel, the chemical industry and the agri-food industry. [16]

Another important feature of the Europeanization process and adoption of the *acquis* is the contribution of the financial assistance programme. In the regression model, this variable is operationalized as the annual PHARE transfers for each candidate country, expressed as a percentage of GDP.

The variable included in the regression analysis to capture the impact of twinning is the number of twinning projects in each candidate country on an annual basis. Although a crude measure of the impact of twinning on the process of *acquis* adoption and implementation, this variable captures the impact of *acquis* adoption and implementation. As with the Europeanization index, the implementation of the *acquis* may have both positive and negative economic effects, and hence the sign of the estimated coefficient is theoretically ambiguous.

Table 4.1 summarizes the main policy transfer variables, their source and the expected effect of each. Given the conflicting theories regarding state–societal interactions and the impact of external forces on CEECs, several variables have an ambiguous *ex ante* effect. For instance, the comprehensive implementation of the *acquis* within the CEECs may be a double-edged sword. On the one hand, a full implementation requires CEECs to impose EU standards on enterprises and large SOEs. This is primarily the case in such areas as the environment, working conditions, transport, nuclear safety, energy, marketing of food products and the control of production processes, sound commercial practices and large state-owned industrial plants. Such stringent standards and policies may have a negative economic impact because those sectors and companies that are export-oriented and depend to a large extent on the EU market have already adapted to these EU conditions or, if not, would welcome a full implementation of the *acquis*. A sound market environment, with enforced EU standards and commercial practices will insulate these

Table 4.1   Independent policy transfer variables

Independent variable			Expected effect on dependent variable
Symbol	Description	Source	
PHARE	Annual PHARE contributions, as a percentage of GDP	European Commission, various PHARE Annual Reports	+
EUR	Index measuring the annual progress made by CEECs in the adoption of the *acquis*	Author's calculations	+/−
Twin	Number of annual twinning projects	European Commission	+/−
WB	World Bank lending, as a percentage of GDP	World Bank Country Reports	+
IMF	Dummy variable, with a value of 1 if a stand-by agreement was in place, 0 otherwise	IMF	+/−
FDI	FDI levels (as % of GDP), as a proxy for policy diffusion through market forces	World Bank World Development Indicators	+

companies from various non-tariff measures that EU might otherwise impose on CEECs exports.

The impact of globalization

The important role played by the IMF in the region (in particular for Bulgaria and Romania) has been operationalized in the form of a dummy variable, taking a value of 1 if the country is engaged in a stand-by loan with the IMF, and 0 otherwise. The assumption behind this choice is that, unlike the World Bank programmes where conditionality is softer, in the case of IMF policy the transfer depends more on the existence/non-existence of an IMF programme and its rigid conditionality rather than the actual amount disbursed.

In contrast, both the World Bank and other bilateral aid programmes are often operational programmes, whose relative size may be important for growth prospects. Therefore, to control the World Bank activities in the region, the regression included the total lending activities of the Bank in each country. The expected sign of the coefficient is ambiguous, because causal relationships can run in both directions. On the one hand, the ability of a transition economy should increase as a result of financial and technical assistance from the Bank. On the other hand, the Bank is expected to reduce its contribution and allow the country to 'graduate' once its institutional reform advances towards EU standards. The first effect is positive, while the second is negative.

As for the other vectors of globalization, given the nature of the dependent variable and the difficulty of quantifying other effects, the impact of market forces has been proxied by foreign direct investment data, expressed as a percentage of GDP.

Control variables

Since external factors shaping the process of policy transfer are not the only variables affecting economic performance, the model incorporates several *control variables* accounting for domestic factors which, as seen in Chapter 2, can influence the process. Therefore a number of domestic conditions will be controlled for. The main domestic macroeconomic variables are investment share, inflation, and unemployment.

Unemployment is not a widely used variable in growth regressions,[17] so, the rationale for its inclusion needs to be explained at some length. One justification for using unemployment is found in the work of Okun (1962). Okun's law suggests that unemployment has a high cost in terms of forgone output.[18] Okun's law may not apply, however, in CEECs. The relationship between unemployment and growth may also be affected by wage-setting institutions. The distribution of income and wages depends on the institutional framework governing an economy. A whole range of sociological, political and other factors, in turn, may explain this. Therefore, in this framework, unemployment may account for a wide range of issues of potential importance for the functioning of the economy. The precise nature of the wage relation, as emphasized in the literature on models of capitalism, determines the nature of the relation between growth and unemployment. If wages grow in line with productivity, there is a positive relation between growth and unemployment (Toche 2001). However, if wage moderation occurs too late, then a trade-off between growth and unemployment may arise.

In the context of transition economies, an argument that can run against Okun's law is that during the communist period, unemployment was underestimated due to a policy of hidden unemployment in the state-owned enterprises. During the post-communist period, job destruction has largely been reform-driven (structural adjustment programmes, privatization and other market-oriented reforms).[19] Therefore, CEECs that undertook more radical reforms probably had higher unemployment.

Moreover, job creation is primarily determined by the conditions affecting the labour market and private sector incentives to hire redundant workers. In CEECs, both processes may positively affect growth: eliminating hidden unemployment significantly improves the prospects of former SOEs; job creation has an obvious positive impact on economic growth. Therefore, even if job creation does not offset job destruction, the relationship between unemployment and economic growth can be positive.

The overall quality of policies is captured by the Index of Economic Freedom. The index is based on country-by-country analyses and the most up-to-date data available on foreign investment codes, taxes, tariffs, banking regulations, monetary policy, black markets, and so on.[20] Higher values indicate more restrictive policies and therefore the estimated coefficient for this index should be negative.

Two variables were added to capture the institutional legacy of initial conditions. Two time-series variables that serve this purpose are found in de Melo *et al.* (1997). These composite variables are constructed using principal component analysis and contain information on institutional characteristics of transition economies. One such variable, referred to as IN1 in this study, and which corresponds to PRN1 in de Melo *et al.* (1997), is an index for the degree of economic distortions at the beginning of the transition period. It includes information about state independence prior to 1989, market memory, black market premium, location and proximity to market economies, trade openness, and repressed inflation. The other variable used, IN2, captures the overall level of development. It is constructed based on initial levels of per capita income, urbanization, overindustrialization, natural resource endowments, and prior economic growth rates.[21]

Finally, another domestic variable that is expected to be influential is the electoral cycle. In an electoral year, it is expected that politicians and parliamentarians in particular are more interested in re-election and electoral campaigns than in sound economic policies. Thus a dummy variable, with a value of 1 for electoral years and 0 otherwise, is included in the regression analysis. The expected sign of this variable is negative.

Table 4.2 summarizes the domestic and control variables. Following these clarifications, the general model expressed in equation (4.1) was estimated for a number of alternative specifications.

The results

Two statistical methodologies are used to fit the econometric model. Apart from the standard ordinary least squares (OLS), the second

Table 4.2   Control variables

Symbol	Description	Source	Expected effect on dependent variable
IN1, IN2	Initial conditions at the beginning of the transition period	de Melo *et al.* (1997)	−
INVSH	Capital formation, as a percentage of GDP	World Bank World Development Indicators	+
INF	Annual inflation rate	World Bank World Development Indicators	−
UR	Unemployment rate	United Nations Economic Commission for Europe	+/−
FREEDOM	Index of Economic Freedom	http://index.heritage.org/	−
ELECT	Dummy variable with a value of 1 for an electoral year in a candidate country, and 0 otherwise	http://www.electionworld.org/	−

method is based on minimizing a 'weighted least squares' criterion. The reason for using weighted least squares in addition to ordinary least squares is that, in the context of panel data, the dependent variable may have different distributional properties for the sample of countries. Use of the weighted least squares procedure will allow the different variance properties of the dependent variable to be reflected in the model. Since least squares techniques are very sensitive to extreme observations that can be highly influential in determining the relationship between the given dependent and independent variables, the sample was checked for the existence of possible outliers and influential points.[22]

A significant number of regressions were performed, based on a wide range of combinations between the main independent variables and other control variables, using a stepwise selection method. Out of the various regressions performed, 13 specifications were selected and finally included. For all of them, the dependent variable is the growth rate. The estimated results of the various models are reported in Table 4.3.[23]

Two types of regressions were performed: one set with a common intercept and another with fixed effects.[24] Although the right-hand side variables, tested explicitly in the various model specifications, were numerous and based on theoretical grounds, they may not exhaust the list of factors that may determine the policy choices of transition economies. Individuals, ideas, historical, cultural and socio-political factors may also play an important role. As the World Bank (1996, p. 11) argued, 'most decisive reforms have reflected the vision of one leader or a small and committed group'. One way to assess the importance of such factors for individual countries is to split the intercept into country-specific fixed effects, as in models 7–13.[25]

Before turning to the interpretation of each variable, it should be noted that the explanatory power of the model is very high, with values for the adjusted R-squared statistic ranging from 0.57 to 0.87. A Wald test for the goodness of fit rejected the null hypothesis that all regression coefficients, except the constant term, are 0. The coefficients measuring the contribution of the independent variables to the dependent variable are, with few exceptions, statistically significant at 1 per cent, 5 per cent, and 10 per cent confidence levels.

In all regression models, several policy transfer variables have shown statistically significant and robust effects across all specifications. Lagged IMF has a significant positive effect on the growth rate.[26] However, IMF at current levels did not have any statistically significant effect.[27] The Europeanization variables also have a significant impact on growth rates. For instance, an average 0.10 percentage points increase in the annual PHARE contribution (expressed as a percentage of the recipient country's GDP) corresponds to an increase in the growth rate of between 0.65 and 0.78 percentage points, depending on which of the models reported in Table 4.3 is used. Similarly, with other effects being held constant, a 5-point increase in the Europeanization index in the current year would correspond to up to a 0.95 percentage points increase in the growth rate. A similar increase in the previous year would add between 0.6 and 1.8 percentage points to the growth rate. This shows that the positive impact of adoption of the *acquis* (as well as the IMF stabilization programmes) on growth needs time to materialize.

As noted in Chapter 2, foreign direct investment has a significant positive impact on economic performance. An increase of 2 percentage points, for instance, in the share of FDI (expressed as a percentage of GDP) would result in an increase in growth rates of between 0.66 and 1.94 percentage points. The impact of World Bank lending activities (WB) was statistically significant at the 10 per cent level in model 9 only, but the results are very sensitive to model specifications.

Particularly interesting are the results for twinning. As mentioned in Table 4.1, between *acquis* adoption and the decision of candidate countries to engage in twinning projects the relationship is ambiguous and could run both ways. In OLS estimates, twinning had a negative sign but was statistically insignificant. In GLS estimates, twinning had a

Table 4.3 Regression results

Independent variables	OLS estimates											GLS estimates	
	1	2	3	4	5	6	7	8	9	10	11	12	13
Intercept	−11.04***	−4.89*	−10.90***	−11.43***	−2.32	−6.85**							
PHARE							7.88**	7.33**	6.86*				6.49*
IMF (−1)	2.77**		2.97**	2.83**	3.27***	2.84**	5.03***	4.01***	4.76***	5.09***	5.08***	3.91***	3.38***
EUR		0.10*	0.10*	0.19**					0.16**		0.11		
EUR(−1)					0.14*	0.22***		0.36***		0.21**		0.20***	0.27***
TW								−0.14					−0.06*
FDI	0.33*						0.43**						
WB								1.54	1.33**			1.5	1.05
INF	−0.01***	−0.02***	−0.01***	−0.01	−0.01***	−0.01***	−0.01***	−0.01***	−0.01***	−0.01***	−0.01***	−0.017***	−0.01***
INVSH	0.25**	0.13	0.26***	0.27***	0.18*	0.16*	0.27	0.34*	0.36*	0.38*	0.41**	0.18	0.19*
UR	0.42***	0.27**	0.37***	−0.01***	0.51***					0.35	0.35		

FREEDOM					−2.81*		−7.44***						
IN1						−1.66**							
Fixed Effects													
BG							11.59	−17.77	−17.06	−16.31	−16.06	−8.39	−13.16
CZ							5.63	−13.03	−13.19	−14.47	−15.21	−6.59	−7.92
ES							1.62	−18.61	−18.39	−16.63	−17.10	−8.66	−12.7
HU							12.15	−13.38	−12.53	−15.73	−15.72	−6.39	−8.56
LA							5.67	−18.97	−18.28	−17.28	−17.31	−10.65	−14.14
LT							10.06	−17.61	−17.47	−16.70	−17.15	−8.98	−12.47
PL							16.8	−9.51	−9.11	−13.21	−13.7	−3.68	−5.06
RO							11.72	−16.96	−16.68	−17.46	−17.48	−9.59	−12.04
SK							11.62	−13.64	−14.04	−18.22	−19.16	−6.35	−8.01
SN							20.43	−7.63	−7.43	−11.73	−12.29	−2.23	−3.63
Adj. R^2	0.59	0.57	0.59	0.60	0.61	0.59	0.66	0.64	0.62	0.62	0.61	0.87	0.86
F-test	27.2***	30.7***	27.45***	28.57***	24.81***	27.2***	38.5***	29.6***	32.93***	40.22***	38.8***	162.88***	96.42***

All entries are estimates with panel-corrected standard errors. A Wald test for the overall goodness of fit rejected the null hypothesis that all the regression coefficients except the constant term are 0.

*** 1% level of confidence, ** 5% , * 10% (two-tailed test).

statistically significant negative coefficient. Both coefficients suggest that twinning had a negative impact on economic performance. One explanation for this effect lies in the importance of implementing the *acquis*. As mentioned earlier, some parts of the *acquis* could have a short-term negative impact on economic activities. This is not reflected in the adoption of the *acquis* but rather in the variable capturing its implementation. A careful examination of the breakdown of twinning projects by economic sector and *acquis* chapter reveals that a large majority of twinning projects have taken place in adopting stricter, EU-compliant agricultural standards and internal market regulations, both having potentially a negative impact on economic performance on the short-term.

Among the control variables, INF, INVSH and UR also show robust and significant effects. Overall economic policies, as captured by FREEDOM, also have the expected sign. However, the magnitude of the coefficient is less robust across specifications. Adverse initial conditions (IN1) have a significant negative effect on growth, as theoretically expected. However, the results are less robust across different specifications, compared to other control variables. The estimates for the alternative initial conditions variable (IN2), as well as the importance of electoral years (ELECT), while having the expected signs, were not statistically significant. Therefore, these specifications are not reported.

Lastly, the country fixed-effects are negative across all specifications (with the exception of model 7). These results suggest that country fixed effects capture the impact of omitted variables that may negatively affect the economic performance of CEECs.[28] As for model 7, where fixed effects are positive, this may be the impact of introducing FREEDOM, which in this model seems to underestimate the progress made by CEECs towards market economies.

Conclusions

This chapter has shed further light on the different mechanisms of policy transfer which affect institutional transformation and economic performance in transition economies. By unpacking external policy transfer into its main components, the impact of Europeanization and globalization forces on transition economies in Central and Eastern Europe became clearer. The theoretical foundation laid out in Chapter 1 was further operationalized and tested empirically. The analysis covered a number of variables introduced to capture the impact of Europeanization and institutionalized globalization on growth rates, as well as the direction and magnitude of such influences.

Several findings are noteworthy. The empirical results show that Europeanization has the most significant impact on economic output in transition economies. The broader implication of these results is that various elements of the Copenhagen criteria (a well-functioning market economy and legal harmonization) are mutually reinforcing. The statistical estimates also lend empirical support to the argument that the IMF adjustment policies improve the rate of growth of real GDP. However, the results suggest that IMF policies need time to produce positive effects.

In sum, the Europeanization process and its policy transfer capacity has the highest impact on economic performance in the region. In the case of laggard acceding countries that are still dependent on IMF funds, such as Romania and Bulgaria, the IMF (as the lender of the last resort during a financial crisis) also has a very high degree of influence on macroeconomic policies. However, given the fact that the World Bank is involved in sectoral projects rather than large-scale reform of state–societal interactions, the impact of its policy transfer capacity on economic performance seems more limited. Indirectly, the econometric results also seem to support the intuitive argument that more coercive policy transfer mechanisms (such as the ones used by the EU and IMF) are more growth-inducing than other less coercive policy transfer mechanisms. The need for coercion is also supported by the fact that in many cases the policy prescriptions and institutional framework advocated by IFIs are opposed by growth-inhibiting domestic factors.

A more detailed framework of analysis that could shed more light on the ways in which Europeanization and globalization may change growth-inhibiting state–societal interactions, such as those identified in the emerging 'cocktail capitalism' in CEECs, is provided in the next chapter. Chapter 5 will relate these econometric findings to other empirical evidence through several case studies on the impact of Europeanization and globalization on actual policy implementation, and the sectoral changes that have taken place in CEECs as a result of the policy transfer mechanisms identified so far.

5
External Factors and Models of Capitalism: The Romanian Experience

The cross-country and time-series analysis undertaken in Chapter 4 concluded quite convincingly that external factors generally have a positive impact on institutional transformation and economic performance in CEECs. At the same time, the analysis carried out in Chapter 3 showed that, in comparative perspective, Romania has been lagging behind other CEECs both in terms of economic performance and institutional transformation; several domestic factors accountable for this evolution have been identified.

The econometric analysis presented in Chapter 4 has already taken into account and analysed the interaction between domestic and external factors across CEECs. The purpose of the empirical evidence contained in this chapter is to enable an examination in greater detail, using specific examples from Romania's experience with the Europeanization and institutional globalization processes. The main objective pursued was to identify the direction and extent of Bretton Woods institutions. In the following pages these issues will be examined in greater detail through a qualitative approach based on case-study analysis of the interactions between external and domestic factors. In particular, this part will assess the effectiveness and direction of change induced by the various European policy transfer mechanisms. In addition, in the case of Romania, two other external factors (the IMF and the World Bank) also played a significant role. The influence of each external factor is assessed against the institutional landscape and the problems associated with the emerging type of capitalism in Romania along the lines of the three main institutional arrangements discussed in Chapter 3 (state–industry, state–labour and state–financial relations).

The impact of the Europeanization process

As indicated in Chapters 1 and 4, the influence exerted by EU institutions and policies was one of the main driving forces of change in CEECs. The impact of the EU on acceding countries is two-fold: on the one hand, legal and institutional harmonization, as measured by the CEECs' progress in the adoption and implementation of the *acquis*, and on the other, the financial assistance made available to the CEECs during the accession period.

The conditions for accession to the EU involve a large number of very detailed and demanding obligations. For instance, financial institutions in acceding countries are expected to perform to high standards of financial strength and transparency, demonstrating that they are well regulated by government while at the same time showing independence in their allocation of credits. EU rules for social dialogue are of particular significance for enterprise restructuring and private investment.

This section will present evidence of the impact of Europeanization on Romanian state–societal interactions, with particular emphasis on privatization, social dialogue and banking regulations, in an effort to determine the extent to which the enlargement process favours institutional choices that are specific to a certain model of capitalism. Apart from the direction of change, the other objective of this section is to assess the extent to which EU influence was effective in addressing the growth-inhibiting institutional patterns identified earlier in the book.

The EU and state–industry relations

State–industry relations and industrial policies in CEECs were considered by the EU as one of the areas that required the most urgent action during the accession process.[1] Cooperation between the EU and candidate countries in the field of industrial cooperation was part of the Europe Agreements. During the subsequent period of preparing the accession negotiations, the EU became increasingly involved in the adjustment and restructuring programmes aimed at increasing the competitiveness of CEECs in an enlarged EU. The impact of the EU on state–industry relations in Romania can be summarized within three broad areas: privatization, enterprise restructuring and competition policy.[2] The EU, through its PHARE programme, has assisted Romania in its privatization efforts both by providing support for general policy development via national privatization institutions and by providing direct support for individual enterprises. PHARE provided the professional skills required for private enterprise development and management at a time when they were in very short supply in Romania. PHARE technical assistance produced a variety of outputs, such as advisory services, the transfer of skills through formal training and more informal 'learning-by-doing'. Institution-building consisted of support to a number of agencies that were, over time, directly involved in the process of privatization: the State Ownership Fund and its successor, the Authority for Privatization and Administration of State Ownership (APAPS), Private Ownership Funds, and the Ministry of Privatization. With PHARE technical assistance, many of these agencies developed a framework for privatization, worked on strategies and policies, developed the legal and institutional framework for privatization transactions in most cases, and initiated the first pilot privatization transactions. PHARE funds were also used in conjunction with financial assistance from IFIs. An important associated PHARE activity was support for public awareness campaigns in most countries, ensuring that citizens would claim the certificates or vouchers available to them under the mass privatization programmes (APAPS 2002a).

The effectiveness of PHARE support largely depended on the receptivity of the prevailing political environment.[3] In Romania, prior to 1997, PHARE technical assistance had been easily discarded when the policy advice did not correspond to political priorities. The pre-1996 Romanian governments were only half-heartedly committed to a sustained privatization strategy. At some point, governments downgraded the privatization process and the agencies that had been charged with implementing them, forcing PHARE programmes to underperform for a while. Due to the high stakes involved, enterprise restructuring has remained a sensitive issue even in recent years. In some cases political opposition delayed the establishment of the necessary institutional arrangements for PHARE implementation to take place. Thus, the implementation phase of the Industrial Restructuning and Professional Re-conversion Programme (RICOP)[4] was postponed by one year, due to the inability of the Romanian government to appoint a national coordinator and set up appropriate domestic institutional arrangements for the implementation of the various activities envisaged within RICOP.

This example confirmed the EU's concern that enterprise restructuring has been a very difficult area for interventions by PHARE (EC 1998b). To avoid such difficulties and political sensitivities, initially only broad industry-sector studies to determine comparative advantage and provide a framework for both restructuring and new industrial development were undertaken, but with mixed results.[5] Despite the initial implementation problems, RICOP also delivered good results (APAPS

2002b, p. 1). One element of the RICOP, launched in June 2000, consisted of various job-creation strategies targeted at the 60,000 workers laid off within the World Bank's Private Structural Adjustment Loan programme (Cotidianul 2001b, p. 15). One notable success involves a joint PHARE–EBRD project for the evaluation of all state-owned commercial companies to identify those that had a better chance of being sold to strategic investors. Another successful joint project involved an analysis of the bad loan/arrears problem, with the objective of identifying core issues and proposing viable solutions that would prevent the recurrence of the problem and the risk of additional bailouts. In addition to PHARE technical assistance, which was aimed at improving the institutional arrangements in the area of state–industry relations, another major shaping force was the policy transfer process stemming from legal harmonization.

One such EU policy transfer that has had a far-reaching impact on state–industry relations in CEECs was competition policy. Competition policy rules are important because the legacy of central planning is concentrated in market structures where strong pressures for state assistance to enterprises in difficulty could not be resisted. The case of competition policy requires particularly close scrutiny, because it is the one area of single market policy that many had hoped could serve multiple purposes in the transition towards EU accession. The adoption of EU competition rules on state aid, abuse of dominance, monopolization or merger control, for instance, had a significant impact on the old clientelistic state–industry relations, such as those described in Chapter 3. It is, however, arguable that in some areas of competition policy, the needs of the CEECs are for a less stringent regime than in the EU, as a transition economy such as Romania might want to apply softer competition laws in order to encourage investment.

A few competition cases from Romania illustrate this point. For instance, in the case of LETEA Bacau (the only Romanian producer of special printing paper), the privatization deal concluded by the SOF after a two-year search for a potential buyer was not allowed by the Romanian Competition Council. The issue surfaced after the SOF argued that the only way it could attract a strategic foreign investor for LETEA was to sell all of its shares, accounting for 75 per cent of LETEA's equity, the remaining shares having been distributed during the MPP. Given the monopolistic position of LETEA in the production of newspapers, the Competition Council had to approve the deal, in accordance with EU regulations. The SOF selected a rather obscure Cypriot company from all the interested investors. Soon afterwards the Competition Council received a complaint that, in fact, the Cypriot company was owned by one of the largest Romanian media companies, and therefore the deal would create a dangerous business agglomeration in this sector (Bibire 2001). As a result of this, the Competition Council asked to examine the ownership and corporate structure of the Cypriot company. At the end of the investigation, the Competition Council announced that it had decided to cancel the privatization deal, even though the contract was already signed.

Another case in which competition policy played a decisive role in influencing state–industry relations is the distribution of spirits. In 2000, after a few rounds of negotiation between the Minister of Finance (an ex-manager of a state-owned alcohol factory) and domestic alcohol producers, the government issued an ordinance whereby the distribution of refined alcohol would become a state monopoly.[6] The Competition Council argued that this new regulation contravened Romanian competition law and the EU *acquis* (David 2000). The state-owned alcohol producers argued that Romania should not be more stringent on competition issues than EU members themselves and threatened that without the new regime they would stop all production and would go bankrupt (Mitroi 2000). In many instances, such pressures were accommodated by the Romanian government. Despite the close state–industry links, the weight of the arguments related to the EU *acquis* and other international commitments helped the competition authorities to impose their viewpoint. In other instances, however, irrespective of competition policy considerations, the stakes were simply too high for the Competition Council to take a strong stance. This was true in the case of the privatization deal between DACIA, the national carmaker, and Renault, at the end of 1999. Renault made its investment conditional upon a number of facilities that were questionable from a competition policy perspective. The Competition Council investigated the impact of exclusive deals between Renault–DACIA and traditional Renault parts providers on domestic sub-contractors. Other measures investigated were the impact of trade preferences extended to Renault on imported intermediate inputs, and the fiscal facilities extended to other domestic carmakers, in particular Daewoo-Romania. The Competition Council finally gave its unconditional approval in September 1999.

Overall, despite a few cases such as those described above, the Europeanization of state–industry relations in Romania was aimed at creating a functioning market economy through privatization, enterprise restructuring and strengthened competition policies. As in the case of the IMF and the World Bank, in terms of effectiveness, the track record of EU influence in each of these areas is mixed.[7] Regarding the type of state–industry relations promoted by the EU in Romania, the evidence suggests that EU policies in Romania have predominantly favoured an Anglo-Saxon model of state–industry relations. By focusing on privatization and strict competition rules, the typical strong state–business relations found in developmental states have been discouraged. Likewise, there is little evidence that EU policies have promoted a Continental participatory framework for the design and implementation of industrial policies such as those mentioned above.[8] At times, the EU PHARE programme promoted closer relations between national business and professional associations and their EU counterparts, as a means of enhancing the capacity of CEEC business associations, but such actions had little impact on the overall institutional settings in Romania.[9] One reason for the limited evidence of EU projects encouraging business or leading professional associations to become *formally* involved in policy making might be the institutional weaknesses of these associations.[10] Furthermore, the predominant clientelistic access of major businesses to policy makers, described at length in this book, reduced the desire of business associations to engage in formal relationships with state agencies involved in industrial policy making, as in the Continental model of capitalism.

The EU and state–banking relations

As shown in Chapter 1, Romanian banking was dominated by a small number of large state-owned and formerly state-owned specialized banks, which were controlled legally (or, in fact, by the state) and run largely for political gain. They lent mainly to state-owned enterprises, they were conservative and they were greatly overstaffed, yet they were also underequipped and largely unfamiliar with the skills of modern banking in a market economy.[11] The weakness of the Romanian banking system and its surveillance by the National Bank of Romania (NBR) were major factors in delaying progress in the negotiation of several chapters of the *acquis*: free movement of services, economic and monetary union, and budgetary provisions. For these reasons, reform of the financial sector was a high priority in the EU assistance package. The banking sector is one in which PHARE has had substantial involvement in all CEECs. The main activities included in the PHARE package of assistance for Romania were aimed at strengthening the supervisory capacities of the NBR and operational activities of commercial banks.[12] Since 1997, the PHARE programme has become 'accession-driven' and, from 1998 onwards, PHARE programmes were effectively driven by the provisions included in the Accession Partnerships (APs), indicating the areas of the *acquis communautaire* where candidate member states needed to make further progress before accession. PHARE financial assistance was conditional upon implementation of the conditions introduced in the Accession Partnership. In the 1998 Accession Partnership for Romania, reform of the banking system and privatization of two banks were explicitly mentioned as short-term conditions (EC 1998c).

Prior to the Accession Partnerships, the various PHARE banking sector projects were aimed at strengthening all aspects of bank management functions. Policy-learning mechanisms were put in place, such as commercial banks being twinned with a commercial bank inside the EU. Potential positive spillovers related not only to banking technology transfers but also to enhanced credibility through 'corporate culture' transfers and commercial advantages from networking between banks.[13] Special projects were devoted to bad debt management, an inherent feature of the Romanian banking system, as well as in other transition economies. Finally, PHARE resources were assigned to projects aimed at establishing and strengthening banking supervision systems at the level of NBR, a necessary feature to limit the types of clientelistic relations described in Chapter 3. Other institution-building activities under PHARE activities targeted other institutions. For instance, the State Ownership Fund benefited from Enhanced Pre-Accession Strategy funds in order to strengthen its institutional capacity to fulfil the EU conditions related to speeding up the privatization of state-owned banks, included in the Accession Partnership and its subsequent amendments (EC 1997b).[14] Other instances of successful transformation more closely followed the pattern of lesson drawing. One such example is provided by the reform of the regulatory framework for cooperative banks. The new rules are based on the principles of cooperative banks as applied in a number of European countries. The credit cooperatives and popular banks had to meet all the prudential requirements commonly imposed in EU countries.

The 2000 national PHARE programme for Romania also contained a project aimed at strengthening the functioning of the Romanian stock market. Despite early efforts and financial assistance from various donors to set up a well-functioning stock market, the activity of the two stock markets in Romania (the Romanian Stock Exchange and RASDAQ) remained marginal compared to the overall economic activities.[15]

However, apart from these successful activities, other PHARE activities in this sector were not effective. An area where PHARE programmes had marginal impact or none at all was in the assistance to banking associations, primarily due to a lack of receptiveness. A different example, at the bank level, is the case of assistance to the Romanian Development Bank.

Overall, as a result of concerted actions from the EU and Bretton Wood institutions, progress has recently been made towards a stable financial system. According to EC (2001a), the regulatory framework adopted in Romania broadly follows the Recommendations of the Basel Committee on Banking Supervision and the relevant EC directives. Despite this recent progress, the financial sector remains fragile so it remains to be seen if the regulatory and supervisory framework will be consistently applied over time.

Regarding the overall orientation of PHARE programmes in the field of state–finance relations, as noted previously the IMF and the World Bank have been at the forefront of macroeconomic policy advocacy on financial and monetary aspects in Romania throughout the 1990s. Consequently, a substantial part of the EU assistance was undertaken in collaboration with other IFIs and had to follow a similar Anglo-Saxon orientation.[16] As in the case of inter-enterprise arrears, the EU policy advocacy followed the line suggested by the IMF and the World Bank. Unlike the case of the Continental model of capitalism, state-owned banks in Romania were not encouraged to acquire majority stakes in industrial companies. Similarly, debt-for-equity swaps in the case of bad loans were handled by a state agency. However, despite these Anglo-Saxon influences, Romania remains a bank-based economy, due to the underdevelopment of the Romanian stock market.

EU and state–labour relations in Romania

The process of Europeanization requires not only legislative harmonization through the adoption of the *acquis communautaire* but also changes in the interest-articulation mechanisms between the state and societal groups. The implementation of EU provision on social dialogue relies on rather elusive behavioural and organizational characteristics of state and non-state actors such as leading employer associations and trade unions. The Amsterdam Treaty requires that social dialogue be promoted, and gives additional quasi-legislative powers to the social partners.[17] The candidate countries are, therefore, encouraged to give the importance required to social dialogue issues, including consultation with social partners on legislative drafts relating to the harmonization and implementation of the employment and social policy *acquis*. One necessary condition for meaningful participation and effective social dialogue is that the social partners are sufficiently developed. The development of not only tripartite structures but also of autonomous, representative bipartite institutions for social dialogue is an important aspect of the future involvement of the social partners in the social dialogue activities developed at European and national level.

The EU's social policy, comprising a set of directives laying out the minimum requirements for consultation procedures between employers and workers' groups has been gradually introduced in many Economic Commission for Europe countries. However, given the 'soft' characteristics of the *acquis* on social dialogue, the European Social Dialogue co-exists with diverse national institutional arrangements within current EU member countries and therefore it is not clear to what extent the EU social dialogue model would direct the institutional setting at a national level in Eastern Europe towards a 'European model'.

The European Works Council (EWC) Directive provides one such example. As with most of the EU candidate countries in Eastern Europe, Romania had already had some form of social dialogue in place since the early 1990s, though the European Commission, in its regular report on Romania, considered that tripartite negotiations still fall short of EU standards (EC 2001a).[18] To address the inadequacies found in state–labour relations, one of the measures included by the Romanian government in the National Programme for the Adoption of the *Acquis* (NPAA) was the harmonization of national legislation with the EWC Directive. The EWC Directive requires EU companies to set up works councils at European level If they employ at least, 1,000 employees in a member country, or at least 150 employees in each of two countries. The EWC Directive also stipulates that the management must keep the works council constantly informed about company developments, and give immediate notification of restructuring plans and other decisions that are likely to affect workers.

According to the NPAA commitments, the provisions of the European Works Council have been included in the 2002 Labour Code Draft in Romania. However, there is already evidence that certain trade unions opposed the introduction of works councils, out of fear of competition. But faced with declining membership, some of them saw the work councils as a way to justify their utility at firm level.[19]

Irrespective of the trade union's attitude, it is questionable whether the EWC will change the predominant type of Romanian industrial relations so as to include more involvement of organized labour in corporate decision-making at enterprise level, as in the case of Continental capitalism. Both private firms and SOEs are still unprepared for an effective implementation of the EWC Directive. Private employers are not well organized, and the government often plays too big a role in industrial relations and corporate governance, due to high levels of state ownership and to the fact that many union leaders are involved in politics, for the works councils to fulfil their roles.

In addition to the EWC Directive, the EU influence on state–labour relations in Romania was manifest in the PHARE programme, in particular through those projects aimed at establishing or strengthening formal structures for social dialogue. An important institution supported by PHARE funds is the Romanian Economic and Social Council (CES), the main tripartite consultative body between state, business and organized labour.[20] Initially it was unclear whether the Council would be a tripartite or multipartite body. One possibility promoted was a replica of the EC Economic and Social Council, which would involve social groups such as pensioners, farmers and consumer groups, as well as unions and employers. The proponents of this formula wanted to create a forum that would have a role in discussing broad economic and social issues.[21] However, trade unions argued that it would be hard to reach a consensus on issues such as industrial policy in a structure that has the potential of becoming, at best, a 'talking-shop' and, at worst, a means of slowing the languid pace of economic reform. Moreover, trade unions and employer associations argued that other social groups had no place in negotiations over issues such as labour laws, dispute resolution and minimum wages.[22] Therefore the EU supported this view, and trade unions and employer associations managed to use the EU rhetoric to improve their position in the newly emerged state–societal arrangement.[23]

The EU's support for the formation of the CES also prompted the strengthening of employer associations. Thus, after several attempts, the Romanian Employers' Associations (Patronatul Roman) managed to group together several smaller entities and now accounts for about 75,000 enterprises and 60 per cent of the total labour force.[24] However, despite these actions oriented towards a 'European' model of state–labour relations, the impact of EU support on state–societal relations did little to redress the problems with state–labour interactions, as identified in Chapter 3: lack of representativity, low membership, fragmentation along political lines, clientelism, the fusion between state and employer representatives in the public sector, and so on.

One reason for this limited influence on organized interest groups is that in the pre-accession stage domestic interest groups have fewer reasons to shift their attention and their demands towards the EU level, simply because the EU institutions do not have direct jurisdiction and competencies over the territories of non-member states. The EWC Directive, for instance, was not legally binding on the participation of worker representatives from Romanian subsidiaries of European MNCs in European works councils.

However, there were few instances when the power weights and type of interactions between state and societal interest groups changed as a result of Europeanization. For example, the EU decided to entrust the Economic and Social Council (ESC) with monitoring prerogatives on the use of EU funds. In doing so, the EU implicitly strengthened the position of the ESC and its social partners in state–societal institutional arrangements in Romania.[25]

Another illustration of the impact of Europeanization on social dialogue institutions is the change in policy style used by Romania in industrial relations. In general, successive Romanian governments since 1989 have demonstrated an inconsistent commitment to strengthening the role of trade unions in social and political life. Some governments, recognizing that social peace and partnership are indispensable for implementing economic and social reforms, signed social pacts with the social partners. The stated objective of these initiatives was to establish a consensus on issues such as macroeconomic stability, social policy, employment, social protection and fiscal measures. From the government's perspective, social pacts were not so much driven by the desire to have societal interest groups involved in policy formulation, but rather by the desire to ensure that serious labour conflicts would be less likely to occur. Consequently, in the absence of genuine attempts at cooperation, social pacts were usually short-lived (Nitu 2002).

Gradually however, state–labour and tripartite relations in Romania moved from open conflict towards a more institutionalized and cooperative approach. The reforms started by the various governments were aimed at drafting a new Labour Code, as well as amending the legislation on trade unions (Law 54/1991) and social dialogue (Law 109/1997) to bring them into line with European standards. Significant progress in adopting the institutional *acquis* and in bringing the policy style more into line with the cooperative attitude promoted at EU level has been achieved only in recent years. A primary objective in the 2000 Romanian National Programme for the Adoption of the *Acquis* was the setting-up of a tripartite Council for Economic and Financial Coordination, under the direct supervision of the Prime Minister. The overall strategy of European integration has, since 2001, been discussed in a Commission for Social Dialogue, within the Ministry of Integration.

At the working level, commissions for social dialogue have been created within all ministries and prefectures. The commissions are consulted on draft sectoral legislation, as well as economic restructuring and privatization issues. Despite these initiatives, the role and the recognition of trade union activities in private enterprises remains weak. Bipartite social dialogue at enterprise level is not sufficiently developed, and this problem is magnified because the employers' movement remains divided (EC 2001a).[26]

In parallel, social dialogue partners in Romania have tried to use the EU integration to enhance their capabilities. The Romanian trade union confederations have tried to use their membership of the European Trade Union confederation (ETUC) as a means to boost their legitimacy in tripartite negotiations and to increase membership. In addition, they are particularly keen to establish a stronger presence in the Romanian MNC subsidiaries, where so far they have failed to gain a foothold.[27] While retaining part of their inherited membership in state-owned firms, which have been bought by foreign investors, unions have failed to make inroads in greenfield investments. Trade union leaders complained that many employees of multinational companies worry that joining a trade union may be seen as a sign of corporate disloyalty and thus jeopardize their jobs.[28] In such cases, EU social directives are unlikely to offer much solace in situations where trade unions have failed to gain worker recognition in MNCs. Without cooperation from the management side of MNC subsidiaries, Romanian trade unions would find little advantage in trying to use the EWC Directive as a means to encourage unionization in greenfield production sites because trade union involvement in works councils is not required by EU law.

In sum, the preceding analysis demonstrates that, unlike the IMF and World Bank programmes in the field of state–labour relations, the EU tried to advance more systematically a 'European' model of industrial relations that incorporates several typical features of Continental capitalist models. Various domestic factors restricted the effectiveness of such influence in Romania. As argued in Chapter 1, one weakening factor is the inability of business and labour interest groups to engage in formal coordination mechanisms with the state. Instead, both preferred to pursue their interests through clientelistic relations or, if these failed, through open conflict. Another constraint on the EU ability to promote a more consensual framework for Romanian industrial relations was the dualist policy style adopted by the Romanian government. Contradictory influences of external factors, as described in this chapter, contributed to the persistence of such duality.

The impact of the International Monetary Fund on domestic institutions in Romania: aid, conditionality and policy transfer

The role of the IMF in the international economy has been under intensive scrutiny in the last few decades.[29] As the IMF began to play a central role in the management of international debt crises in the 1980s, the policies advocated by the IMF stirred up a controversy that moved to centre-stage in political as well as economic debates.[30] The IMF's mandate, as mentioned in its founding statute is, *inter alia*, 'to facilitate the expansion and balanced growth of international trade, and to contribute thereby to the promotion and maintenance of high levels of employment and real income ... of all members as primary objectives of economic policies'.[31]

Most of the debates, both within academic circles and at policy level, have focused mainly on the adequacy of the Fund's 'economic stabilization programmes'[32] in addressing the problems associated with the general mandate of the IMF, as spelled out in the IMF statute. By pointing to the negative economic, social and political consequences in the 'beneficiary' countries, its critics attacked the 'orthodoxy' of the Fund's economic doctrine and the developmental impact on countries under IMF programmes.[33]

This controversial role and the economic policy conditions accompanying loans granted by the IMF received considerable attention in Romania as well. Romania's relations with the IMF date back to the 1970s, beginning during the oil crises of the 1970s when, due to its large petrochemical sector, Romania was faced with acute balance of payment problems. Figure 5.1 illustrates the use of IMF funds by Romania in historical perspective. The use of IMF funds started to decrease after 1984, when IMF conditionality was deemed unacceptable by the communist government. During the late 1980s, the balance of payment problems persisted but they were addressed through a massive reduction of import and domestic consumption. During the 1990s, once again the reliance on IMF funds increased rapidly and, along with the European Union, the IMF was a major player in terms of funds disbursed to Romania.

As will be shown in the following pages, such relatively strong dependence on IMF aid reduced the room for manoeuvre available to domestic political forces and increased the role played by the Fund in shaping key macroeconomic policies in Romania. While the terms of IMF agreements, and the conditionality attached to them, place the

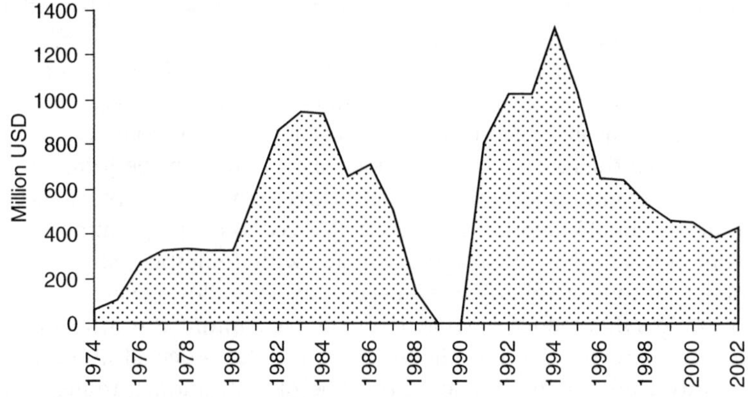

Figure 5.1   Romania's use of IMF funds: 1974–2002
Source: World Bank (2004a).

Fund in a good position to influence domestic macroeconomic policies, the impact of IMF on domestic institutions is – in addition to its well-known preference for neoliberal arrangements – less obvious.

Several arguments support of the idea that the IMF can easily influence policies, but domestic institutions less so. First, as many authors have argued, due to its mandate the IMF can only indirectly influence institutional arrangements.[34] Furthermore, official rhetoric at the Fund and the Bank often emphasizes that relations with borrowing governments are apolitical, consensual and non-interventionist (IMF 1999b). Moreover, judging by its mandate, the Fund is a technocratic organization. Its three main functions are also very technical: administration of a code of conduct concerning exchange rate policies and restrictions on payments for current account transactions, the provision of financial assistance to member countries correcting imbalances, and the creation of a platform for continued consultation and cooperation. The Fund has repeatedly stressed that it takes decisions according to a 'doctrine of economic neutrality', regardless of factors such as international politics and the nature of the regimes in developing countries, but many critics argue that politics often play a role in the IMF decisions.

Second, the Fund does not initiate on new financial assistance instruments; instead, it is the country that comes with a request for funding for a proposed programme. As in any other financial institution, the Fund has the right to accept or decline the proposal and, according to its established criteria, attach certain conditions. Moreover, even when approached, the Fund cannot influence the undertaking of a stabilization programme. As practice has shown, in many cases, the implementation of IMF conditionality has not been effectively enforced.[35]

All these reasons would suggest that the impact of the IMF on policy transfer and models of capitalism should be limited. However, an equal number of reasons suggest the contrary. There are three main reasons to assume that the role of the IMF is not only linked to the performance of purely economic tasks, but that it also offers a cover for the pursuance of an institutional blueprint. First, every IMF economic programme is, as a result of its complexity, intimately linked with domestic political issues that are at the core of any market economy. By imposing various policy constraints that reduce the role of the state to a minimalist influence on the economy, the Fund implicitly drives the state–societal interactions towards a minimalist, Anglo-Saxon type of institutional arrangement (Gowan 1995). The Fund's implicit neoliberal, market-friendly policy advocacy is carried out by means of conditionality, as well as by surveillance of compliance with its principles and rules by its members. The IMF can do this because it is an international organization that has considerable influence, primarily *vis-à-vis* its members seeking funding. It has the power to do so because it can grant or deny the resources that the member states have pooled at its disposal. What gives it most influence, however, is the fact that it is the only lender of last resort on the international financial market; it enjoys a sort of monopoly power, allowing it to impose its own conditions. Moreover, the approval of debtor countries' economic policies has also become a precondition for other debt agreements, as commercial banks and official creditors link rescheduling agreements to IMF-endorsed creditworthiness. Confronted with such a forceful bargaining power, borrowing countries do not have much choice in designing and following their macroeconomic restructuring plans.

Second, the actual decision-making procedures within the Fund, as well as the weighted voting system, suggest that there is room for politically motivated decisions to be pushed through, given the privileged position enjoyed by several key developed countries.

To assess the extent to which IMF activities, as described above, have an impact on institutional transformation in Romania, the following section empirically examines several IMF programmes implemented in Romania. The investigation covers issues within which the IMF was traditionally involved, such as financial and monetary issues, budget reform, privatization, and so on. Another section will look into the 'new' IMF role, in particular the impact of the IMF programmes on labour issues, as evidenced in the case of Romania.

IMF and Romanian state–industry relations

After 1989, the contact between Romania and the IMF meant that other macroeconomic conditions deemed crucial for the evolution of the transition process, were added to the balance of payment issues. One key area of concern for the IMF was the fiscal deficit and the easy access to state funds that SOEs enjoyed. Reducing fiscal deficits implicitly meant that SOEs would become subject to tight budget constraints. Once such conditions were in place, the problematic aspects of state–industry relations identified in Chapter 3 would fade away, complementing the positive results expected from the restructuring and privatization of SOEs. For instance, as part of the stand-by arrangement with the IMF, the government discontinued the practice of financially supporting state-owned enterprises with receipts from the privatization process (IMF 2001c, p. 2).[36]

However, throughout the post-1989 period, the restructuring of SOEs remained a daunting task for both the Romanian governments and international organizations involved in the transformation process.[37] According to the IMF, all five stand-by arrangements concluded by Romania and the IMF during the 1990s decade failed (to different degrees) to implement the agreed reform programme, mainly due to the government's inability to impose tight budget constraints on large SOEs (IMF 2001b, p. 4).

A telling example of such difficulties is the Romanian isolation programme. As part of its conditionality on state–industry arrangements, the IMF advocated an enterprise isolation programme which had been implemented in several transition economies. Such programmes usually involved restructuring measures aimed at preparing large loss-making SOEs for privatization. As part of the project, the Agency for Restructuring was created to implement, in close coordination with the SOF and responsible line ministries, technical assistance measures and financial packages aimed at restructuring these loss-making SOEs. Initially, the aim was to restructure about 300 loss-making SOEs but this ambitious plan had to be scaled down under union pressure, and eventually only 73 industrial firms and 74 agricultural SOEs were included in the programme (GOR 1994).[38] Despite the initial objectives of the programme (reduction in losses, state subsidies, and excess employment), SOEs included in the programme performed poorly on all indicators. At the end of the project in 1997, out of 174 SOEs included in the isolation programme, only four firms had successfully implemented the objectives of the programme.[39]

The fact that instead of being liquidated or severely restructured the enterprises included in the isolation programme were actually receiving more state funds and specialized management expertise led other companies to request their inclusion in the programme, despite their initial opposition.[40] Since the enterprise isolation programme was aimed at reducing the losses and, whenever possible, avoiding the bankruptcy of companies either fully or partially owned by the state, this was perceived as discrimination against loss-making firms that were left out of the programme. Furthermore, several companies argued against the unfair competition introduced by the preferential conditions granted under the isolation programme.

Therefore, despite IMF conditionality, the systemic problems affecting state–industry relations identified in Chapter 3 persisted. Several reasons for the failure of the enterprise isolation programme to attain its objectives can be found in the institutional arrangements. The main institutional weakness was the lack of coherent strategies and conflicting interests of the institutions involved. As mentioned in Chapter 3, the institutional framework developed in Romania to deal with the privatization process was quite complex, involving the SOF, five POFs, and branch ministries. The provisions included in the isolation programme that were aimed at enhancing cooperation between the SOF, line ministries, and the newly created Agency for Restructuring were a positive development, but in practice they had little impact. Soon after its setting-up, the Agency for Restructuring disagreed with the SOF on the orientation of the restructuring programme, so there was little actual progress made.

Another case that clearly illustrates the limited success of IMF advice in Romania are inter-enterprise arrears (IEAs). IEAs plagued Romania and posed a heavy systemic burden on many competitive enterprises. To a limited extent, inter-enterprise arrears affected various CEECs but they became a serious problem in Romania after 1990 (Daianu 1994; Rostowski 1994).[41] At the end of 1991, IEAs amounted to about 50 per cent of GNP (Rostowski 1994, p. iii). In contrast, in the same period, IEAs constituted only 18 per cent of GDP in Czechoslovakia and Poland (Rostowski 1994, pp. 8–9).

Both the IMF and the World Bank have acknowledged the importance of this issue and have tried to design appropriate solutions for its elimination. Several options were suggested for tackling the issue of inter-enterprise arrears. The obvious strategy was to introduce credible and efficient bankruptcy procedures, but this proved to be a difficult and lengthy process in many CEECs. In the meantime, several other solutions to the IEA problem were proposed.

One strategy, adopted in Poland, sought to create favourable conditions for IEAs to be transferred into equity. One option was for creditor companies to acquire a stake in the debtor company, in exchange for their debts. Banks were also involved in these debt-for-equity swaps, in cases when creditor companies preferred liquidities. The result of these debt-for-equity schemes in Poland resembles the cross-ownership networks that characterize Continental and developmental forms of capitalism, as described in Chapter 1. This argument is supported by the findings of Pinto and Wijnbergen (1994) on the important role that Polish banks played in strengthening financial discipline among SOEs and reducing IEAs.

In contrast, the Romanian scheme offered few incentives to Romanian banks to act against the propagation of IEAs (Perotti and Carare 1997). The strategy adopted by Romania was to cancel out as many IEAs as possible and then cover the remaining net IEAs with credit from the central bank. One argument in favour of this scheme was that such an approach would break the vicious links between debtor and creditor SOEs. The various Romanian governments and the National Bank of Romania, with the agreement of the IMF and the World Bank, have tried to set up such a 'one-off' clearing mechanism for IEAs.[42] Under that mechanism, arrears will be settled multilaterally across all SOEs affected, with the net amount of remaining debts being covered by the NBR (Clifton and Khan 1993).[43] However, the inherent tendency to continue the settlement of IEAs with credit from the NBR increased the magnitude of the IEAs in the Romanian economy (Daianu 1994).[44]

Unlike the Polish case, where market mechanisms were used to promote not only the elimination of IEAs but also production networks and cross-ownership between major business partners, the Romanian example shows that despite the adherence to the policy advice given by IFIs, the final outcome was not the expected outcome. Moreover, policy learning from the success of the developmental-oriented strategy adopted in Poland did not occur in the case of Romania. Whether the Polish experience could have been successfully transposed to Romania is difficult to say. The evidence provided in Chapter 1 showed that, unlike other CEECs, in Romania informal networks and interlocking structures involving various companies and state actors were not growth enhancing.[45]

In sum, the evidence provided above suggests that the IMF programmes (and as the following sections will show, the World Bank and EU programmes on state–industry relations) were promoting reform strategies based on rapid privatization and arm's length state–industry relations. Privatization was seen as having a positive influence on fiscal deficits, reducing the losses in the public sector and increasing the state revenues through privatization receipts. However, as argued in Chapter 1, such strategies had to face the opposition of vested domestic interest groups that benefited from close state–industry relationships. As a result of the strength of such opposing domestic institutional arrangements, the effectiveness of external influences was significantly affected.[46] Furthermore, the example of inter-enterprise arrears suggests that, unlike other CEECs, there is little evidence suggesting that the growth-inhibiting state–industry relations in Romania could have been transformed into growth-enhancing, developmentally oriented institutions.

The IMF and Romanian state–finance relations

As mentioned in the previous sections, during 1999 Romania had to implement a broad set of policies, prior to the approval of another stand-by agreement with the IMF. The main conditions were imposed on fiscal and monetary policies. On fiscal policies, the IMF agreement provided for the removal of tax exemptions and investment incentives, the introduction of wage limits in the public sector, increased wage taxes, a ceiling on government borrowing and on state-owned bank lending to SOEs, as well as a reduction in inter-enterprise arrears. The Fund also required increased transparency of fiscal policy and fiscal institutions. This evaluation is conducted against a set of principles of fiscal transparency. The assumption is that lack of transparency is an indication of a lower-quality public sector and that this lack of transparency promotes inefficiency and various problems of governance.

On monetary issues, the agreement introduced targets for broad money and ceilings on the domestic and foreign assets of the National Bank of Romania and other Romanian banks. Several conditions were also attached to other policies such as bank privatization and restructuring. Specific conditions were aimed at improving the institutional capacity for banking supervision of the National Bank of Romania and the legal framework (IMF 1999d; IMF 2001b, p. 54).

All these policy constraints implicitly had an indirect impact on state–finance relations and the institutions governing these interactions. Even though the IMF directly addressed institutional aspects only marginally (strengthening the NBR banking supervision, fiscal disciplines, etc.), the IMF also influenced the relative balance of power between the various actors involved in state–finance relations in Romania. Stronger banking supervision rules gave more leverage to the NBR in limiting the type of clientelistic relationships described in Chapter 3 that were so pervasive in Romania. Both managers of state-owned banks and politicians felt less inclined to engage in looting, soft loans and asset-stripping activities before an IMF evaluation of performance under a stand-by arrangement. Nevertheless, despite the fact that Romania has been under IMF supervision throughout the last decade, the extent to which IMF conditionality can alleviate such institutional weaknesses seems limited. The IMF stand-by arrangements stressed the importance of a strengthened supervisory and regulatory framework in the financial sector. The implementation of the Basel Core Principles as well as international accounting standards were key recommendations (IMF 2001b, p. 19). However, the financial sector in Romania, despite some recent improvements, remains affected by structural weaknesses.

The IMF stand-by arrangements also included conditions related to the privatization of the banking sector. In those cases where the IMF's policy advice was included as conditionality in the stand-by agreement, the IMF influence was effective.[47] The 2001–3 arrangement required Romania to draft a privatization strategy for the largest state-owned bank, Banca Comerciala Romana (BCR), *before* the stand-by arrangements could be approved.[48] This led the Romanian government to speed up the privatization process of BCR and agree on the complete sale of the bank and transfer of control to a strategic investor by the end of 2002. In other cases, even though the specific IMF policy advice was not literally adopted, the overall pressure for change induced by the IMF remained crucial for the continuation of sustained reform in the banking sector.

In summary, the IMF tried to promote two main types of changes to state–finance relations in Romania. First, IMF conditionality included measures aimed at strengthening the NBR capacity to enforce standard prudential and supervision rules on the banking sector. Second, by promoting the rapid privatization of state-owned banks, the IMF tried to reduce political influence on banking activities. In doing so, the IMF, as well as the World Bank and the EU, tried to eliminate all of the negative aspects of close state–banking relationships for the stability of the financial system. Although some forms of state–finance interactions proved to be growth-enhancing, as the literature on developmental capitalism argues, the IFIs viewed the state and market institutions as antithetical. In addition, given the reliance of the Romanian economy on the banking sector as its major source of capital for investment activities, the emerging financial system in Romania was far from an Anglo-Saxon model, where the stock markets play a prominent role.

The IMF and labour issues in Romania: advocating a developmental model of state–labour relations?

Traditionally, the IMF was perceived as a strong promoter of market mechanisms, and as taking a minimalist approach towards the role of the state in economic activities. However, despite this reliance on neoclassical economics, the position of the IMF on labour issues in Romania is in marked contrast with the free market principles guiding the policy advocacy of the IMF. Moreover, the IMF strategy seems to have evolved recently, at least at the level of rhetoric, away from a neoliberal model based on a minimalist approach to state–society interactions and towards a more socially embedded policy advocacy. Michel Camdessus, the former IMF Director General, acknowledged that the stabilization policies and structural reforms are truly effective only when the political actors and interest groups (labour organizations, employers, etc.) are committed to change (Camdessus 1999, p. 1).

Given this change in vision by the IMF, this section tries to elucidate, based on empirical evidence, the extent to which IMF programmes have pursued a neoclassical, Anglo-Saxon model of state–labour relations or, as recent statements seem to suggest, a Continental model of state–labour relations based on a partnership between the state and societal actors.

As a departing point in this analysis, a close examination of various IMF documents suggests that the Fund does not have the primary responsibility and expertise on social policies. Therefore, in implementing its programmes, the IMF relies on close cooperation with those organizations that are more specialized in this field. Between the Bretton Woods institutions, this expertise lies with the World Bank. Other international institutions, such as regional development banks, UN agencies (ILO, UN Development Programme, etc.), bilateral donors and Non-governmental organizations, are also identified as major partners in assisting the Fund on social policy advice.

Nevertheless, given the content of the IMF programmes, the impact of the IMF on state–labour relations was not merely marginal or indirect, but rather quite significant for the outcome of state–societal interactions. A typical condition advocated and supported by the IMF in the region refers to the minimization of the budget deficit, including the share allocated to social instruments.[49] Since in transition economies the size of the state-owned sector remains considerable, it also follows that the share of wages within the state budget is an important element. Consequently, the IMF often advocated some form of policy conditionality on wage-setting policies and labour restructuring.[50] In the various stand-by arrangements between Romania and the IMF, wage restraint remained one of the core performance criteria on which IMF loan disbursement depended.[51]

The IMF strongly advocated wage restraint and deflationary policies, sometimes at any cost. Moreover, the IMF believed that organized labour is a major aggravating element in the inflationary spiral. IMF (2001d) argues that wages are the most plausible cause for the high inflationary pressure during the past decade in Romania. The IMF report goes on to say that 'the combination of wage levels well above those justified by productivity (even if those wages are low in absolute terms), especially in conjunction with widespread overstaffing and ... the failure to enforce financial discipline has clearly done much to fuel inflation' (IMF 2001d, p. 26).

However, wages in Romania have remained at lower levels than in most other CEECs (with the exception of Bulgaria) throughout the post-1989 period. Even in recent years real wages in Romania are about five times lower than in Poland and eight times lower than in Slovenia. Morevoer, Schadler *et al.* (1995b) produced evidence that real wages in Romania were not only the lowest in the region but also lower than wages in lesser developed countries in Africa. At the same time, the productivity level was relatively high in Romania. Table 5.1 contains several indicators supporting this conclusion. The level of wages denominated in US dollars (as a proxy for real wages), even though an imperfect indicator, suggests that, based on 1992 figures – a year when real wages were among the highest – Romania had the lowest level of real wages in the region, even lower than the average wages in Africa. In addition, a rough

Table 5.1   Indicators of labour competitiveness, 1992

Country	Average monthly earnings, in US dollars	Wage/Output per capita (Index OECD = 100)
Central Europe	186	101
Bulgaria	179	138
Czechoslovakia	168	76
Hungary	286	98
Poland	214	113
Romania	**83**	**78**
OECD	1848	100
Africa	130	358
Latin America	376	211
Asia, excluding NICs	120	129
Asian NICs	857	86

NICs = newly industrializing countries.

Source: Schadler *et al.* (1995b), p. 119.

measure of labour productivity and unit labour costs is the ratio of wages to gross national product (GNP) per capita. A lower ratio indicates a more competitive labour force. By this measure, Romania was more competitive than most other countries in the region (with the exception of Czechoslovakia) or Asian newly industrializing countries, and was far more competitive than Africa and Latin America.

In addition, as Figure 5.2 shows, there is little evidence that wage growth was a major inflationary factor. Wage increases usually lead to inflation when they are higher than labour productivity increases. With the exception of 1998, real wage increases were lower than the positive changes in labour productivity. Moreover, in 1994, 1999 and 2000 real wages declined, despite improvements in labour productivity.

In contrast to these economic indicators, the IMF continued to include tough conditionality on wage policy in its stand-by arrangements with Romania. For 2001, for instance, Romania and the IMF agreed to lower employment in the public sector and to reduce real wages by 3 per cent (IMF 2001b, p. 18). The stand-by arrangement also requested the government to ensure that the 2002 social pact with trade unions was consistent with these objectives.

Apart from wage restraint, the IMF also pushed for ambitious targets on labour shedding. According to the 2000 Memorandum between Romania and the IMF, economic restructuring during 2000 should have brought a considerable reduction in the labour force in the public sector (23,000 employees), defence, public order and national security

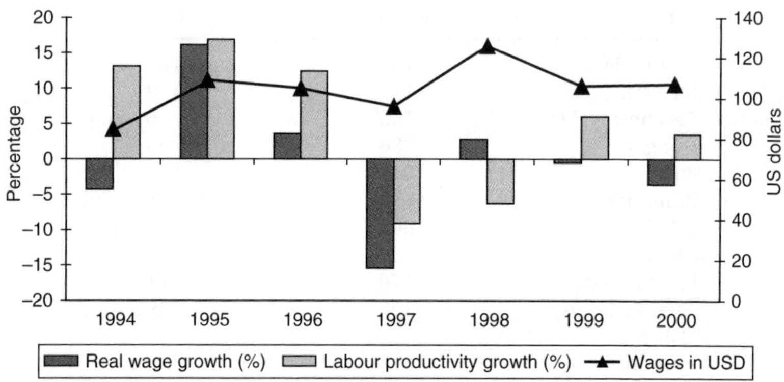

Figure 5.2 Real wages and productivity in Romania, 1995–2000
Source: Author's calculations, based on IMF (2001b), p. 187.

(22,000 employees), education (23,000 employees), and electric energy production and distribution (20,000 employees). If the workers laid off from the major SOEs liquidated during the year 2000 are added to this, this would represent almost 2 per cent of the total number of employed workers registered in Romania.[52]

Unsurprisingly, during the transition period, the IMF and organized labour had different views on the right labour restructuring and wage-setting policies and the various Romanian governments faced a tough choice between IMF conditionality and supporting of organized labour.[53] Given the fact that the IMF conditionality included a number of provisions with direct impact on labour, seeking the support of social partners for the terms included in the agreements with the IMF was a constant objective of the various Romanian governments.[54] For instance, in the stand-by agreement with the IMF agreed in 2001, the Romanian government committed to the IMF on various labour-related issues that contravened the agreement reached with trade union confederations during the 2000 electoral campaign.[55] The text of the agreement stated that the Romanian government:

> decided to resist firmly any pressure from enterprises for wage increases in the remaining period of 2001. For 2002, we decided to implement a much stronger control over wages in the public enter-prises ... We will also ensure that the social pact that we intend to sign with trade unions and other partners is not inconsistent with this programme. (IMF 2001b, pp. 52–3)

However, such commitments were made without prior consultation with social partners, a constant critique made by trade unions. When the government tried at all costs to reach a social pact with organized labour, this contravened IMF conditionality and was criticized by the IMF (Cotidianul 2001b, pp. 4–6). The government therefore systemati-cally lost any degree of confidence due to ambiguous messages.[56] All of these contradicting commitments triggered strong reactions from trade union confederations against IMF policy advice and conditionality.[57] On other occasions, the trade unions refused to enter into an agreement with the government, knowing that the value of such an agreement would be diminished by subsequent discussions between the IMF and the Romanian government (Media Uno 2002, pp. 1–2).

As a result of this lack of coordination, the government's attempts to justify unpopular measures such as IMF conditionality were highly inef-fective, and they often exacerbated labour protests. Although all parties considered consensual state–labour relations as a major precondition for a relaunch of the economy, such pacts were short-lived.

Overall, it can be argued that the impact of the IMF on Continental-style state–labour relations in Romania was negative, drastically reducing the room for negotiation between the government and trade unions. In terms of models of capitalism, by insisting on a strong role for the state in maintaining wage controls, the impact of the IMF on state–labour relations was not towards a market-based Anglo-Saxon model but, quite paradoxically, towards state–labour relations that were more similar to those usually found in a statist developmental model. Despite the general move to reliance on market mechanisms in CEECs during the 1990s, the IMF advocated state-controlled wage determination in which state–labour relations were based on strict wage controls previously agreed between the Romanian government and the IMF. Moreover, the above analysis suggests that, in contrast to the official rhetoric, IMF conditionality in Romania did little to improve the participatory features of state–labour relations.

The World Bank: between Anglo-Saxon capitalism and mezzo-corporatism

Not only was the role of the IMF in the international architecture intensely debated, but also the impact of the World Bank's policy prescriptions on beneficiary countries.[58] One point in the debate is the very position held by the World Bank *vis-à-vis* the role of the state in the economy. Until the early 1990s, there was little disagreement within the 'Washington consensus' and its laissez-faire policies. However, after the spectacular success of the East Asian countries, the World Bank started to question its position on the role of the state in the economy. The World Bank acknowledged that those countries maintained both various forms of strategic state intervention and high growth rates. The World Bank report also mentions that the successful Asian economies also had in place 'formal institutions that facilitate communication and co-operation between private and public actors' as an 'institutionalized form of wealth sharing aimed primarily at winning the support and co-operation of business elites' (World Bank 1993, p. 181). However, this position was amended in the following years, by saying that the positive role of the state is based on 'good governance' rather than state intervention per se. The World Bank (1992, p. 1), for instance, defines governance as 'the manner in which power is exercised in the management of a country's economic and social resources for development'.

Good governance would therefore mean any political institutional arrangement that improves a country's development prospects. However, the World Bank's interpretation of good governance involves minimalist government intervention, a stable economic environment, and transparency and accountability of public institutions. Therefore the various strategic policies and institutions associated with the Asian developmental state were perceived either as superfluous or even negative (World Bank 1995, 1997).

To assess whether this view influenced the activities of the World Bank in Romania, the most fruitful approach is to look into various projects implemented by the Bank in Romania since 1991 and examine them against this orthodox paradigm. The World Bank's project portfolio in Romania targeted various economic and social challenges of transition: strengthening the social safety net, improving health and education, enhancing the effectiveness of public service, and protecting the environment.

Several World Bank projects bundled policies that addressed both the industrial restructuring and banking and financial sector. For instance, the 1999 Private Sector Institutional Building Loan (PSIBL) provided technical assistance for case-by-case privatizations of large SOEs. In addition, the project also targeted the restructuring of state-owned banks and the establishment of a secondary market for Government securities. Other structural adjustment programmes covered a large array of macroeconomic policies aimed at achieving a stable economic environment. Such a comprehensive framework imposed itself not only due to the systemic nature of the economic difficulties crippling the Romanian economy, but also, as shown in Chapter 3, due to the clientelistic nature and the iron triangles formed between the state, business and financial sectors.

For instance, as shown in Table 5.2, the structure of the Private Sector Institutional Building Loan (PSIBL) is illustrative of the integrated approach adopted by the Bank in reforming the Romanian economy. The project devotes a significant proportion of total funds to each of the three dimensions of state–business–finance relations. Furthermore, in recognition of the lesson learned from the failure of the Financial and Enterprise Sector Adjustment Loan (FESAL) project, the Bank understood that enterprise privatization is essential for the success of the overall project.[59] Therefore, almost half (43 per cent) of the project funds were devoted to enterprise privatization and corporate restructuring.[60]

However, apart from one notable exception aimed at enhancing the export potential of Romanian industry, there is very little evidence of

Table 5.2 The structure of the World Bank Private Sector Institutional Building Loan programme, by sector

Sector	Indicative costs (US$ million)	% of total costs	Bank contribution (US$ million)	% of total sectoral costs	% of Bank contribution
Privatization	10.8	33	10.8	100	43
Financial sector	8.4	25	7.9	94	32
Institutional development	4.4	13	4.4	100	18
Other (administrative costs, fees, etc.)	9.5	29	1.9	20	7

Source: World Bank (1999b).

World Bank projects attempting to draw lessons from the success of the Asian developmental state and to transpose, at least partially, the conclusions of the *East Asian Miracle* study. Similarly, evidence of World Bank projects encouraging effective state–societal institutions is scarce. One such case is the restructuring of the mining sector, where the World Bank project promoted a transitory institutional framework that resembled a mezzo-corporatist arrangement. Both cases will be discussed at length in the following sections.

Below we will turn to some specific examples of how the World Bank projects managed to address the problematic issues mentioned in Chapter 1, state–industry, state–finance and state–labour relations.

The World Bank and state–industry institutional arrangements

For decades, the World Bank financed specific investment projects around the world, particularly in industries with good export potential. In addition, the Bank, in its structural adjustment loans (SALs), provided financing for export expansion and industrial restructuring (World Bank 1986, p. 7). The World Bank, as an investment project lender, concentrated a great deal of its efforts on 'institution building' at the enterprise and sectoral level. Such efforts in the case of transition economies involved removing the management weaknesses resulting from political interference in SOE operational activities (soft loans, subsidies, administered prices, asset-stripping, etc.).

Faced with major macroeconomic challenges, the Romanian government entered into consultations with the World Bank to explore the technical assistance opportunities available. Following these consultations, the Romanian government requested a FESAL in the early 1990s.

The FESAL programme was launched in 1992 to remove structural impediments to growth (World Bank 1999a). Its objectives included, among others, the acceleration of privatization, enforcing hard budget constraints on remaining SOEs, privatizing the remaining SOEs, and improving the business environment.

PSAL and the PSIBL were designed to build on and complement the reforms initiated under the FESAL (which ended in April 1998 with policy measures incomplete and the final tranche of US$100 million not disbursed), and were aimed at supporting the government's efforts to stabilize the macroeconomic situation by accelerating structural and banking sector reforms, including the privatization of state-owned enterprises, and the creation of an environment conducive to private sector growth and development (World Bank 1999a). The PSAL also assisted the government in the process of reducing the sizeable losses of several state enterprises and in ensuring that the social protection programme became more streamlined and efficient. The PSIBL was specifically targeted at strengthening the domestic institutional infrastructure involved in the other restructuring and privatization programmes. With the successful completion of the PSAL in June 2000, a new PSAL-II programme has been designed to continue and deepen these reforms.

One objective in the PSAL was the privatization of three major state-owned companies: SIDEX, ALRO and ALPROM. SIDEX was a major target for the World Bank restructuring and privatization strategy, due to the significant losses incurred by the steel plant and all the associated negative effects (soft budget constraints, budget deficits, clientelistic relations) described in Chapter 3.[61] Given the reluctance of the Romanian government to restructure and privatize SIDEX prior to the PSAL programme, the World Bank's involvement was intended to induce a 'lock-in' effect on the commitment of Romanian authorities towards the privatization of large loss-making SOEs.[62] Faced with an anti-developmental, clientelistic institutional arrangement that was favoured by vested domestic interest groups, the World Bank's Anglo-Saxon policy advocacy, based on a rapid privatization, represented an important determinant.

Eliminating losses incurred by large SOEs was not the only rationale behind the World Bank's policy on privatization. Privatization was also a means of maintaining or improving the efficiency of profitable SOEs. One strategy advocated by the World Bank, and fully supported by the IMF, was the privatization of the main SOEs in the energy sector. Thus the two gas distribution companies, as well as two of the eight electricity companies, were included in the government's privatization programme for 2002. The World Bank also advocated the privatization of other large SOEs in the aluminium sector and the national oil distribution company. In many of these cases there was evidence of asset stripping and the World Bank privatization programme was indirectly aimed at addressing such issues.[63]

Thus, the World Bank tried to promote state–industry institutional arrangements and policies typical of an efficient Anglo-Saxon model of capitalism and discouraged the existing relations that favoured political patronage of SOEs, without any attempt to transform them into growth-enhancing relations that could have led to an 'Eastern European miracle'.

The impact of the World Bank on state–finance relations

As mentioned earlier, the World Bank strategy of addressing the institutional weaknesses of Romania evolved towards an integrated approach, dealing with both industrial and financial aspects simultaneously. Apart from state–industry relations, in the financial sector FESAL projects were aimed at strengthening the supervisory and enforcement capacity of the NBR, and assisting the development of capital markets in Romania through the opening of the Bucharest Stock Exchange and the creation of the over-the-counter market, RASDAQ.

However, despite the assistance of the World Bank, the Romanian financial market remained one of the most underdeveloped in the region. The fragility of financial supervisory institutions was another persistent problem on which the World Bank concentrated significant resources, both on preventive measures and on crisis management, but with little success.[64] Despite these preventive measures aimed at building the capacity of Romanian institutions to effectively manage the financial sector, Romania remained prone to domestically generated financial crises.

In addition, the World Bank carried out two separate PSALs in Romania. The PSALs supported several broad areas of activity: (1) privatizing a few state-owned banks and restructuring several poorly performing state-owned banks in order to prepare them for eventual privatization, (2) strengthening the bank regulatory and supervisory framework; and (3) assisting the development of government securities markets.

In all components, the World Bank had clearly spelled out objectives that related to major policy failures, such as those identified in Chapter 3. In the financial sector for instance, in the aftermath of two of the major financial scandals – the case of BANCOREX and Banca Agricolathe – World Bank played a major role in ensuring that the liquidation of BANCOREX and the restructuring of Banca Agricola were carried out in an appropriate manner. In particular, the World Bank helped the NBR to put in place the regulatory framework necessary for a sound banking system.

As in other projects, the World Bank imposed strict conditions in order to ensure that the monitoring of the project could be easily carried out. Similar tangible performance indicators were set for enterprise restructuring and privatization of many SOEs, accounting for a significant proportion of the SOF's total equity portfolio (World Bank 1999b, pp. 14–17).

Despite strict built-in conditionality[65] and financial incentives associated with the impact of World Bank activities on the path of transition in Romania, inherent problematic features of the domestic factors largely hampered such potential positive impact. According to the World Bank's own evaluations, the FESAL project in Romania largely failed to achieve its other operational objectives (World Bank 1999a, p. 2).[66] The privatization process of state-owned banks was not accelerated as planned, even after the 1996 elections when a centre-Right coalition government came into power.

One other failure was the inability to improve the regulatory framework with regard to credit cooperatives. According to the World Bank, the project was hampered by major difficulties within the governing coalition and by the loss of commitment to reform (World Bank 1999a, p. 2). In some cases, the strategy adopted for bank restructuring and privatization turned out to be based on a somewhat incomplete assessment of the situation. Particularly troublesome was the fact that the precise financial condition of the state banks could not be determined.[67] Hence, despite its financial and technical assistance to Romania since the early 1990s with regard to the banking sector, the World Bank was unable to prevent or predict the successive banking crises that hit Romania throughout the period. While it is true that banking crises were not unique to the region and can be seen throughout the world, this category of bank collapse due to bank mismanagement, usually associated with fraud by the owners and managers of banks and by some degree of regulatory or policy failure on the part of government, proves the limits of any policy transfer that is not backed by a commitment to reform by domestic institutions.

The evidence discussed earlier therefore suggests that both in the case of the banking system and financial markets, the World Bank advocated the introduction of institutional practices and policies that are major prerequisites for a functioning Anglo-Saxon capitalist system. In this context, the existing state–finance relations were largely considered detrimental, and consequently the main policy advocacy was the privatization of state-owned banks and the reduction of the role of the state to a more effective regulator.

Despite the fact that a number of World Bank projects did not achieve their stated objectives, based on speed and results of reform undertaken prior to and after the World Bank assistance, it can be argued that often the impact of World Bank programmes was quite significant. As in a large number of World Bank projects worldwide, not all Romanian projects had the same degree of success in implementation. Some of them were highly unsatisfactory (such as the FESAL projects). Others, like one discussed below on a key aspect of state–labour relations in Romania (the Mines Closure and Social Mitigation Project), were quite successful not only in reshaping institutional arrangements but also in diffusing a tense social issue.

The World Bank and state–labour relations in the mining sector: from perverted to social mezzo-corporatism

Unlike the IMF, the World Bank was more involved in developing a cooperative atmosphere between state and labour. For instance the Comprehensive Development Framework (CDF) initiative was designed to be a participatory approach, soliciting input from a broad spectrum of stakeholders in the country's future. Such broad dialogue has helped to generate more continuity in the Bank's strategy for state–societal relations in Romania.

One important complementary component of this strategy was to ease the social costs of transition. World Bank projects tried, for instance, to improve the safety nets available to redundant workers. One instance of this was a comprehensive strategy linking the liquidation of loss-making SOEs and the creation of social safety nets which was applied in the mining sector. The mining sector represents an illustrative case study for Romania for a number of reasons. First, as was shown in Chapter 1, the mining sector in general has high visibility in Romania and has been the cause of considerable political unrest. The state–societal relations maintained in the mining sector had a strong influence on the overall political and economic transition process in Romania. State–labour relations in the mining sector were of particular importance, as was the overall evolution of the sector. Romania had a sizeable reserve of metals (gold, silver, combined metals, copper) as well as salt, uranium, lignite and hard coal. The sector increased its relative economic and social importance; at its peak more than 10 per cent of the population was dependent in some way on the mining sector. The mining industry is the most heavily subsidized sector in Romania. In 1996, production subsidies received by the mining industry from the state budget amounted to almost $400 million. In 1997, the sector received more than 50 per cent of the subsidies provided to SOEs.[68] Chapter 3 highlighted some of the major characteristics of the organized labour in coal mining and their close ties with the pre-1996 Leftist governments; it also analysed in some detail the evolution of this perverted relationship, and the systemic consequences that this state–labour interaction inflicted upon the emerging capitalist system in Romania.

Second, as a result of assistance received from external sources (in this case mainly the World Bank), the mining sector brings evidence of a successful change in the institutional mechanism regulating the sector from perverted state–societal relations to something which very much resembles an effective social corporatist mechanism.

Taking into account the political problems and the economic importance of the mining sector both in terms of employment and of subsidies received from the state budget, the importance given to this sector in the World Bank's Country Assistance Strategy (CAS) is not surprising. As mentioned in Chapter 3, the centre-Right coalition that came into power in 1997 decided for both economic and political reasons to reduce the size of the mining sector and to stop all mining activities that were not economically viable. To this end, the government designed a restructuring strategy which tried to reform the mining sector in a comprehensive manner. Apart from making the mining industry economically sound, the strategy was aimed at phasing out the government's direct involvement and encouraging private investments in the sector. In addition, the government sought to put in place a social safety net for those negatively affected by the closure of unviable mines. The government offered not only generous separation payments but also re-training schemes and facilities for entrepreneurship. By December 1998, however, about 50 per cent of the workforce (83,000 miners out of a total of about 173,000) had decided to accept the voluntary layoff scheme and its benefits (World Bank 1999c).

The laying off of so many workers precipitated a sharp decline in the overall economic activity of the mining regions and a high rate of unemployment. Despite the promises of labour redeployment and social safety nets that were made to labour unions in order to gain their acceptance of the redundancy package negotiated in 1997, the results were far from satisfactory. Unhappy with the results of the restructuring strategy, by January 1999 labour unions had begun once again to march on Bucharest.[69] Despite some attempts to build an appropriate institutional framework to deal with the situation, none of the institutions involved in the implementation of the restructuring of the mining sector had any previous experience with the complex tasks involved. This situation triggered the assistance of the World Bank through a loan of around US$45 million to the government of Romania to help deal with the mine closures and social mitigation costs (World Bank 1999c). The World Bank project targeted a sample of the mines to be closed and offered technical assistance and financial support for the implementation of all of the measures involved in the national restructuring strategy.[70]

One particularly noteworthy aspect of the World Bank involvement in this restructuring strategy is that the Bank redefined the institutional arrangements used to carry out the social component of this painful downsizing. Although the government was the initiator of this reform, the Bank empowered and redefined the role of the National Agency for Programme Development and Implementation for the Reconstruction of the Mining Regions (NAD) in such a way that NAD became the major player in the restructuring process. The Bank's strategy called for strengthening the capacity of NAD to implement the mandate given by the Ministry of Labour and Social Protection. In so doing, the World Bank reduced the role played by the government in general, and also by the Ministry of Labour and Social Protection and other government agencies. Instead, the World Bank redefined the implementation of the project, requiring NAD to work in close cooperation with local government, mining management and the trade unions to obtain timely information and take appropriate support measures.

At the local level, NAD facilitated the formation of tripartite Local Consultative Committees (LCCs) consisting of members of local administration, labour union representatives and mine managers. These committees played an important role in NAD's work, not only in identifying and prioritizing specific actions but also in providing feedback to NAD on actual implementation.[71]

Thus the World Bank project effectively tried to reduce the role of the government and, indirectly, the predominant forms of state–labour relations in this sector by decentralization and the introduction of a social partnership. These new tripartite relations, which were built on a more equal footing between local government, organized labour and employers under the overall coordination of a quasi-independent state agency, come very close to a typical social corporatist arrangement in the mining sector. This mezzo-corporatist institutional arrangement became quite effective in coordinating all the actors involved at different state (local and central) and societal (trade unions, entrepreneurs, etc.) levels.

This conclusion is rather puzzling, given the common wisdom that World Bank policies would support a neoliberal model of state–labour relations. One explanation for this strategy may be found in the transitory character of this institutional arrangement, which more closely resembles a mechanism for crisis management than a sustainable, long-term arrangement.[72] In the long term, the World Bank strategy was to gradually expose the mining sector to market forces, with no more state–labour coordination mechanisms than in other sectors. Therefore it remains questionable whether the mezzo-corporatist solution was a deliberate institutional choice of a particular model of interest intermediation specific to the Continental capitalist model or just a crisis-management device to ensure the success of the project, given the strong trade unions active in the mining sector.

Conclusions

This part empirically assessed the extent to which external factors had an impact on the direction and speed of transformation from communism to a capitalist economy. It has shown that although the influence of external factors was not always very effective, the pace of reform in Romania was influenced to a large extent by external factors.[73]

These external influences were exerted by using various degrees of conditionality. As shown above, conditionality and coercion took different forms in each of the main external actors involved in the economic transformation in Romania. The IMF would be more inclined to interrupt financial assistance, if targets were missed by the Romanian government. In the case of the World Bank, programmes were carried out even when it was clear that the outcome would be less than satisfactory. As for the EU, there was no instance of PHARE funds being denied as a result of lack of compliance.

Despite conditionality, domestic factors tried to derail many attempts at reform, and external factors had to adopt a pragmatic and flexible approach to the design and monitoring of assistance programmes. During the early 1990s, the World Bank, for instance, realized that the various Romanian government officials, SOE and bank managers were quite reluctant to follow the 'therapy' advocated by the Bank. In other cases, rather than opposing the Bank and breaking the conditionality attached to its programmes, domestic interests found it more lucrative to adapt to the new environment while preserving their old networks and style of interactions. The 'rules of the game' changed fairly quickly from overt state involvement and political clientelism towards more invisible corrupt practices. Consequently, the Bank had to accept that 'bureaucrats are still in business', even when the policies advocated by the Bank were, at least formally, put in place. As a result, both the World Bank and the IMF changed their strategy in the mid-1990s and started to concentrate a larger share of their efforts and funds on the eradication of corruption. However, as shown by various quantitative indicators and case-study evidence provided in Chapter 3, corruption levels did not decline as much as expected. There is now a widespread perception that a commitment to reform on the part of domestic institutions and actors is most important for the successful implementation of World Bank and IMF policies. Furthermore, there is by now strong evidence that it is not possible to substitute for that ownership with conditionality (World Bank 1992, 1998, 2000a; IMF 2001a). Most importantly, as Dollar and Svensson (1998) argued, governments that are inclined to reform must be identified and cannot be created by international organizations.

Overall, the EU enjoyed much more legitimacy in setting priorities and conditionality than the World Bank or the IMF. However, in many instances, the 'goodness of fit' (Risse, Cowles and Caporaso 2001) between European and domestic institutions was low enough to create friction and a great deal of resistance to Europeanization. In certain cases, EU adaptational pressure on domestic policy making in Romania was even openly criticized by domestic actors.[74] Even though this conditionality was framed in strict terms under the Accession Partnership, the extent to which institutional transformation took place was equally driven by Romania's desire to maintain the gap with the more advanced CEECs in the EU accession process.

More specifically, the effectiveness of external policy advocacy varied across issues. On privatization, as Chapter 3 has shown, Romania was lagging behind other CEECs. The privatization of large SOEs, and loss-making enterprises in particular, never gained sufficient momentum. This situation was largely due to the capture of the state by vested domestic interests. Yet the evidence provided in this chapter has suggested that the pace and final results of reform would have been even more modest without external assistance. Consequently, because the preferences of domestic actors were in favour of a slow reform or no reform, any acceleration of the process can be legitimately attributed more to the impact of external factors than to an endogenous transformation induced by domestic forces.

In the banking sector, despite some progress made over the last five years thanks to technical assistance from various sources (including the IMF, the World Bank and the EU), the regulatory framework and the surveillance mechanisms of the NBR remain fragile compared to European and international standards and practices. Even though in certain cases external factors were successful in effectively addressing the types of negative aspects identified in Chapter 3, the Romanian financial system remains prone to domestically generated crises.

Apart from the extent to which external influences were determining factors for the speed and effectiveness of institutional transformation in CEECs, the analysis carried out in this chapter has also tried to determine the direction of this influence, from a models of capitalism perspective.

Thus, in certain policy areas such as state–industry and state–finance relations, the degree of cooperation between the three main external factors in promoting a neoliberal, Anglo-Saxon model based on a minimalist state was significant. The World Bank and IMF programmes in Romania, as in other CEECs, are closely coordinated with the EU. The Accession Partnership between the EU and Romania continues to provide the single framework through which the priority areas for further work are identified regarding progress to be made by Romania towards membership of the EU, the financial means available to implement these priorities and the conditions that will apply to that assistance. The Bank is also party to a Memorandum of Understanding with the EC and other institutions to coordinate in support of accession, including the co-financing of EU accession related investments. The EU policy advocacy in the region shows a great deal of coordination between the EU, IMF and the World Bank with regard to macroeconomic policies, thus supporting the neoliberal influence of Europeanization (World Bank 2001a).

On state–labour relations, the impact of external factors is mixed. Unlike other policy areas examined in this chapter, state–labour relations has been an area where the EU influence was more oriented towards a 'European' model based on social dialogue and other features inspired by the Continental model. While encouraging transition economies to establish institutions of social dialogue and consultation between policy makers and social partners in conformity with the EU *acquis*, the EU was more in favour of bipartism than of state-led tripartism (EC 2001a).

In contrast, Bretton Woods institutions favoured other institutional arrangements for state–labour relations. Unlike other policy areas where the IMF was advocating minimalist state intervention, the IMF encouraged the government to adopt a more prominent role and a tougher stance in its relations with organized labour, a position similar to that found in developmental states.

The World Bank, in contrast, favoured a more market-based model, with the state playing a role only in the provision of social safety nets and poverty alleviation measures. In practice, however, the case of the mining sector showed that, when necessary, the World Bank projects can promote even transitory mezzo-corporatist arrangements as a means of achieving a market-based model.

In conclusion, building on the analysis carried out in Chapter 4, this chapter has presented further evidence in favour of the idea that the EU and Bretton Woods institutions not only had an impact on the economic performance of CEECs as a result of their financial assistance, but they also played an important advisory role in Romania, addressing institutional weaknesses and shaping the direction of transformation towards a combination of various models of capitalism. However, their influence was not always pointing towards the same model of capitalism and this contributed to the emergence of 'cocktail capitalism' in Romania.

6
Conclusions

The hypothesis tested at length in this book through a combination of quantitative and qualitative methodologies was that institutions are the underlying determinant of the long-run performance of economies. To that end, several preliminary questions had to be answered. A first step in the analysis was to amass the necessary theoretical tools needed for the understanding of a complex institutional transformation such as the one that has been taking place in CEECs (see Chapter 1). Based on this theoretical framework the next step was, first, to identify the types of capitalism that are emerging in the CEECs and, second, to analyse their capacity to enhance the economic performance of the region. These questions were addressed in Chapter 2. The first question was answered through an exploratory operationalization of the models of capitalism theory in the case of CEECs, while the second was dealt with in a cross-country and time-series quantitative analysis. For this purpose, an econometric model was worked out based on panel data for ten transition economies from Eastern Europe. Various economic and institutional indicators were tested for their impact on growth rates in the CEECs.

Another key finding of Chapter 2 that runs across the entire book is that apart from the institutional choice of one model of capitalism or another, more important than the actual choice is the consistency of such choices. 'Cocktail capitalism', whereby various pieces of a complex institutional puzzle do not match each other, is a recipe for failure.

Based on these findings, the next step was to engage in an in-depth analysis of the specific types of state–societal institutions that are accountable for this negative impact on economic performance in CEECs. Using Romania as a case study, Chapter 3 looked at state–industry relations and concluded that all types of privatization methods applied in Romania – Anglo-Saxon style mass privatization, Continental MEBO, or developmental-style strategic privatization – had some institutional deficiencies and hence failed to contribute significantly to an improvement in Romania's economic performance. The problems associated with partial privatization were perpetuated because powerful insider 'winners' preferred to preserve this 'transition period' rather than completing the reform process. Moreover, although privatization in Romania shared features common to all three capitalist systems, the emerging type of capitalism in Romania never managed to emulate the efficient mechanisms of the main models of capitalism described (markets, tripartite relations, developmental state). Instead, the Romanian 'cocktail capitalism' is a model of partial reforms in which 'winners take all'. Rather than creating incentives and political support for further reforms and the emergence of growth-oriented elites, Romanian 'cocktail capitalism' maintained the incentives for private rent-seeking and the clientelistic reallocation of assets.

Chapter 3 also examined state–labour relations and described the mixture of clientelistic and state-dominated relations that emerged in Romania after 1989. An extreme example of state-dominated relations was provided by the case of the mining sectors, where perverted corporatist relations between the state and organized labour had a destabilizing impact on state–societal relations throughout the decade. Thus it was shown that state–labour relations in Romania are far from being corporatist as in the Continental model, regardless of what prefix is attached to it: 'state', 'neo', 'liberal', 'democratic' or 'social'. State–labour interactions are not developmental either, since the lack of a strong performance-based work ethic for trade unions and the non-existence of an export-oriented strategy for the state hampered any effort to promote economic development. Furthermore, the state is paradoxically too much involved in bargaining with labour at enterprise level to consider the Romanian state–labour interaction as following the Anglo-Saxon model. The trade unions are more powerful and organized than in a typical Anglo-Saxon capitalist economy, and social democratic values are stronger. Hence what really characterizes state–labour relations in Romania is a 'cocktail' model of capitalism, based on political clientelism, short-termism and a rent-seeking behaviour manifested in a 'subsidy and wage increase for silence' equilibrium between state, business, and labour.

Lastly, Chapter 3 provided a comprehensive examination of state–finance relations and argued that the banking system in Romania was plagued by government intervention, corruption and clientelistic ties.

Instead of becoming a major engine for Romania's economic recovery, the Romanian banking system was a major contributor to the constant economic decline in the last decade. When looking at the functioning of the Romanian financial system in more detail, the predominant features are insider trading, self-loans and straightforward theft, as evidenced by the numerous cases exposed above. These flaws were either politically driven or simply a result of the weak regulatory capacity of the state (as the owner of the banks) and lax monitoring by the central bank (as the central authority entrusted with the responsibility of maintaining a properly-functioning banking system). This book has presented evidence that, in Romania, political factors intrude far more prominently on banking than in more mature democracies. These political factors often determine banking behaviour at the expense of profit-oriented business and prudential concerns.

The next two chapters assessed the impact of external influences on the institutional transformation taking place in CEECs. Chapter 4 used a quantitative analysis to map the influences of external factors such as the IMF, the World Bank and the EU in terms of the various streams of literature that were introduced in Chapter 1. Then, based on this reconceptualization, it examined the impact of the external factors on the economic performance of CEECs during the last decade. The empirical results suggest that the assistance of Bretton Woods institutions, and in particular the EU, have had a positive impact on economic performance. This positive influence is in contrast with the negative impact of several domestic institutional arrangements that create inflationary pressure and support corrupt activities.

This clash between the institutional preferences of external factors and the incentives of domestic factors to maintain inefficient institutions was further explored in Chapter 5. Ample evidence showed that in the case of Romania, this conflict of interests largely contributed to the emergence of an inefficient 'cocktail capitalist' model, where incomplete and inconsistent institutions reduce the potential for economic growth. Based on these findings, the analysis has shown that the negative economic performance of Romania can be largely explained by the fact that external influences clashed with the institutional choices of domestic factors. The preferences of domestic state and societal actors were oriented towards either a perverted corporatist model (as in the case of the mining sector) or, more often, anti-developmental, growth-inhibiting clientelistic relations centred on state and political elites.

As shown throughout the book, the emerging type of capitalism in CEECs contained elements of all the three models of capitalism reviewed in Chapter 1. The resulting model of capitalism was often poorly adapted to promoting sustainable economic development when it ran against domestic vested interests. Despite certain differences in vision between external factors (on state–labour institutional arrangements in particular), this is not the main reason why the emerging institutional arrangements in Romania are growth inhibiting. The problems stem rather from the anti-reformist incentives of the winners of incomplete reforms (Hellman 1998) and, as the previous chapters highlighted, inconsistent institutional choices.

As the literature surveyed has indicated, these characteristics are of course not only found in Romania, as most other transition economies display varying degrees of these institutional weaknesses. Yet, as the case-studies and examples provided in the book showed quite clearly, what really explains the poor economic performance of Romania in comparison to other Central European countries is that that all too often Romanian 'cocktail capitalism' omits the ingredients which would favour the creation of institutions and coalitions to support overall growth. What differed in the case of Romania, compared to other CEECs, was the role that each of these factors played. In Romania, growth-inhibiting institutions supported by domestic interests were more resistant to transformational pressures than was the case in other CEECs. This supports the argument that, unlike other CEECs, external influences in Romania did not find sufficient support across domestic forces to implement a growth-enhancing model of capitalism or to combine in a positive way institutional features from various models of capitalism.

In sum, various forces promoted a certain institutional blueprint, each of them having a different impact on economic performance. Figure 6.1 presents schematically the impact of domestic and external factors on the emerging models of capitalism and their economic performance. Three main vectors of change are singled out: Europeanization, institutionalized globalization, and domestic forces. These influences are placed in bi-dimensional space defined by a political continuum (horizontal axis) and an economic continuum (vertical axis). As found in Chapters 2 and 3, domestic factors favour a state-centred clientelistic capitalism and have a predominantly negative impact on economic performance, placing them in the lower-right corner. EU factors promote a mixture of Anglo-Saxon and Continental institutional features with a more limited state role, and their influence has strong positive economic effects (upper-right corner). For instance, a 5 percentage point increase in the Europeanization index would correspond, *ceteris paribus*,

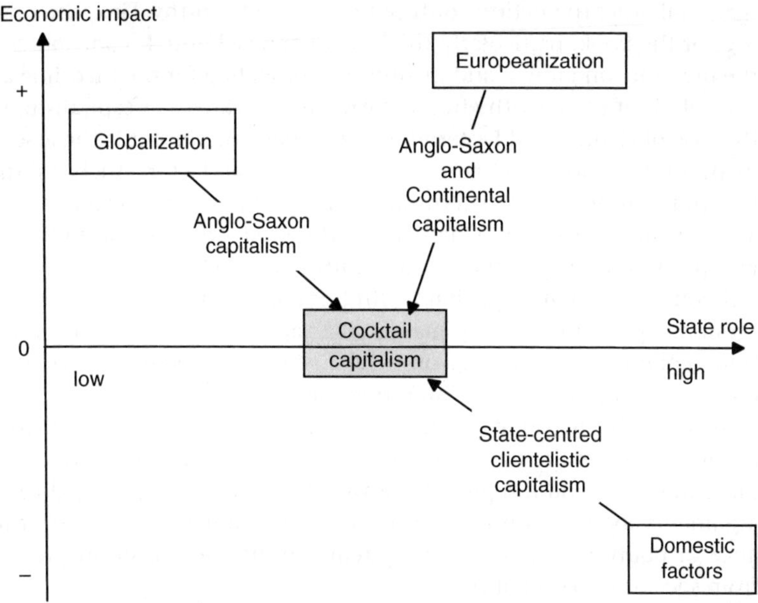

Figure 6.1 'Cocktail capitalism': main determining factors and direction of change

to up to an additional 1 percentage point increase in the annual growth rate. Finally, institutionalized globalization forces (Bretton Woods institutions and global market forces) promote primarily an Anglo-Saxon model of capitalism with a minimalist state role and a positive economic impact (upper-left corner). The result is a 'cocktail capitalism' model, whose final position on both the vertical and horizontal axes will depend in each CEEC upon the strength of each determining factor.

Figure 6.1 also summarizes the theoretical framework that guided the overall research. The book relied on a fruitful cross-fertilization of various streams of literature: models of capitalism, interest-intermediation, policy transfer, Europeanization and globalization. In particular, the analysis reconceptualized the transition process as a case of policy transfer from various levels (global, European, sub-regional) using different mechanisms, each having various degrees of effectiveness. By showing that CEECs did not adopt a uniform Anglo-Saxon model of capitalism, the book also adds to the existing evidence that the pressure for institutional convergence from increased globalization interacts with strong domestic factors, and thus varieties of capitalism persist.

Several other theoretical contributions are noteworthy. First, the findings of the book, particularly those of Chapters 2 and 4, contribute to the literature on growth and institutions, providing for the first time an evaluation of the growth effects of each major variety of capitalism, in the case of Central and Eastern Europe. Equally important is the assessment of the growth effects of major external factors such as the Europeanization and globalization process in the context of CEECs. The analysis undertaken in Chapter 4 also used an original index of Europeanization that can be used in further research.

Second, the detailed qualitative findings on institutional change and economic performance in Romania fill a gap in the literature on transition economies by focusing on a relatively underresearched country, compared with other transition economies.

In synthesis, this book has tried to answer a number of questions that are at the core of the transformation processes which have been taking place in CEECs and has provided a wealth of methodologically diverse arguments about institutional choices and their impact on the performance of political and economic systems during the transition process from socialism to capitalism.

At the end of this analysis, looking ahead towards the accession of Bulgaria and Romania, a more general view of the dynamics of the whole process described in this book and its relevance for the years to come seems in order. All the evidence reviewed here clearly suggests that Europeanization should not be narrowly conceived as something chiefly related to the accession process. Europeanization is a gradual process that does not stop with the signing of the EU Accession Treaty. Unlike accession negotiations, the Europeanization of CEECs is a long-drawn-out process that is far from complete, even for existing members. In the future, European integration will enter new fields and become more encompassing in the fields already covered. For new or old EU members the process of Europeanization is here to stay. Therefore many of the issues tackled in this book will remain to a great extent valid for many years when former CEECs (by then EU members with full rights) will shape, and still be shaped by, Europeanization forces.

Notes

Introduction

1 International political economy and institutional economics as research fields emphasize the methodological breadth, drawing on a variety of perspectives including case study analysis, simulations, game theory, statistics, etc.

1 Theoretical Considerations

1 Each of the concepts mentioned above has generated an extensive literature. Within the limits available, this introduction cannot purport to provide a comprehensive analysis of this literature. A comprehensive review of these publications is found in Kubicek (2000). For studies using a political culture approach see, for instance, Alexander (2000) and Reisinger *et al.* (1994) for the case of the former Soviet Union, or Przeworski (1996) for Poland. For a comparison of rational choice and the political culture approaches and a test of their explanatory power in the Eastern European transformation process, see Whitefield and Evans (1999) and Bates, de Figueiredo and Weingast (1998). Brubaker (1996) and Verdery (1996) are examples of works using theories of nationalism in the context of Eastern Europe. For a collection of post-structuralist studies challenging the dominant neoliberal discourse of transition, see, for instance, Pickles and Smith (1998). Blanchard (1997) offers a neoclassical analysis of the economics of transition. An influential political economy analysis of 'partial reforms' is found in Hellman (1998). A review of institutionalist perspectives on transition is offered in Kovacs (1993). For studies advocating a 'transitology' approach, see, for instance, Schmitter and Karl (1994) and Przeworski (1991). For a critique of this approach see Bunce (1995) and Wiarda (2001).
2 Olson (1982) emphasizes the negative impact of institutional sclerosis on economic performance. Lange and Garret (1985) discuss the conditions under which Leftist governments and organized labour enhance economic performance. Hart (1992, pp. 273–5, 281–3) argues in favour of the importance of strong coalitions either between state and business (as in the case of Japan) or between business and labour (as in the case of Germany) for sustained economic growth. Knack and Keefer (1995) adopt a neoclassical approach and test the importance of rule of law and property rights. Hicks and Kenworthy (1998) test a number of key hypotheses put forward in the earlier literature about the importance of state–societal interactions on economic redistribution and growth.
3 Arthur Bentley and David Truman are often cited as being among the first scholars to coin the pluralist interest group theory (Bentley 1908; Truman 1951). See, for instance, Dahl (1956) and Lindblom (1965) for an early account of pluralist theories. Almond (1983) provides a very good review of the pluralist literature and its interaction with the neocorporatist literature.

4 The literature on lobbying is extremely vast. See, for example, Ziegler and Baer (1969), Malbin (1979), and Hayes (1981).

5 For a study of American business groups that contradicts the pluralist assumptions, see Neustadtl and Clawson (1988). Overall, their evidence lends stronger support to the class rather than the pluralist perspective.

6 A good summary of the extensive literature on corporatism can be found in Cawson and Ballard (1984).

7 Throughout this thesis, corporatism, liberal corporatism and neocorporatism are used interchangeably in a contemporary sense.

8 For both theoretical and empirical investigations on these issues, see, for instance, the collection of studies in Cawson (1985).

9 Many studies explore the relationships between neocorporatist policy-making mechanisms and the welfare state, while other authors view neocorporatism as a third approach between capitalism and socialism (Winkler 1976) or as a post-capitalist state–societal arrangement (Lawson 1985).

10 Among the numerous studies where various hypotheses advanced in the corporatist literature are tested quantitatively, see, for instance, Schmitter (1981), Hicks and Kenworthy (1998), Lehmbruch (1984) and Paloheimo (1984).

11 It is beyond the scope of this literature review to give a comprehensive overview of all the approaches towards policy networks and network analysis. More extended literature surveys are found in Wilks and Wright (1987), Jordan and Schubert (1992), Rhodes and Marsh (1992) and Marin and Myantz (1991).

12 Some authors have even defined policy networks as an umbrella concept that would encompass both pluralist and neocorporatist arrangements (Atkinson and Coleman 1989; van Waarden 1992).

13 A related argument is made by van Waarden (1992), who argues that policy making has become a complex system of governmental and non-governmental actors in search of legitimacy in the making of public policies.

14 See Rhodes and Apeldoorn (1997, pp. 177–8) for examples of common network-related features of Germanic and Latin models.

15 For comprehensive overviews and empirical applications of the theories of the state see the classical work of Block (1987), and that of Evans, Rueschmeyer and Skocpol (1985). A very comprehensive collection of studies on the role of the state in the economy may be found in Samuels (1989).

16 The comparison is more difficult with the developmental state because of the latter's state authoritarianism combined with extensive corporate welfare schemes and the active role of workers at the shop-floor level.

17 On the features of French capitalism that place it within the European capitalism model see Grosse and Luger (1994) and Adams and Stoffaes (1986). For an opposite view, see, for instance, Woolcock (1996).

18 Other observers who have seen evidence of corporatist patterns of interest in group–government contacts are Crouch (1978) and Schmitter and Lehmbruch (1979). In addition, Keeler (1987) shows quite convincingly how the agricultural sector acts as a corporatist enclave in the French political economy.

19   Unlike other Western democracies, the importance of trade unions is specifically mentioned in the German Constitution. Article 9 (Freedom of association) reads as follows:

> The right to form associations to safeguard and improve working and economic conditions is guaranteed to everyone and to all trades and professions. Agreements that restrict or seek to hinder this right are null and void; measures directed to this end are void and the measures taken in this respect illegal. The measures taken in accordance to articles 12a, 35, para 2 and 3, 87a, para 4, and 91, cannot be directed against work conflicts initiated by associations, as defined by the first phrase of the present paragraph, in order to maintain and improve the working conditions and economic welfare.
>
> (Author's translation from the German original)

20   Recently, however, the differences between Anglo-Saxon and Continental banking have become less pronounced.

21   On the concept of stakeholder capitalism, the meaning of stakeholding and various refinements of the concepts (stakeholder state, the stakeholder society, stakeholder company, stakeholder economy), see Kelly, Kelly and Gamble (1997) and Hutton (1999).

22   Dittus and Prowse (1996, p. 24) bring evidence in support of this argument. Germany has the highest share concentration ratio (42%), compared with the USA (25%) and Japan (33%).

23   For an elaboration of the developmental state concept as well as a collection of case studies on developmental experiences in East Asian countries, Brazil, India and France, see, for instance, Woo-Cummings (1999). For an account of the role of government in the economic development of Japan, see Johnson (1982); for South Korea, see Jones and Sakong (1980), Mukerjee (1986) and Amsden (1989); for Taiwan, see Wade (1990); for Singapore, see Rodan (1989). For a comparative analysis of the Asian newly-industrializing economies, see Castells (1992), Weiss and Hobson (1995, pp. 133–95). For a cross-regional comparison, see Ettlinger (1994). A good description of developmental states in Japan and France is also found in G.K. Wilson (1985).

24   On the pathological embeddedness of state bureaucracy and rural oligarchs in Brazil, see Hagopian (1994). Similar evidence on Thailand is provided by Doner and Ramsay (1997).

25   Polanyi (1944/1999) originally coined the term 'embeddedness' to characterize the manner in which market interactions are inextricably bound in pre-existing institutional and normative frameworks. Granovetter (1985) provides a more contemporary discussion on how state–business interactions are embedded in previously existing social norms.

26   For a good collection of studies analysing the economic policies applied by several successful and less successful developmental states, see the *Third World Quarterly*, Vol. 17, No. 4, pp. 583–839.

27   Wade (1990) and Shafer (1997) produce convincing evidence about the role of the Korean state in spurring international competitiveness and promoting the emergence of new comparative advantage in new industries. Several

other studies have analysed the economics of developmental states in Taiwan and South Korea (White 1988) and other East Asian countries (Vogel 1991).

28 To a lesser extent, some Latin American states have also succeeded in 'midwifing' the emergence of new, more sophisticated industrial activities (Evans, Rueschmeyer and Skocpol 1985; Jenkins 1991; Shapiro 1994; Evans 1995).

29 According to Dittus and Prowse (1996), institutional cross-shareholding as a result of the *keiretsu* system attained 73% of all listed companies. Major bank-based *keiretsu* include Mitsubishi, Mitsui and Sumitomo. Major industrial-based *keiretsu* include Toyota and Matsushita (Ozawa 1996).

30 A similar argument is made by Stark and Bruszt (1998), who argue that the emergence of a developmental model of capitalism in certain CEECs may be held accountable for better economic performances during the transition process.

31 The common view on networks in Eastern Europe as being reallocative rather than wealth-creating mechanisms is well evidenced in Staniszkis (1991), Szalai (1991) and Voszka (1995).

32 That networks are not unambiguously welfare-enhancing mechanisms is also made quite clear by Stark and Bruszt themselves when noting that 'strong networks ... have the capacity to be agencies of development or rent-seekers depleting the public treasury and inhibiting economic growth' (Stark and Bruszt 1998, p. 129).

33 Similar instances of incoherence in the reform process have been described in Dittrich, Schmidt and Whitley (1995) in other transition economies.

34 So far, there have been few attempts to provide a theoretical approach that will encompass political, economic and institutional issues of key relevance for the systemic transformations taking place in CEECs. A notable exception is Pop (2002a).

35 For an attempt to provide a conceptual framework linking domestic, European and global levels in the case of EU's Common Agricultural Policy, see Hennis (2001).

36 For recent bibliographic surveys exploring the range of conceptual nuances of Europeanization and the various sub-fields in which the concept has been applied, see, for instance, Olsen (2002) and Featherstone (2003).

37 For an argument in favour of the convergence thesis, see, for instance, Wessels (1996). For an argument against, see, for instance, Schmidt (1995, 2002), Wright (1996) or Blaschke (2000).

38 Among the numerous studies on these issues, see, for instance, Schmidt (2001) for a good summary of the current debate.

39 See, among others, Berger and Dore (1996), Crouch and Streeck (1997), Hollingsworth and Boyer (1997), and Schmidt (2001).

40 For an investigation of the role played by EU conditionality on democratization and political transformations in selected CEECs, see, for instance, Vachudova (2005).

41 As such, this argument also assumes that Europeanization is a direct effect of or reaction to globalization, at a regional level.

42 See Swank (1998) for evidence of taxation decline in contemporary Europe. For a refutation of this structural dependency theory, see Cooke and Noble (1998).

43 Hix (1998) argues that a primary reason for European diversity is to be found in the lack of redistributional competence and regulatory power at the supranational level. McGowan and Wallace (1996) argue that the EU supranational regulatory impact on national capitalist institutions is mitigated by member states, leading to uneven convergence.

2 Institutions and Economic Growth in Central and Eastern Europe: A Quantitative Analysis

1 However, Fischer, Sahay and Végh (1996) argued against this sharp economic decline by suggesting that the data (especially in the early years of transition) are of poor quality and that the post-transformation GDP level is underestimated relative to its pre-transformation level because output prices have dramatically declined and also because the underground economy has considerably increased. Others have argued that a more accurate picture of the economic trends in transition is obtained by using purchasing power parity (PPP) values of GDP (Halpern and Wyplosz 1997).
2 For an argument in favour of the 'big bang', see for example, Lipton and Sachs (1990), Balcerowicz (1994) and Aslund, Boone and Johnson (1996). For a discussion on the virtues of gradualism see, for instance, Dewatripont and Roland (1992).
3 For an earlier study on the importance of institutions for economic development see, for instance, Scully (1988). Posen (1998) conducted a more recent study. For a historical account see, for instance, David (1994). Empirical analyses of growth and institutions are found in Barro (1991), Knack and Keefer (1995), Knack (1996) and Brunetti (1997). For a general survey of the studies on growth and institutions, see Aron (2000).
4 The most notable studies are the research projects conducted under the auspices of the World Bank and EBRD, where data were gathered through surveys and research on the ground. A significant number of publications produced by these institutions has spurred the debate about institutions and economic performance.
5 This debate builds upon an earlier stream of literature concerned with the relationships between financial systems and economic performance. For a survey of that literature see, for instance, Carlin and Mayer (1999). See also Crama *et al.* (1999) for an argument based on detailed firm-level empirical evidence that the Continental model of corporate governance increases the financial performance of firms.
6 In addition to the transition process itself and the societal transformations associated with it, the globalization of the economy and the Europeanization process advanced in the 1990s has drawn renewed interest in the persistence of national specificities with regard to capitalist systems and their institutional arrangements. This topic will be further explored in Chapters 4 and 5.
7 It should be mentioned, however, that even though the coefficients were statistically insignificant, a Wald test rejected the null hypothesis that both coefficients are equal to zero in model 7.

3   Domestic Institutions and Economic Performance: 'Cocktail Capitalism'

1   Different models of capitalism also have different shares of private owner-ship in the national economy. The Anglo-Saxon system favours limited state ownership, with the exception of the Keynesian period when the models tended to converge on the extent of public ownership. For an extensive sur-vey of corporate ownership see La Porta, Lopez de Silanes and Shleifer (1999).
2   On the importance of property rights in the formation of a capitalist econ-omy see also Anderson and Hill (1975) and Gould (1999). More generally, on the importance of institutions for economic performance see Eggertsson (1990) or the classical study by North (1990).
3   The Czech mass privatization process was, from the very beginning, intended to create an Anglo-Saxon type of capitalism (Gould 1999, p. 12).
4   This conclusion came across from several interviews with POF officials.
5   For a more complete discussion on the different national aspects of corpo-ratism in Europe see also Schmitter (1977, 1981).
6   Similar arguments about patron–client relations and their impact on eco-nomic growth are made by Scott (1977) and Hutchcroft (1997)
7   Olson argued that a key factor making collective action difficult in large groups such as thousands of SOE individual owners was the inability of such groups to monitor the behaviour of members who might be tempted to free ride. A good review of the literature on collective action is that of Kratochwil and Mansfield (1994).
8   For a comparison of different methods of privatization in Eastern Europe, see Estrin and Stone (1996), pp. 8–9.
9   Based on the SOF database 1992–2000 and interviews with SOF officials.
10   Several studies have pointed out the methodological problems associated with those attempts to estimate the impact of privatization on enterprise per-formance. In certain cases, insiders (both employee and managers) colluded and stripped the company of valuable assets before privatization, in order to reduce the purchase price of the company. On other hand, it is frequently difficult to establish the counterfactual. What would have happened with the same company, had it not been privatized? It might be argued that the company could have performed equally well in the absence of MEBO priva-tization, either as an SOE or by attracting foreign investors.
11   Based on a confidential interview with a POF official.
12   The dramatic reduction in the value of the debt/equity ratio for trade and tourism is probably due to the special case of trading companies. First, after 1990, they gradually received back their strong currency reserves, which improved their financial situation. Second, their book value was very small in comparison to other companies (since there were very few fixed assets), which did not require the employees and managers to take a bank loan for the purchase of the stock package.
13   The contradictory effects of different privatization methods are illustrated by the World Bank position towards MEBO privatization in Poland. Dabrowski, Gomulka and Rostowski (2000) describe how the World Bank representatives were against the Polish workers' councils, being in favour of government-appointed supervisory boards for SOEs. The Polish negotiating team was

surprised to see 'statist' advice coming from the World Bank and argued that state-appointed managers would replicate the flaws built into the socialist system.

14 See Evans (1995) for a detailed description of various mechanisms through which the state plays an active role in promoting investment.

15 Information based on confidential interview.

16 Information based on confidential interview.

17 For a definition of the state capture concept and a cross-country quantitative analysis of this phenomenon in CEECs, see Hellman *et al.* (2000). For a detailed account of the privatization process undertaken by the *Treuhandanstalt* and the complex state–societal mechanisms governing its activities, see Czada (1996).

18 Based on confidential interview with a former SOF official.

19 Summing all the premiums and benefits, a director in the State Ownership Fund could earn an annual income of 3,737,433,510 lei (around US$170,000: confidential interview with a former SOF official).

20 There is little wonder that the Ministry of Finance complained about its inability to collect taxes from SOEs when the financial audit for these companies was carried out by the same civil servants supposed to enforce tax collection measures on debtors.

21 Based on interviews with several SOE managers.

22 A chronological list of interventions and interpellations made in the Romanian Parliament is available online at http://www.cdep.ro.

23 Moreover, restructuring programmes not only did little to improve the efficiency of SOEs but they also drained further resources from the state budget to cover the additional government subsidies, loans, operational costs of restructuring programmes, technical assistance and services of foreign consultants involved in these programmes (Djankov 1998, p. 10).

24 The only notable exceptions from the SOF asset portfolio were around 800 autonomous state companies scattered in sectors considered strategic, such as transportation, telecommunication, energy, raw material extraction and processing, etc. (Laws 15/91 and 58/9).

25 The *Treuhandanstalt* ministerial agency in charge of privatizing the formerly state-owned and managed enterprises sold these off to the highest bidder, often below market value (Czada 1996).

26 The increase in real wages and sharp reduction in unemployment in 1996 is not necessarily a result of good economic performance but rather due to the fact that that year was an electoral year.

27 The costs of macroeconomic restructuring were also shifted to politically less powerful or less organized groups, such as small business, farmers, public administration, education, research and development, etc.

28 The initial discussions between the government and trade unions on the idea of a tripartite council had been stalled since 1994. However, as will be argued later, the EU has been instrumental in the setting-up of the Economic and Social Council.

29 As reported to the authors by various ministry officials and local representatives.

30 Evidence of this infiltration was occasionally reported in the post-1989 Romanian press, especially after a number of Securitate files were released to the press in the mid-1990s.

31   This information is based on various reports from people in the press that allegedly had privileged access to the Securitate files on infiltrated agents and collaborators. However, at the time of writing, most of the Securitate files have still to be made public.

32   *Mineriada* is a term that has been used in the Romanian media to describe the violent interventions of coal miners in Bucharest during 1990.

33   Iliescu's political campaign, based on the idea of honesty and compassion, contributed to his image as a charismatic leader and remained one of the foundations for his regime's legitimacy.

34   In other mining sectors, where the trade unions were much weaker, the restructuring went at an even greater pace than the government could handle. In 1997, the then Minister of Industry and Trade, C. P. Tariceanu, asked the Parliament to urgently adopt a draft law for limiting the number of voluntary layoffs, after 50,000 people claimed the compensatory layoff package (Vera and Manta 1997, p. 1).

35   The case of *Mineriadas* in Romania is to some extent similar to the protest arising from the events of May 1968 in France and in Italy in 1969 (see Salvati 1981).

36   This pattern of asset-stripping is by no means limited to SIDEX. Boariu and Roua (2001) offer similar evidence of the existence of asset-stripping by managers and trade union leaders in the case of Alro, a major aluminum producer.

37   Just to give an illustration of the magnitude of SIDEX's impact on the Romanian economy, the debts of SIDEX towards the budget are almost half the annual salaries of all teachers in Romania.

38   A similar conclusion about the anti-developmental nature of state intervention is reached by Stark and Bruszt (1998, p. 152) in their discussion of the policies adopted in Hungary in the early 1990s.

39   Based on information provided during various interviews conducted with trade union leaders at SIDEX.

40   See, for instance, the literature on East Asia's state-led direct credit programmes for strategic industrial sectors. Good examples are found in Johnson (1982) and Vittas and Cho (1995).

41   For a detailed discussion on the cosy relationships between bankers and politicians in transition economies see, for instance, Roe, Siegelbaum and King (1997).

42   The literature on the determinants of banking system structure is very limited, not only for Central and Eastern Europe but also for more developed economies. The exceptions are two quantitative microeconomic studies on the banking structure in the USA (Kaufman and Mote 1994; Berger, Kashyap and Scalise 1995) and several qualitative studies on the European banking systems, looking mainly at the impact of financial integration in the EU (Kaufman 1992; Dermine 1993; Lewis and Pescetto 1996).

43   In the United States, for instance, during the 1990s stock market capitalization reached a peak of about 150 per cent of GDP. Similarly, the ratio is higher than 100 per cent in the UK. In many other Western European countries, stock market capitalization ranges between 30 and 60 per cent (World Bank 2004b).

44   For a good discussion on the debate about financial repression, as well as a comparative discussion of financial systems, see Fry (1988), Haggard (1990) and Haggard, Lee and Maxfield (1993).

45 A closer look at monthly nominal interest rate data revealed a large fluctuation from one month to another, with interest spreads as high as 40 per cent.

46 Hellman, Murdock and Stiglitz (1995) stress that, for financial restraint policies to create such positive effects, a number of conditions must be present, including a stable, low-inflation macroeconomic environment, non-excessive taxation of the financial sector, and positive real interest rates.

47 There is a large volume of theoretical and empirical literature on identifying the causes and channels of soft budgets. The theoretical literature is summarized in Kornai (1998). Empirical studies include Bonin and Schaffer (1995) on Hungary, Claessens and Kyle (1997) on Bulgaria, Perotti and Carare (1997) on Romania, and Schaffer (1998) on the Czech Republic, Hungary, Kazakhstan, Poland, Romania and Russia.

48 This is perhaps explained by the political cycle. The year 1996 was an electoral year and the new reformist government that took office in 1997 should have had an impact on the magnitude of non-performing loans. Various explanations may account for this lagged evolution in 1997. First, many institutional and bureaucratic changes introduced by the new government did not take immediate effect in 1997 and thus the legacy of the Iliescu government persisted into 1997. Alternatively, one may assume that the nature and extent of political pressure exercised by the new reformist government were not very different from those of the previous regime.

49 In fact the number of soft loans, bank frauds and other irregularities was overwhelming. In only a few years, BANCOREX, the flagship Romanian bank specializing in foreign transactions, became bankrupt. For further details on specific cases of bank fraud, soft loans and bank crashes in Romania see, for instance, Cernat (2004).

50 The greater a bank's capacity to deal with creditworthiness on neutral banking criteria, the greater will be its ability to avoid bad borrowers (adverse selection) and to screen and limit excessive risk-taking by those borrowers that it does accept (moral hazard). When credit decisions are politically motivated, these mechanisms do not function.

4 External Policy Transfer and Economic Growth: Reconceptualizing External Influences

1 Two notable exceptions are Grabbe (1999) and Goetz (2000), who have made a first attempt at looking at these issues in the context of enlargement.

2 Ladrech (1994, p. 69) defines Europeanization as 'an incremental process reorienting the direction and shape of politics to the degree that EC political and economic dynamics become part of the organizational logic of national politics and policy-making'.

3 IMF (1984) provides the terms of cooperation between the IMF and the Bank in their operations. This confirms the practice instituted in 1970 for ad hoc, selective attendance at discussions of countries in which both the Fund and the Bank have programmes of financial assistance.

4 Cross-conditionality refers to linkages between financial assistance programmes from one agency and the implementation of conditionality imposed by some other agency. This policy has been used by the IMF and the World

Bank, as well as other institutions (such as the EU, for instance) in their financial assistance programmes.

5   For a survey of the factors affecting these interactions, see, for instance, Whitley (1998).

6   The attempts by various national governments to attract multinationals to their countries led to an absurd contest, with each government seeking to outbid the others in offering greater incentives in the form of loans, subsidies and such like. As Servan-Schreiber (1968, p. 14) plaintively described the position of one host country, 'we pay them to buy us'.

7   Some questions related to enlargement have nevertheless found thorough answers in the already-existing theoretical frameworks. For instance, the club theory explains quite parsimoniously what drives the desire for enlargement, both for existing and aspiring members. In this basic formulation, this theory argues that a club expands when the benefits are higher than the costs for both existing and acceding members.

8   Economics is a notable exception. Studies of economic integration of CEECs into the global economy or the EU (both in terms of trade and investment flows) are a major source of analytical approaches to enlargement.

9   Out of the official 31 chapters of the *acquis communautaire*, only 29 are 'real' chapters, covering specific areas of the *acquis*. Unlike other chapters, most of the *acquis* in chapters 30 and 31 do not require specific legal approximation and implementation measures by the CEECs prior to accession.

10   For a review of the literature that addressed the conditionality and the impact of IMF and World Bank programmes on economic performance, see, for instance, Tsikata (1998) and Schadler *et al.* (1995a, b).

11   The focus on *implementation*, rather than just *adoption* of the *acquis communautaire*, as a crucial element of the overall integration process has been emphasized in particular for the 'second wave' candidate countries. See, for instance, EC (1997a, p. 38).

12   With regard to the use of the Europeanization variable, one particular advantage of the current model should be noted. In the Europeanization debate concerning existing EU member states, several authors (e.g., Howell 2004) consider that the interaction between EU and national levels is mutual and therefore the distinction between the dependent and independent variable becomes a two-way relationship. If this is the case, obviously the econometric analysis becomes more complicated. However, this impediment does not apply to CEECs, as there is no formal mechanism through which non-members could significantly influence the EU integration process. Therefore, Europeanization is a one-way process in which CEECs adapt existing national structures and policies and adopt new ones in order to comply with the requirements imposed by the accession process.

13   Throughout the entire period all countries received a score of 3 for chapters 30 and 31, given the fact that there was no *acquis* adoption process involved during the accession period.

14   The methodology used is based on Piazolo (1997), who used this procedure in a similar context.

15   A high degree of harmonization with regard to internal market procedures removes the costly conformity assessment requirements, anti-dumping, countervailing duties, quotas, or other protective measures.

16 For instance, the Association Agreements provide for restrictions on state aid in particular sectors. The issue is extremely politicized because these sectors are of fundamental importance in the sectoral structure of transition economies, and to their overall export potential to the EU.

17 Unemployment is not included in studies aimed at testing a wide set of potential explanatory variables used in growth regressions, such as those by Levine and Renelt (1992) and Sala-i-Martin (1997).

18 For an econometric analysis and a survey of various methods of estimating the relationship between growth and unemployment see, for instance, Barreto and Howland (1993).

19 Successful adjustments rely mostly on cuts in transfer programmes and in government wages and employment. Unsuccessful adjustments rely primarily on increases in taxes, leaving transfer programmes, government wages and employment untouched, or even increased.

20 For details on the methodology used in the construction of this index, see *The 2000 Index of Economic Freedom*, available online at http://www.heritage.org/index/2002/chapters/chap5.html.

21 For full details on the construction of this index, see de Melo *et al.* (1997).

22 The method adopted for this followed standard econometric graphical procedures. No observations appeared as potential outliers.

23 The robustness of the model was tested against omitted variables. Since other variables that are not directly related to the adoption of the *acquis* may influence or be correlated with the degree of policy transfer captured by the dependent variable, they were also included as control variables in the model. Thus it was suggested in the literature that proximity to the European core or common borders represent an advantage for a more rapid integration. Based on this argument, distance between CEECs' national capitals and Brussels and the number of common borders between each transition economy and an EU member were used as a proxies for these variables. None of them turned out to be statistically significant and the results for the other core variables remained unaffected.

24 Using fixed effects is a good way to account for potential country-specific omitted variables.

25 A second method of assessing the importance of omitted variables is to look at the regression residuals. These capture the deviations of estimated growth rates from what could be viewed as 'normal' levels, based on the set of independent variables used in the model.

26 On different datasets including developing countries, other studies have found insignificant effects (Killick 1995) or a negative impact of IMF programmes (Przeworski and Vreeland 2000).

27 This is not surprising, given that IMF-sponsored economic stabilization programmes involve comprehensive economic measures that need time to take place before achieving a viable economic environment. Similar insignificant results were also obtained by Pastor (1987).

28 A second method of assessing the importance of omitted variables is to look at the regression residuals. These capture the deviations of estimated growth rates from what could be viewed as 'normal' levels, based on the set of independent variables used in the model.

5   External Factors and Models of Capitalism: The Romanian Experience

1   See the various Regular Reports of the European Commission on candidate countries.
2   Enhancing competitiveness is a key element of the EU industrial policy. Competition policy is another guiding principle of EC industrial policies that cut across various domains, including market access, trade policy and state aids. Among the numerous EC documents on this subject, see, for instance, EC (1994).
3   The impact of PHARE programmes on the privatization effort has been extremely significant, at least where the politically charged environment was conducive to privatization. According to an assessment report on the programme in Poland, PHARE contributed to 'the successful implementation of the Polish Government's privatization strategy'. Without the PHARE programme, a lack of skills would have been an obstacle to the implementation of the reforms agreed under the IMF and World Bank.
4   RICOP (Industrial Restructuring and Professional Re-conversion Programme) had five principal objectives: social assistance measures for massive layoffs (around €28 million); public works (€14 million); job creation activities (€9 million); SME development (€30 million); other social safety nets (€10 million; see APAPS 2002b, pp. 1–3).
5   Unlike other CEECs (e.g., Poland or Slovenia), EU-sponsored enterprise restructuring strategies and studies in Romania were too general and were mostly shelved (based on confidential interview with a former SOF official).
6   The ordinance introduced several restrictive measures such as a guaranteed minimum price, production and import quotas.
7   In the last Regular Report on Romania, however, it is deemed that the overall impact of PHARE has been positive, particularly in the fields of industrial restructuring and privatization (EC 2001a, p. 11).
8   As mentioned in Chapter 1, in the Continental model, leading business associations and other societal interest groups are key players in the formulation of policies affecting them.
9   An example of PHARE activities aimed at strengthening business associations is the twinning programme financed by the PHARE Business Support Programme to enhance the capability of Central and Eastern European Chemical Industry Federations to represent the interests of their associate companies, and to prepare themselves for European Union enlargement (CEFIC 2001).
10   A similar explanation is advanced in the next section about the impact of the PHARE programme on banking associations.
11   The precarious situation of the Romanian banking system was mentioned in several EC regular reports on Romania (EC 1998a and 1999).
12   Typical assistance to commercial banks included strategic and restructuring studies, expert assistance for management development, reinforcement of credit departments and human resource development (EC 1998b).
13   As regards twinning activities, the EU was in a privileged position, compared to the IMF and the World Bank. Neither of them was in a position to provide such assistance on a similar scale and on a grant basis.

14 For instance, PHARE technical assistance provided the SOF with the necessary skills for auditing bank portfolios, enterprise management and industrial restructuring of state-owned enterprises (EC 1997c, p. 19).

15 During 1994–8, the British Know-How Fund and the Canadian International Development Agency (CIDA) provided technical assistance to the National Securities Committee and the Romanian securities market on a bilateral basis (EC 2000c).

16 In addition to the Bretton Woods institutions, other projects were implemented jointly with the EBRD. One such project targeted the elimination of bad loans given by many state-owned banks to cover SOE arrears.

17 Cf. Articles 138 and 139 of the Treaty of Amsterdam.

18 Limited progress in the field of social dialogue is more the norm than the exception across CEECs. The implementation of EU legislation covering social dialogue issues, as well as the setting-up of appropriate tripartite and bipartite institutional arrangements, is uneven across CEECs. Only Slovenia and the Czech Republic conform fairly well to EU standards in terms of legislative harmonization, institutional settings and actual policy making. Others, such as the Baltic countries, have only recently adopted the required legislation and institutional setting (especially for bipartite social dialogue). In countries such as Hungary, despite a longer experience with tripartite arrangements, autonomous social dialogue between workers and employers remains limited, and trust between the social partners and government at the tripartite level is still lacking (EC 2001b).

19 Interview with trade union leader.

20 Several other projects were aimed at strengthening the capacity of sectoral associations, through cooperation between EU-level sectoral associations and their Romanian counterparts. Other programmes promoted seminars on various social policy and social dialogue issues, involving Romanian trade unions, business associations, professional associations and European interest groups.

21 Based on interviews with Economic and Social Council staff members.

22 Based on interviews with trade union representatives in the Economic and Social Council.

23 Ibid.

24 Based on an interview with an official from Patronatul Roman.

25 This decision was based on the recommendations made during the inaugural meeting of the Joint Consultative Committee of the ESC of the EU and the Romanian ESC, held in Bucharest in February 2000.

26 As in several other CEECs, bipartite relations fall short of EU standards. Particularly problematic in the case of Romania, however, is the EU–Romanian Joint Consultative Committee with the European Economic and Social Council, which was built on the ILO model and thus includes government representatives, which contravenes the EU's preference for bipartite relations.

27 Based on an interview conducted in Bucharest with a FamiliaConstruct representative, March 2002.

28 Ibid.

29 The literature on IMF policies and its impact on developing countries is vast and goes beyond the purpose of this book. For a recent survey see, for example, Dicks-Mireaux, Mecagni and Schadler (2000).

30 In essence, the IMF relies on the so-called demand conditionality, based on a monetary approach to the balance of payment. Typical IMF conditionality includes measures aimed at reducing fiscal deficits (by cutting spending and/or increasing taxation), currency devaluation, raising interest rates, and trade liberalization.

31 Article I(ii) of the Articles of Agreement of the International Monetary Fund, available online at www.imf.org.

32 Economic stabilization is a programme of comprehensive economic measures designed to achieve a viable balance of payments within the context of improved long-term economic growth and price stability.

33 For a critical analysis of IMF programmes see Spraos (1986), Gowan (1995) and Calomiris (1998).

34 See, for instance, Kahler (1989) and Stiles (1991), among others.

35 An overall assessment of IMF conditionality can be found in IMF (2001a, 2001e). See in particular the comments by Bird, Joyce, Rodrik, Alexander, Oxfam International, The Netherlands Ministry of Finance and the Netherlands Central Bank, Galbis and Mahmood.

36 These measures primarily involved government guarantees for SOEs, used as collaterals for bank loans (IMF 2001b, p. 16). In addition, tax arrears were settled through debt-for-equity swaps, which led to an implicit re-nationalization. According to the IMF-agreed programme, such debt-for-equity swaps have to be eliminated, and the state should sell its claims of SOEs to potential private investors interested in debt-for-equity swaps (IMF 2001c, p. 3).

37 Even among the leading reformers, bail-outs in the form of soft bank loans (the Czech Republic), bank loan write-offs (Hungary), tax write-offs and the use of government contracts (Slovakia), and directed subsidies (Poland) existed. See Djankov and Murrell (2000) for a survey of these issues in CEECs.

38 According to a trade union official, the unions feared that the inclusion of their companies in the project would lead to labour shedding.

39 Djankov and Hayperuma (1997) compare the pool of companies included in the programme with similar companies that were left outside the isolation programme. They conclude that labour restructuring took place at a slower pace in isolated firms, despite access to redundancy payments (Djankov and Hayperuma 1997, p. 15). Likewise, firms included in the isolation programme made more use of state subsidies than other companies. Based on these indicators, Djankov and Hayperuma (1997) show quite clearly that the enterprise isolation programme failed in all aspects.

40 When the Romanian state authorities refused their inclusion, several companies even sued the Romanian Government in the Constitutional Court, on the grounds that the enterprise isolation programme contravened the constitutional obligations of the Romanian state not to discriminate against different forms of property. See, for example, the various decisions of the Constitutional Court on the *Agrocom* versus *State* case (Curtea Constitutionala 1996).

41 The issue of inter-enterprise arrears in Romania is well documented in the academic literature. See, for instance, Begg and Portes (1993), Clifton and Khan (1993) and Perotti and Carare (1997).

42 The World Bank made one of its Structural Adjustment Loans to Romania subject to strict adherence to the rules laid out for the scheme, and to an

overall ceiling on IEAs as a percentage of SOE turnover (Clifton and Khan 1993, p. 692). The IMF also insisted on the elimination of successive central bank bail-outs on IEAs (Perotti and Carare 1997, p. 9).

43 However, as the literature on inter-enterprise arrears suggests, inherent in such an approach is the tendency to increase the contribution from the state budget to settle arrears. See Rostowski (1994) for an elaboration of this argument.

44 This increase in IEAs continued even though the Romanian government actively encouraged large creditors (in particular those in the energy sector) to form alliances against large debtors and to stop the supply of essential inputs (Daianu 1994).

45 For a detailed analysis of growth-enhancing networks in Hungary, see, for instance, Stark and Bruszt (1998).

46 For a detailed account of the evolving nature of Romania and Bretton Woods institutions, see, for instance, Pop (2002b).

47 Based on an interview with a former NBR economist, Bucharest, August 2002.

48 This condition is also included in the World Bank and EU financial assistance programmes to Romania.

49 IMF (1999b, p. 13) notes that transition economies had high levels of social spending that were poorly targeted, and therefore the policy objective would be to streamline them. Since better targeting is often difficult due to institutional weaknesses in transition economies, in practice the IMF advice frequently translated into a reduction in social spending in line with strict financial targets.

50 The IMF advocacy in favour of wage controls is not unique to the Romanian case. Wage controls were part of the stand-by arrangements with Hungary, Poland, Bulgaria, Czechoslovakia and Yugoslavia. Unlike Romania and Bulgaria, they were eliminated in the other CEECs by the mid-1990s (Schadler *et al.* 1995b).

51 See, for instance, Annex B of IMF (1999d).

52 For further details about Romania–IMF relations, see the documents available on the IMF website at http://www.imf.org/external/country/ROM/index.htm, in particular Romania Letter of Intent, Memorandum on Economic Policies and Technical Memorandum of Understanding, 16 May 2000.

53 In Romania, as in many other cases, the IMF programmes were perceived as having a negative social impact, particularly on labour. Vreeland (2002) brings compelling empirical evidence that IMF programmes had negative effects on income distribution, reducing the labour share of income in favour of capital owners. According to Vreeland, in countries that enter into IMF programmes labour income declines once countries are under IMF guidance, and it takes about 10 years to catch up with countries that do not take part in IMF programmes (Vreeland 2002, p. 127).

54 See, for instance, the support from bussiness associations for the government-led macroeconomic reform programmes during the negotiations with the IMF (CCIR 2001).

55 The Romanian government committed itself to cutting around 10,000 jobs in state-owned loss-making companies in the second half of 2001. In addition,

for about 116,000 people, half of the December bonuses were cut (IMF 2001b, p. 52).

56   BNS carried out a study aimed at highlighting the inconsistencies between Romanian domestic commitments and those included in the stand-by arrangement with the IMF (BNS 2000b).

57   BNS, for instance, sued the IMF in a local court for the inconsistencies between the conditionality of the stand-by arrangement with Romania and several articles from the IMF statute (BNS 2000a).

58   A summary of some of these criticisms is found in Phelan (2001), for instance.

59   It should be noted that a similar FESAL project has been successfully implemented in Poland. However, when the Bank tried to replicate the success in Romania, the FESAL project failed.

60   The World Bank has come to realize gradually that successful reform requires operating on these three fronts simultaneously and in an integrated framework. The failure of the initial FESAL programme that was designed in 1992 was largely attributed to this shortcoming.

61   The restructuring process prior to privatization was hampered by the ability of clientelistic networks to adapt to the new environment. Allegations of clientelistic asset-stripping activities persisted for a long time and almost compromised the conclusion of the privatization deal (Ursu 2001).

62   To ensure that the Romanian government takes all the necessary measures to complete the privatization process at SIDEX according to the schedule agreed with the World Bank, the privatization of SIDEX was included in the conditions introduced by the IMF in the stand-by arrangement for 2001–2 (IMF 2001c).

63   See Boariu and Roua (2001) for information on asset-stripping by managers and trade union leaders in the aluminium sector.

64   For instance, the World Bank was called upon by the Romanian authorities to assist them in addressing the governance issues that led to the collapse of the largest mutual investment fund in Romania.

65   For instance, illustrative for the strict built-in conditionality is that the FESAL programme contained 27 disbursement conditions. When the programme failed, 41 extra conditions were added.

66   Two principal causes were identified as responsible for this failure. On the one hand, the project conditionality relied on 'soft' indicators that could not be effectively monitored; on the other hand, the Romanian institutional conditions were much more adverse than initially thought.

67   One telling example is the case of Dacia Felix Bank which, after two formal audits and portfolio reviews, was positively evaluated by the World Bank and included as a reliable financial intermediary to carry out one of its industrial development projects. Soon afterwards, the bank collapsed spectacularly due to gross mismanagement.

68   Interview with an official in the Ministry of Industry, Bucharest, May 2002.

69   The agreement reached with the trade unions mentioned the creation of a specialized agency for social mitigation and job creation in the mining regions, the designation of mining regions as disadvantaged regions, providing tax incentives to future investors in the region, and the creation of new jobs for mine workers.

70 A study conducted by the Bank at the beginning of the project found that there were a number of problems with the restructuring strategy pursued so far by the government. Despite the fact that the voluntary redundancy package was quite generous (twice the amount given to workers in other sectors), the lack of alternative employment opportunities remained a source of discontent. The redundancy package made reference to micro-credit lines for enterprise development and SMEs but, due to restrictive banking rules for loans to SMEs and new enterprises, this never materialized.

71 For instance, the LCCs were a useful state–societal intermediation mechanism in identifying investment opportunities and formulating proposals that were later incorporated into the EU's regional development plans for the Jiu Valley and Gorj County, and in designing social safety nets.

72 Another explanation might be that, as the World Bank acknowledges, past experiences in Romania with projects in the social field demonstrated that the Ministry of Labour and Social Protection was not able to implement projects effectively, due to its insufficient social embeddedness (World Bank 1999c, p. 17).

73 A similar argument was made by Brucan (2002), who argued that the vast majority of reforms implemented by the various Romanian governments, regardless of their political colour, were initiated only under the pressure of Bretton Woods institutions.

74 The Romanian Minister of Agriculture openly criticized EU pressure for subsidies to domestic tobacco producers to be eliminated, declaring that EU integration should not be pursued blindly at any cost (Burtan 2002).

Bibliography

Adams, W. and Stoffaes, F. (1986) *French Industrial Policy*. Washington, DC: Brookings Institution.

Adevarul (1998), No. 2457(March), Bucharest.

Adevarul (1999), No. 2461 (February), Bucharest.

AFP (1999a) 'Romanian miners' leader kicked out of right-wing party', *Agence France Presse*, 28 January.

AFP (1999b) 'New convictions for jailed Romanian miners' leader', *Agence France Presse*, 4 March.

Akerlof, G. and Romer, P. (1993) 'Looting: the economic underworld of bankruptcy for profit', *Brookings Papers on Economic Activity*, 2, 1–73.

Albert, M. (1993) *Capitalism vs. Capitalism*. New York: Four Wall Eight Window.

Alexander, J. (2000) *Political Culture in Post-Communist Russia: Formlessness and Recreation in a Traumatic Transition*. London: Macmillan and New York: St Martin's Press.

Almond, G. A. (1983) 'Corporatism, pluralism, and professional memory', *World Politics*, 35(2), 245–60.

Amsden, A. (1989) *Asia's Next Giant: South Korea and Late Industrialization*. New York: Oxford University Press.

Amsden, A. (1990) 'Third world industrialisation: "global fordism" or a new model?', *New Left Review*, 182, 5–51.

Anderson, R. W. and Kegels, C. (1998) *Transitional Banking. Financial Development of Central and Eastern Europe*. Oxford: Clarendon Press.

Anderson, T. and Hill, P. (1975) 'The evolution of property rights: a study of the American West', *Journal of Law and Economics*, 18(1), 163–79.

APAPS (2002a) *Prezentare generala a programelor de privatizare cu finantare externa*. Bucharest: Autoritatea pentru Privatizare si Administrarea Participatiilor Statului. Available from: http://www.apaps.ro/ (accessed May 2002).

APAPS (2002b) *Raport de Activitate RICOP*. Bucharest: Autoritatea pentru Privatizare si Administrarea Participatiilor Statului. Available from: http://www.apaps.ro/programe/raport.htm (accessed May 2002).

Appel, H. (1999) 'Reconsidering the Determinants of Economic Policy-making: lessons from Privatisation in Transition Countries', Paper presented to the 95th Annual Meeting of the American Political Science Association, 2–5 September.

Aron, J. (2000) 'Growth and institutions: a review of the evidence', *The World Bank Research Observer*, 15(1), 99–135.

Arrow, K. (1994) 'The production and distribution of knowledge', in Silverberg, G. and Soete, L. (eds), *The Economics of Growth and Technical Change*. Aldershot: Edward Elgar.

Aslund, A., Boone, P. and Johnson, S. (1996) 'How to stabilize: lessons from post-communist countries', *Brookings Papers on Economic Activity*, 1, 217–314.

Atkinson, M. M. and Coleman, W. D. (1985) 'Corporatism and industrial policies', in Cawson, A. (ed.), *Organized Interest and the State*. London: Sage, pp. 22–45.

Atkinson, M. M. and Coleman, W. D. (1989) 'Strong states and weak states. Sectoral policy networks in advanced capitalist economies', *British Journal of Political Science*, 19(1), 47–67.

Bache, I. (1998) *EU Regional Policy-Making: Multi-Level Governance or Flexible Gatekeeping?* Contemporary European Studies Series. Sheffield: UACES/Sheffield Academic Press.

Balcerowicz, L. (1994) 'Common fallacies in the debate on the transition to a market economy', *Economic Policy*, 19, 18–50.

Bankcoop (2001) *Statutul Bancii*. Bucharest: Bankcoop.

Barreto, H. and Howland, F. (1993) 'There are Two Okun's Law Relationships between Output and Unemployment', Department of Economics Working Paper, Wabash College.

Barro, R. J. (1991) 'Economic growth in a cross section of countries', *Quarterly Journal of Economics*, 106(2), 407–43.

Barro, R. J. and Sala-i-Martin, X. (1995) *Economic Growth*. Boston, MA: McGraw-Hill.

Bates, R. H., de Figueiredo, R. J. P. Jr and Weingast, B. R. (1998) 'The politics of interpretation: rationality, culture, and transition', *Politics and Society*, 26(2), 221–57.

BBC (1990) 'Iliescu addresses victory square meeting on unrest', *BBC Summary of World Broadcasts* (Bucharest Home Service), 14 June.

BBW (1999) 'Kvaerner in trouble', *Bucharest Business Week*, 19–25 April.

Beach, W. and O'Driscoll, G. (2002) 'Explaining the factors of the index of economic freedom', in O'Driscoll, G., Holmes, K. and O'Grady, M. A. (eds), *The 2002 Index of Economic Freedom*. Washington, DC: The Heritage Foundation, pp. 59–77.

Beck, T., Demirgüç-Kunt, A. and Levine, R. (1999) *A New Database on Financial Development and Structure*. Washington: World Bank.

Begg, D. and Portes, R. (1993) *Enterprise Debt and Economic Transformation: Financial Restructuring of the State Sector in Central and Eastern Europe*. CEPR Discussion Paper No. 695. London: CEPR.

Bentley, A. (1908) *The Process of Government*. Chicago, IL: University of Chicago Press.

Berger, A., Kashyap, A. and Scalise, J. (1995) 'The transformation of the US banking industry: what a long, strange trip it's been', *Brookings Papers on Economic Activity*, 2, 55–218.

Berger, S. (1981) *Organising Interests in Western Europe: Pluralism, Corporatism, and the Transformation of Politics*. Cambridge: Cambridge University Press.

Berger, S. and Dore, R. (1996) *National Diversity and Global Capitalism*. Ithaca, NY: Cornell University Press.

Besancenot, D. and Vranceanu, R. (1999) 'A trade union model with endogenous militancy: interpreting the French case', *Labour Economics*, 6, 355–73.

Bibire, R. (2001) 'Privatizarea de la Letea va fi reluata', *Monitorul*, 21 March, Bacau. Available from: www.monitorul.ro (accessed 10 August 2001).

Birker, E., Cooper, C., Molander, P. and Pochard, M. (2000) *Report on an Assessment of the Twinning Instrument under Phare*, July, available online http://europa.eu.int/comm/enlargement/pas/twinning/pdf/assesm_july.pdf (accessed 21 May 2005).

Blanchard, O. (1997) *The Economics of Transition in Eastern Europe*. Oxford: Clarendon Press.

Blaschke, S. (2000) 'Union density and European integration: diverging convergence', *European Journal of Industrial Relations*, 6(2), 217–37.

Blaszczyk, B. (1999) 'Moving ahead: privatisation in Poland', *Economic Reform Today*, 2. Available from: http://www.cipe.org/publications/fs/ert/e32/e32_04.htm (accessed 12 June 2001).

Block, F. (1987) *Revising State Theory*. Philadelphia, PA: Temple University Press.

Bloomestein, H. J. and Spencer, M. G. (1994) 'The role of financial institutions in the transition to a market economy', in Caprio, G. Jr, Folkerts-Landau, D. and Lane, T. (eds), *Building Sound Finance in Emerging Market Economies*. Washington, DC: International Monetary Fund and World Bank, pp. 139–89.

BNS (2000a) *BNS has begun a Lawsuit against the IMF*. Bucharest: Blocul National Sindical. Available from: http://www.bns.ro (accessed July 2002).

BNS (2000b) *Programul de Guvernare versus Memorandumul cu privire la politicile economice şi financiare ale Guvernului convenit cu Fondul Monetar Internaţional*. Bucharest: Blocul National Sindical. Available from: http://www.bns.ro (accessed July 2002).

Boariu, A. and Roua, E. (2001) 'Sindicatele cer ca Alro si Alprom sa ramana sub controlul statului', *Adevarul* 3406, 30 May. Available from: http://adevarul. kappa.ro (accessed 06 June 2001).

Bonin, J. P. and Schaffer, M. E. (1995) *Banks, Firms, Bad Debts and Bankruptcy in Hungary 1991–94*. Discussion Paper 234. London: London School of Economics, Centre for Economic Performance.

Borish, M. S., Ding, W. and Noël, M. (1996) *On the Road to EU Accession. Financial Sector Development in Central Europe*. Washington, DC: The World Bank.

Börzel, T. A. (1998) 'Organizing Babylon – on the different conceptions of policy networks', *Public Administration*, 76, 253–73.

Börzel, T. and Risse, T. (2000) *When Europe Hits Home: Europeanization and Domestic Change*. European Integration online Papers (EIoP) Vol. 4, No. 15. Available from: http://eiop.or.at/eiop/texte/2000-015a.htm.

Boycko, M., Shleifer, A. and Vishny, R. W. (1996) 'A theory of privatisation', *The Economic Journal*, 106, 309–20.

Brom, K. (1997) 'A Review of Romanian Privatisation', mimeo.

Browne, W. (1990) 'Organised interests and their issue niches: a search for pluralism in the policy domain', *The Journal of Politics*, 52(2), 477–509.

Brubaker, R. (1996) *Nationalism Reframed: Nationhood and the National Question in the New Europe*. Cambridge: Cambridge University Press.

Brucan, S. (2002) 'Interview with Frederic Mitterrand', *TV5 Monde*, Sunday 28 April.

Brunetti, A. (1997) 'Political variables in cross-country analysis', *Journal of Economic Surveys*, 11(2), 163–90.

Brunetti, A., Kisunko, G. and Weder, B. (1997) *Institutions in Transition: Reliability of Rules and Economic Performance in Former Socialist Countries*. World Bank Research Working Paper, No. 1809.

Bulmer, S. (1994) 'Institutions and policy change in the European Communities: the case of merger control', *Public Administration*, 72, 423–44.

Bulmer, S. and Burch, M. (2000) 'The "Europeanization" of central government: the UK and Germany in historical institutionalist perspective', in Aspinwall, M. and Schneider, J. (eds), *The Rules of Integration*. Manchester: Manchester University Press, pp. 73–96.

Bunce, V. (1995) 'Should transitologists be grounded?', *Slavic Review*, 54, 111–27.

Burtan, R. (2002) 'Ilie Sarbu nu stie ce a facut guvernul cu ordonanta care dadea facilitati Societatii Tutunul Romanesc', *Evenimentul Zilei*, 27 February, Bucharest.

Businessweek (2002) 'The Crisis in Corporate Governance: Special Report', *BusinessWeek*, 6 May. McGraw-Hill Inc. Available from: http://www.businessweek. com/magazine/toc/02_18/B3781govern.htm (accessed 22 August 2002).

Calmfors, L. and Driffill, J. (1988) 'Bargaining structure, corporatism and macro-economic performance', *Economic Policy*, 6, 13–47.

Calomiris, C. (1998) 'The IMF's imprudent role as lender of last resort', *Cato Journal*, 17, 275–94.

Calvo, G. A. and Coricelli, F. (1992) 'Output collapse in Eastern Europe: The role of credit', *IMF Staff Papers*, 40(1).

Camdessus, M. (1999) 'Second Generation Reforms: Reflections and New Challenges', Opening Remarks to IMF Conference on Second Generation Reforms by Managing Director of the International Monetary Fund, Washington, DC, 8 November.

Cameron, D. (1978) 'The expansion of the public economy: a comparative analysis', *American Political Science Review*, 72, 1243–61.

Caprio, G. Jr (1995) 'The role of financial intermediaries in transitional economies', *Carnegie-Rochester Conference Series on Public Policy*, 42, 257–302.

Carlin, W. and Mayer, C. (1999) 'How Do Financial Systems Affect Economic Performance?', University of Oxford Financial Research Centre Economics Series Paper No. 08, Oxford.

Carlin, W. and Soskice, D. (1990) *Macroeconomics and the Wage Bargain*. Oxford: Oxford University Press.

Cassen, R. (ed.), (1986) *Does Aid Work?* London: Oxford University Press.

Castells, M. (1992) 'Four Asian tigers with a dragon head: a comparative analysis of the state, economy and society in the Asian Pacific Rim', in Appelbaum, R. P. and Henderson, J. (eds), *States and Development in the Asian Pacific Rim*. London: Sage, pp. 33–70.

Cawson, A. (1985) *Organized Interests and the State: Studies in Meso-Corporatism*. London: Sage.

Cawson, A. and Ballard, J. (1984) *A Bibliography of Corporatism*. European University Institute Working Paper no. 115, Florence.

CCIR (2001) 'In dialogul cu FMI, oamenii de afaceri au sustinut politica econom-ica a Guvernului', *Mesagerul Economic*, 26 February–4 March 2001. Bucharest: Camera de Comert si Industrie a Romaniei.

CEFIC (2001) *Partnership for Building up Future Europe and the Enlarged Internal Market*. Brussels: European Chemical Industry Council. Available from: www.cefic.be (accessed 18 June 2002).

Cernat, L. (2001) 'Anglo-Saxon vs. Continental Capitalism: Institutional Aspects of EU-level Participatory Management', Paper presented at Cross-border Mergers and Employee Participation in Europe Conference, Ecole des Mines de Paris, 9 March.

Cernat, L. (2004) 'The Politics of Banking in Romania: Soft Loans, Looting and Cardboard Billionaires', *Government and Opposition*, 39(3), 451–75.

Cernat, L. and Vranceanu, R. (2001) *Trade Openness and Economic Growth: New Evidence from Eastern Europe*. ESSEC Working Paper, No. 24, Paris: Ecole Supérieure des Sciences Economiques et Commerciales.

Cerny, P. G. (1993) *Finance and World Politics: Markets, Regimes and States in the Post-Hegemonic Era*. Aldershot and Brookfield, VT: Edward Elgar.

Cerny, P. G. (1997) 'Paradoxes of the competition state: the dynamics of political globalisation', *Government and Opposition*, 32(2), 251–74.

Chang, H. J. (1993) 'The political economy of industrial policy in Korea', *Cambridge Journal of Economics*, 17(2), 131–57.

Chaplinsky, S., Niehaus, G. and Van De Gucht, L. (1998) 'Employee buyouts: causes, structure, and consequences', *Journal of Financial Economics*, 48(3), 283–332.

Chavance, B. and Magnin, E. (1998) 'National trajectories of post-socialist transformation: is there a convergence towards western capitalisms?', *Prague Economic Papers*, 7(3), 227–37.

Chirovici, E. O. (1998) 'Florin Ionescu a trecut, problemele BANCOREX au ramas', *Curierul National*, 2179, 11 May.

Claessens, S. and Kyle, P. R. Jr (1997) 'State enterprise performance and soft budget constraints: the case of Bulgaria', *Economics of Transition*, 5(2), 305–22.

Clifton, E. and Khan, M. (1993) 'Interenterprise arrears in transforming economies: the case of Romania', *IMF Staff Papers*, 40(3), 680–96.

Coates, D. (1999) 'Models of capitalism in the new world order: the UK case', *Political Studies*, 47, 643–60.

Cole, A. (1998) *French Politics and Society*. London: Prentice Hall.

Cook, J. (1999a) 'Miners' victory sets back reform hopes in Romania', *Financial Times*, 23 January, p. 3.

Cook, J. (1999b) 'Romania. All very sinister', *The Economist*, 6 February, p. 55.

Cook, J. (1999c) 'Romania miners's chief gets jail term', *Financial Times*, 16 February, p. 2.

Cook, J. (1999d) 'Romania tries to climb out of bottomless pit of mine losses', *Financial Times*, 12 March, p. 3.

Cooke, W. N. and Noble, D. S. (1998) 'Industrial relations systems and US foreign direct investment abroad', *British Journal of Industrial Relations*, 36(4), 581–609.

Corvers, F. and van Veen, T. (1995) 'On the measurement of corporatism', *Labour*, 9(3), 423–42.

Cotidianul (1999) *Stiri economice*. Available from: http://www.cotidianul.ro/anterioare/1999/eveniment/even26iul01aug.htm.

Cotidianul (2001a) *Dupa o lunga perioada de tergiversare, Guvernul incearca deblocarea RICOP*, 19–25 February. Available from: http://www.cotidianul.ro (accessed April 2002).

Cotidianul (2001b) *Guvernul, patronatele si sindicatele au semnat ieri pactul pentru un an de pace sociala*. Available from: http://www.cotidianul.ro (accessed February 2001).

Crama, Y., Leruth, L., Renneboog, L. and Urbain, J.–P. (1999) 'Corporate governance structures, control and performance in European markets: a tale of two systems', Tilburg University Centre for Economic Research Discussion Paper, No. 97, Tilburg.

Cristian, D. and Teodor, O. (1999) *Afacerea 'BANCOREX' candideaza la titlul de „jaful secolului"*. Cotidianul, 31 July 1999. Available from: http://www.cotidianul.ro/anterioare/1999/eveniment/even26iul01aug.htm#31 iulie.

Crouch, C. (1978) 'The changing role of the state in industrial relations in Western Europe', in Crouch, C. and Pizorno, A. (eds), *The Resurgence of Class Conflict in Western Europe since 1968*. New York: Holmes & Meier, pp. 197–220.

Crouch, C. and Streeck, W. (eds) (1997) *Political Economy of Modern Capitalism: Mapping Convergence and Diversity*. London: Sage.

Crowther, W. E. (1988) *The Political Economy of Romanian Socialism*. New York: Praeger.

Curtea Constitutionala (1996) 'Decizia no.130 – Recurs impotriva Deciziei Curtii Constitutionale no. 76 din 19 iunie 1996', *Monitorul Oficial*, No. 293, 19 November. Bucharest.

Czaban, L. and Whitley, R. (1998) 'The transformation of work systems in emergent capitalism: the case of Hungary', *Work, Employment and Society*, 12, 47–72.

Czada, R. (1996) 'The Treuhandanstalt and the transition from socialism to capitalism', in Benz, A. and Goetz, K. (eds), *A New German Public Sector? Reform, Adaptation and Stability*. Aldershot: Dartmouth, pp. 93–117.

Dabrowski, M., Gomulka, S. and Rostowski, J. (2000) 'Whence Reform? A Critique of the Stiglitz Perspective', Supplementary Paper prepared for the UN-ECE Seminar, From Plan to Market: The Transition Process after Ten Years, Geneva, 2 May.

Dahl, R. (1956) *A Preface to Democratic Theory*. Chicago, IL: University of Chicago Press.

Dahrendorf, R. (1990) *Reflections on the Revolution in Europe*. New York: Times Books.

Daianu, D. (1994) *Inter-Enterprise Arrears in a Post-Command Economy: Thoughts from a Romanian Perspective*, IMF Working Paper, No. 54. Washington, DC: IMF.

David, P. (1994), 'Why are institutions the "carriers of history"? Path dependence and the evolution of conventions, organizations, and institutions', *Structural Change and Economic Dynamics*, 5(2), 205–20.

David, S. (2000) 'Oficiul si Consiliul Concurentei – impotriva monopolului de stat pe alcool', *Adevarul*, No. 3260.

Daviddi, R. (ed.) (1995) *Property Rights and Privatisation in the Transition to a Market Economy: A Comparative Review*. Maastricht: European Institute of Public Administration.

Davidson, I. (1998) *Jobs and the Rhineland Model*. London: Federal Trust Report.

DCG (2000) *Raport asupra activitatii Fondului Proprietatii de Stat*. Bucharest: Departamentul de Control al Guvernului.

Deacon, B., Hulse, M. and Stubbs, P. (1997) *Global Social Policy: International Organisations and the Future of Welfare*. London: Sage.

Deeg, R. (1999) *Finance Capitalism Unveiled: Banks and the German Political Economy*. Ann Arbor, MI: The University of Michigan Press.

De Jong, H. W. (1989) 'The takeover market in Europe: control structures and the performance of large companies compared', *Review of Industrial Organization*, 6, 1–18.

De Jong, H. W. (ed.) (1993) *The Structure of European Industry*, 3rd edn. Dordrecht and Boston, MA: Kluwer.

De Jong, H. W. (1995) 'European Capitalism: Between Freedom and Social Justice', *Review of Industrial Organization*, 10, 339–419.

Deletant, D. (1996) *Ceausescu and the Securitate: Coercion and Dissent in Romania, 1965–1989*. London: Hurst.

Demirgüç-Kunt, A., Levine, R. and Min, H. G. (1998) 'Opening to Foreign Banks: Issues of Stability, Efficiency, and Growth', *Proceedings Bank of Korea Conference on the Implications of Globalization of World Financial Markets*. Seoul: Bank of Korea, pp. 83–105.

Dermine, J. (1993) *European Banking in the 1990s*, 2nd edn. Oxford: Basil Blackwell.

Dewatripont, M. and Roland, G. (1992) 'The virtues of gradualism and legitimacy in the transition to a market economy', *The Economic Journal*, 102, 291–300.

Deyo, F. (ed.) (1990) *The Political Economy of the New Asian Industrialism*. Ithaca, NY: Cornell University Press.

Dicks-Mireaux, L., Mecagni, M. and Schadler, S. (2000) 'Evaluating the effect of IMF lending to low income countries', *Journal of Development Economics*, 61, 495–526.

Dimitrov, L. (1997) Improvement of the mass privatisation legislation', *IME Newsletter*, April, Sofia: Institute for Market Economics. Available from: http://www.ime-bg.org/news/apr97/mass_priv.pdf (accessed 14 June 2002).

Dittrich, E. J., Schmidt, G. and Whitley, R. (eds) (1995) *Industrial Transformation in Europe: Process and Contexts*. London: Sage.

Dittus, P. and Prowse, S. (1996) 'Corporate control in central Europe and Russia: should banks own shares?', in Frydman, R., Gray, C. and Rapaczynski, A. (eds), *Corporate Governance in Central Europe and Russia*, Vol 1. Budapest: CEU Press, pp. 20–67.

Djankov, S. (1998) Enterprise Isolation Programs in Transition Economies. Policy Research Working Paper No. 1952. Washington, DC: World Bank.

Djankov, S. and Hayperuma, K. (1997) *The Failure of the Government-Led Program of Corporate Reorganization in Romania*. The William Davidson Institute Working Paper No. 139, University of Maryland.

Djankov, S. and Murrell, P. (2000) 'Enterprise Restructuring in Transition: A Quantitative Survey', Department of Economics, University of Maryland, College Park, unpublished manuscript, December.

Dollar, D. and Svensson, J. (1998) *What Explains the Success or Failure of Structural Adjustment Programs?* Policy Research Working Paper No. 1938. Washington, DC: World Bank.

Dolowitz, D. and Marsh, D. (1996) 'Who learns what from whom: a review of the policy transfer literature', *Political Studies*, 44(2), 343–57.

Dolowitz, D. and Marsh, D. (2000) 'Learning from abroad: the role of policy transfer in contemporary policy-making', *Governance*, 13(1), 5–24.

Doner, R. F. and Ramsay, A. (1997) 'Competitive clientelism and economic governance: the case of Thailand', in Maxfield, S. and Schneider, B. R. (eds), *Business and the State in Developing Countries*. Cornell Studies in Political Economy. Ithaca, NY, and London: Cornell University Press, pp. 237–76.

Dore, R. (1987) *Taking Japan Seriously: A Confucian Perspective on Leading Economic Issues*. London: Athlone.

Douglass, M. (1994) 'The "developmental state" and the newly industrialised economies of Asia', *Environment & Planning A*, 26(4), 543–66.

Dyson, K. and Wilks, S. (eds) (1983) *Industrial Crisis: A Comparative Study of the State and Industry*. Oxford: Basil Blackwell.

Earle, J. and Brown, J. D. (1999) 'Evaluating Enterprise Privatisation in Russia', *Russian Economic Trends* 8(3), 25–30.

Earle, J. S. and Telegdy, A. (1998) 'Rezultatele Programului de Privatizare in Masa (I)', *Sfera Politicii*, No. 59. Bucharest, pp. 10–16.

Earle, J. S. and Telegdy, A. (1999) 'Capitalismul romanesc de astazi', *Sfera Politicii*, No. 63. Bucharest, pp. 20–4.

EBRD (1998) *Transition Report 1998. Financial Sector in Transition*. London: European Bank for Reconstruction and Development.

EBRD (1999) *Transition Report 1999*. London: European Bank for Reconstruction and Development.

EBRD (2000) *Transition Report 2000*. London: European Bank for Reconstruction and Development.

EC (1994) *An Industrial Competiveness Policy for the European Union*, COM (94) 319 Final. Brussels: EC.

EC (1995) *White Paper: Preparation of the Associated Countries of Central and Eastern Europe for Integration into the Internal Market of the Union*. Brussels: EC.

EC (1997a) *Commission Opinion on Bulgaria's Application for Membership of the European Union*. Brussels: EC.

EC (1997b) *Enhanced Pre-Accession Strategy – Project Document RO9706*. Available from: http://www.infoeuro.ro (accessed in July 2002).

EC (1997c) *The PHARE Programme: An Interim Evaluation*. Brussels: EC.

EC (1998a) *1998 Regular Report from the Commission on Romania's Progress Towards Accession*. Brussels: EC.

EC (1998b) *An Evaluation of PHARE Restructuring and Privatisation Programmes: Final Report*. Brussels: Commission of the European Community.

EC (1998c) *Romania: 1998 Accession Partnership*. Brussels: EC.

EC (1999) *Regular Report from the Commission on Romania's Progress Towards Accession*. Brussels: EC.

EC (2000a) *Regular Report from the Commission on Estonia's Progress Towards Accession*. Brussels: EC.

EC (2000b) *Agenda 2000*. Brussels: EC.

EC (2000c) *Romania: 2000 National PHARE Program*, Brussels: EC.

EC (2001a) *Regular Report from the Commission on Romania's Progress Towards Accession*. Brussels: EC.

EC (2001b) *Reports on Progress Towards Accession by each of the Candidate Countries*. Brussels: EC.

ECE (2000) *Economic Survey of Europe*. Geneva: United Nations, Economic Commission for Europe.

Eggertsson, T. (1990) *Economic Behaviour and Institutions*. Cambridge: Cambridge University Press.

Elster, J., Offe, C. and Preuss, K. (1998) *Institutional Design in Post-Communist Societies, Rebuilding the Ship at Sea*. Cambridge: Cambridge University Press.

Esping-Andersen, G. (1985) *Politics against Markets*. Princeton, NJ: Princeton University Press.

Esping-Andersen, G. and Friedland, R. (1982) 'Class Coalitions in the Making of Western European Economics', in Esping-Andersen, G. and Friedland, R. (eds), *Political Power and Social Theory*. Greenwich CT: Jai Press, pp. 1–52.

Estrin, S. and Stone, R. (1996) 'A taxonomy of mass privatisation', *Transition*, 7(11–12), 8–9.

Ettlinger, N. (1994) 'The localization of development in comparative perspective', *Economic Geography*, 70(2), 144–66.

Evans, M. and Davies, J. (1999) 'Understanding policy transfer: a multi-level, multi-disciplinary perspective', *Public Administration*, 77(2), 361–85.

Evans, P. B. (1992) 'The state as problem and solution: predation, embedded autonomy, and adjustment', in Haggard, S. and Kaufman, R. R. (eds), *The Politics of Economic Adjustment*. Princeton, NJ: Princeton University Press, pp. 139–91.

Evans, P. B. (1995) *Embedded Autonomy: States and Industrial Transformation*. Princeton, NJ: Princeton University Press.

Evans, P. B. (ed.) (1997) *State–Society Synergy: Government Action and Social Capital in Development*. Berkeley, CA: UC Berkeley.

Evans, P. B. (1979) *Dependent Development: The Alliance of Multinational, State, and Local Capital in Brazil*. Princeton, NJ: Princeton University Press.

Evans, P. B., Rueschmeyer, D. and Skocpol, T. (1985) *Bringing the State Back In*. Cambridge: Cambridge University Press.

Expres 1996. *Stiri politice*, 29 July. Available from: http://www.Expres.ro/arhive/politica/1996/iulie/29Iul/content4.html.

Expres 1997. *Stiri politice*, 17 September. Available from: http://www.Expres.ro/arhive/politica/1997/septembrie/17Sep/content12.html.

Feagin, J., Orum, A. and Sjoberg, G. (eds) (1991) *A Case for Case Study*. Chapel Hill, NC: University of North Carolina Press.

Featherstone, K. (2003) 'Introduction: In the Name of "Europe" ', in Radaelli, C. M. and Featherstone, K. (eds), *The Politics of Europeanization*. Oxford: Oxford University Press, pp. 3–27.

Financial Times (2000) 'Opposition candidate denies party wants to halt privatisation in Romania', 17 November. Available from: www.ft.com.

Fischer, S., Sahay, R. and Végh, C. (1996) 'Stabilization and growth in transition economies: the early experience', *Journal of Economic Perspectives*, 10(2), 45–66.

Flanagan, R. J., Soskice, D. W. and Ulman, L. (1983) *Unionism, Economic Stabilization, and Income Policies: European Experience*. Washington, DC: Brookings Institutions.

Fleetwood, S. (1999) 'The inadequacy of mainstream theories of trade union behaviour', *Labour*, 13(2), 445–80.

Freeman, R. (2000) *Single Peaked vs Diversified Capitalism: The Relation Between Economic Institutions and Outcomes*, NBER Working Paper 7556. Cambridge, MA: National Bureau of Economic Research.

Friedman, T. L. (1999) *The Lexus and the Olive Tree*. New York: Farrar, Straus & Giroux.

Friis, L. (1998) 'And then they were 15: the EU's EFTA-enlargement negotiations', *Cooperation and Conflict*, 33(1), 81–107.

Friis, L. and Murphy, A. (1999) 'The European Union and Central and Eastern Europe: governance and boundaries', *Journal of Common Market Studies*, 37(2), 211–32.

Froot, K. A. (1994) 'Foreign direct investment in Eastern Europe: some economic considerations', in Blanchard, O., Froot, K. A. and Sachs, J. D. (eds), *The Transition in Eastern Europe*, Vol. 2. Chicago, IL: University of Chicago Press, pp. 293–318.

Fry, J. (1988) *Money, Interest and Banking in Economic Development*. Baltimore, MD: Johns Hopkins University Press.

Frydman, R. and Rapaczynski, A. (1994) *Privatisation in Eastern Europe: Is the State Withering Away?* Budapest: Central European University Press.

Frydman, R., Gray, C., Hessel, M. and Rapaczynski, A. (1999) 'When Does Privatisation Work? The Impact of Private Ownership on Corporate Performance in the Transition Economies', *Quarterly Journal of Economics*, 114, 1153–91.

Garrett, C. S. (2001) 'Towards a new model of German capitalism? The Mannesmann–Vodafone merger and its implications for the German economy', *German Politics*, 10(3), 83–102.

Garuda, G. (2000) 'The distributional effect of IMF programs: a cross-country analysis', *World Development*, 28, 1031–51.

Gerlach, M. L. (1992) *Alliance Capitalism: The Social Organization of Japanese Business*. Berkeley, CA: University of California Press.

Gerschenkron, A. (1962) *Economic Backwardness in Historical Perspective*. Cambridge, MA: Harvard University Press.

Gertler, M. (1988) 'Financial structure and aggregate economic activity: an overview', *Journal of Money, Credit, and Banking*, 20(3), 559–88.

Gheorghe, G. and Huminic, A. (2000) 'Istoria mineriadelor din anii 1990–91', *Sfera Politicii*, 67. Bucharest: Fundatia Societatea Civila.

Globokar, T. (1997) 'Eastern Europe meets West: an empirical study on French management in a Slovenia plant', in Sackmann, S. (ed.), *Cultural Complexity in Organizations*. London: Sage, pp. 72–86.

Goetz, K. H. (2000) 'European integration and national executives: a cause in search of an effect?', *West European Politics*, 23(4), 211–31.

Goldsmith, R. (1969) *Financial Structure and Development*. New Haven, CT: Yale University.

Goodhart, C. A. E. (1994) 'Banks and the control of corporations', *Economic Notes by Monte dei Paschi di Siena*, 23(1), 1–18.

GOR (1994) 'Hotarirea Guvernului No. 301/1993', *Monitorul Oficial*, No. 21 (January). Bucharest: Guvernul Romaniei.

GOR (2001) *Cartea alba a guvernarii in luna decembrie 2000*. Bucharest: Guvernul Romaniei.

Gould, A. (1993) *Capitalist Welfare Systems: A Comparison of Japan, Britain, and Sweden*. London: Longman.

Gould, J. (1999) *Winners, Losers and the Institutional Effects of Privatisation in the Czech and Slovak Republics*. EUI working paper no. 99/11. Florence: European University Institute.

Gowan, P. (1995) 'Neo-liberal theory and practice for Eastern Europe', *New Left Review*, 213, 3–60.

Grabbe, H. (1999) 'Transnational Relations and Developing Models of Capitalism: The Political Economy of Integrating Central and Eastern Europe into EU', Paper for the ECPR 27th Joint Sessions of Workshops, Mannheim, 26–31 March.

Grabbe, H. (2003) 'Europeanization Goes East: Power and Uncertainty in the EU Accession Process', in Radaelli, C. M. and Featherstone, K. (eds), *The Politics of Europeanization*. Oxford: Oxford University Press, pp. 303–31.

Grabel, I. (1997) 'Savings, investment, and functional efficiency: a comparative examination of national financial complexes', in Pollin, R. (ed.), *The Macroeconomics of Saving, Finance, and Investment*. Ann Arbor, MI: University of Michigan Press, pp. 251–97.

Granovetter, M. (1985) 'Economic action and social structure: the problem of embeddedness', *American Journal of Sociology*, 91, 481–510.

Grant, W. (1989) *Government and Industry*. London: Edward Elgar.

Grant, W. and Nath, S. (1984) *The Politics of Economic Policymaking*. Oxford: Basil Blackwell.

Gray, V. and Lowery, D. (1988) 'Interest group politics and economic development in the U.S.', *American Political Science Review*, 82, 109–32.

Grosse, E. U. and Luger, H. H. (1994) *Understanding France in Comparison with Germany*. Berne: Peter Lang.

Guitian, M. (1981) *Fund Conditionality: Evolution of Principles and Practices*, IMF Pamphlet Series, No. 38. Washington, DC: International Monetary Fund.

Gurley, J. G. and Shaw, S. (1955) 'Financial aspects of economic development', *American Economic Review*, 45(4), 515–38.

Haggard, S. (1990) *Pathways from the Periphery: The Politics of Growth in the Newly Industrializing Countries*. Ithaca, NY: Cornell University Press.

Haggard, S., Lee, C. H. and Maxfield, S. (eds) (1993) *The Politics of Finance in Developing Countries*. Ithaca, NY: Cornell University Press.

Hagopian, F. (1994) 'Traditional Politics Against State Transformation in Brazil', in Migdal, J. S. *et al.* (eds), *State Power and Social Forces: Domination and Transformation in the Third World*. Cambridge: Cambridge University Press, pp. 37–64.

Hall, P. and Soskice, D. (eds) (2001) *Varieties of Capitalism: The Institutional Foundations of Comparative Advantage*. Oxford: Oxford University Press.

Halpern, L. and Wyplosz, C. (1997) 'Equilibrium exchange rates in transition economies', *IMF Staff Papers*, 44(4), 430–60.

Hansmann, H. (1996) *The Ownership of Enterprise*. Cambridge, MA: Harvard University Press.

Hart, J. A. (1992) 'The effects of state–societal arrangements on international competitiveness: steel, motor vehicles and semiconductors in the United States, Japan and Western Europe', *British Journal of Political Science*, 22, 255–300.

Hayek, F. A. (1949) *Individualism and Economic Order: Essays*. London: Routledge.

Hayes, M. (1981) *Lobbyists and Legislators*. New Brunswick, NJ: Rutgers University Press.

Heclo, H. (1978) 'Issue networks and the executive establishment', in King, A. (ed.), *The New American Political System*. Washington, DC: American Enterprise Institute, pp. 87–124.

Heclo, H. and Wildavsky, A. (1981) *The Private government of Public Money: Community and Policy inside British Politics*, 2nd edn. London: Macmillan.

Helliwell, J. F. (1994) 'Empirical linkages between democracy and economic growth', *British Journal of Political Science*, 24(2), 225–48.

Helliwell, J. F. (1996) *Economic Growth and Social Capital in Asia*, NBER Working Paper, No. 5470. Cambridge, MA: National Bureau of Economic Research.

Hellman, J. (1998) 'Winners take all: the politics of partial reforms in postcommunist transitions', *World Politics*, 50, 203–34.

Hellman, J., Jones, G., Kaufmann, D. and Schakerman, M. (2000) *Measuring Governance, State Capture and Corruption*. Policy Research Working Paper, No. 2312. Washington, DC: World Bank.

Hellman, T., Murdock, K. and Stiglitz, J. (1995) 'Financial Restraint: Towards a New Paradigm', Paper written for the World Bank EDI Workshop on the Roles of Government in East Asian Economies: Rent Creation, Coordination and Institutional Development, Stanford University, 10–11 February.

Henley, A. and Tsakalotos, E. (1993) *Corporatism and Economic Performance*. Aldershot: Edward Elgar.

Hennis, M. (2001) 'Europeanization and Globalization: The Missing Link', *Journal of Common Market Studies*, 39(5): 829–50.

Hicks, A. and Kenworthy, L. (1998) 'Cooperation and political economic performance in affluent democratic capitalism', *American Journal of Sociology*, 103, 1631–72.

Hirschman, A. O. (1958) *The Strategy of Economic Development*. New Haven, CT: Yale University Press.

Hirschman, A. O. (1970) *Exit, Voice and Loyalty: Responses to Decline in Firms, Organizations, and States*. Cambridge, MA: Harvard University Press.

Hirst, P. and Thompson, G. (1996) *Globalization in Question: The International Economy and the Possibilities of Governance*. Cambridge: Polity Press.

Hix, S. (1998) 'ECSA Review Forum: Integrating Left and Right', *ECSA Review*, XI(3), 2–3.

Holder, W. E. (1999) 'Comments on What Role do Legal Institutions Play in Development?', Paper presented at the IMF Conference on Second Generation Reforms, Washington, DC, 8 November.

Hollingsworth, J. R. and Boyer, R. (eds) (1997) *Contemporary Capitalism: The Embeddedness of Institutions*. Cambridge: Cambridge University Press.

Hooghe, L. (ed.) (1996) *Cohesion Policy and European Integration*. Oxford: Oxford University Press.

Hooghe, L. (1998) 'EU cohesion policy and competing models of capitalism', *Journal of Common Market Studies*, 36(4), 457–77.

Howell, K. E. (2004) 'Developing Conceptualisations of Europeanization: Synthesising Methodological Approaches', *Queen's Papers on Europeanization*, No. 3/2004. Belfast: Queen's University.

Hutchcroft, P. (1997) 'The politics of privilege: assessing the impact of rents, corruption, and clientelism on Third World development', *Political Studies*, 45, 639–58.

Hutton, W. (1999) *The Stakeholding Society: Writings on Politics and Economics*. Oxford: Basil Blackwell.

Iankova, E. (2000) 'Accession the the European Union and Institutional Design: The Europeanization of Post-Communist Tripartism', NCEEER Working Paper. Washington, DC: The National Council for Eurasian and East European Research.

Iankova, E. (2001) 'Governed by Accession? Hard and Soft Pillars of Europeanization in Central and Eastern Europe', Working Paper No. 60. Washington, DC: The Woodrow Wilson Centre.

Ibrahim, G. and Galt, V. (2002) 'Bye-bye central planning, hello market hiccups: institutional transition in Romania', *Cambridge Journal of Economics*, 26, 105–18.

ILO (1997a) *World Employment Report 1996–97*. Geneva: International Labour Organization.

ILO (1997b) *World Labour Report 1997*. Geneva: International Labour Organization.

ILO (2000) *LaborSta*. ILO Online Statistical Database. Available from: http://www.ilo.org.

IMF (1984) *The Chairman's Summing Up at the Conclusion of the Discussion on Fund–Bank Collaboration and the Adjustment Process – Issues for Consideration*. Washington, DC: IMF.

IMF (1999a) *Finance & Development*, June. Washington, DC: International Monetary Fund.

IMF (1999b) *IMF Annual Report*. Washington, DC: International Monetary Fund.

IMF (1999c) *Review of Social Issues and Policies in IMF-Supported Programs*. Washington, DC, 27 August.

IMF (1999d) *Romania: Letter of Intent and Memorandum on Economic Policies*, 26 July, Annexes A–D. Available from: http://www.imf.org.

IMF (2000) *Direction of Trade Statistics*, CD-ROM. Washington: International Monetary Fund.

IMF (2001a) *Conditionality in Fund-Supported Programs: Overview*. Available from: http://www.imf.org/external/np/pdr/cond/2001/eng.

IMF (2001b) *Request for Stand-By Arrangement*. IMF country Report, No. 1/204, November. Washington, DC: International Monetary Fund.

IMF (2001c) *Romania: Letter of Intent, Memorandum of Economic and Financial Policies, Technical Memorandum of Understanding*, Washington, DC, 17 October.

IMF (2001d) *Romania: Selected Issues and Statistical Appendix*. IMF Country Report No. 01/16. Washington, DC: International Monetary Fund.

IMF (2001e) *Streamlining Structural Conditionality: Review of Initial Experience. Streamlining Structural Conditionality in Fund-Supported Programs: Interim Guidance Note. Conditionality in Fund-Supported Programs: External Consultations.* Available from: http://www.imf.org/external/np/pdr/cond/2001/eng/collab/econ.htm.

IMF (2002) *IMF Members' Quotas and Voting Power, and IMF Governors*, 11 June. Available from: http://www.imf.org/external/np/sec/memdir/members.htm.

IMF and World Bank (2001) *Strengthening IMF–World Bank Collaboration on Country Programs and Conditionality*. Washington, DC, 23 August.

Inotai, A. (1999) 'Winners and losers in EU integration in Central and Eastern Europe', *Journal of Transforming Economies and Societies*, 6(4), 2–25.

Ionascu, A. (2000) 'Comisia senatoriala de ancheta asupra FPS il gaseste pe Radu Sarbu vinovat in afacerea Polus: Senatorii au gasit grave nereguli in perioada in care Sarbu si Sorin Dimitriu au pastorit FPS', *Cotidianul*, 24 February. Available from: http://www.cotidianul.ro/anterioare/2000/politica/pol2127feb.htm#23%20februarie (accessed 18 December 2000).

Jayasuriya, K. (2001) 'Globalization and the changing architecture of the state: the regulatory state and the politics of negative coordination', *Journal of European Public Policy*, 8(1), 101–23.

Jenkins, R. (1991) 'Learning from the gang: are there lessons for Latin America from East Asia?', *Bulletin of Latin American Research*, 10(1), 37–54.

Jessop, B. (1979) 'Corporatism, parliamentarism and social democracy', in Lehmbruch, G. and Schmitter, P. C. (eds), *Trends towards Corporatist Intermediation*. London: Sage, pp. 185–212.

Jessop, B. (1994) 'Changing forms and functions of the state in an era of globalisation and regionalisation', in Delorme, R. and Dopfer, F. (eds), *The Political Economy of Diversity: Evolutionary Perspectives on Economic Order and Disorder*. London: Edward Elgar, ch. 6.

Jobert, B. and Muller, P. (1987) *L'Etat en action*. Paris: Presses Universitaires de France.

Johnson, C. (1982) *MITI and the Japanese Miracle*. Stanford, CA: Stanford University Press.

Johnson, C. (1995) *Japan: Who Governs? The Rise of the Developmental State*. New York and London: Norton.

Jones, L. P. and Sakong, I. L. (1980) *Government, Business, and Entrepreneurship in Economic Development: The Korean Case*. Cambridge, MA: Harvard University Press.

Jordan, A. G. and Schubert, K. (1992) 'Policy networks', *European Journal of Political Research*, Special Issue 21(1–2), 7–27.

Kahler, M. (1989) 'International institutions and the politics of adjustment', in Nelson, J. M. (ed.), *Fragile Conditions: The Politics of Economic Adjustment*. New Brunswick, NJ: Transaction Books, pp. 139–59.

Katzenstein, P. (1977) 'Conclusion: domestic structures and strategies of foreign economic policies', *International Organizations*, 31(4), 879–920.

Katzenstein, P. (ed.) (1978) *Between Power and Plenty: Foreign Economic Policies of Advanced Industrial States*. Madison, WI: The University of Wisconsin Press.

Katzenstein, P. (1985) *Small States in World Markets: Industrial Policy in Europe*. Ithaca, NY: Cornell University Press.

Kaufman, G. (1992) *Banking Structures in Major Countries*. Norwell, MA: Kluwer Academic.

Kaufman, G. and Mote, L. (1994) 'The politics of neo geographic distribution of financial institutions in Chicago', *Federal Reserve Bank of Chicago Economic Perspectives*, 1st Quarter, January, 10–27.

Keeler, J. T. S. (1987) *Corporatism in France: Farmers, the State, and Agricultural Policymaking in the Fifth Republic*. New York: Oxford University Press.

Kelly, G., Kelly, D. and Gamble, A. (eds) (1997) *Stakeholder Capitalism*. New York: St Martin's Press.

Kenis, P. and Schneider, V. (1991) 'Policy networks and policy analysis', in Marin, B. and Mayntz, R. (eds), *Policy Networks*. Frankfurt: Campus Verlag Westview, pp. 25–62.

Keohane, R. O., Nye, J. S. and Hoffmann, S. (eds) (1993) *After the Cold War: International Institutions and State Strategies in Europe 1989–1991*. Cambridge, MA: Harvard University Press.

Keynes, M. J. (1937) *The General Theory of Employment, Interest, and Money*. New York: Harcourt Brace Jovanovich, reprinted 1953.

Keynes, M. J. (1973) *The Collected Writings of John Maynard Keynes*. London: Macmillan.

Killick, T. (1995) *IMF Programs in Developing Countries: Design and Impact*. London: Routledge.

King, R. G. and Levine, R. (1993a) 'Finance, entrepreneurship, and growth. Theory and evidence', *Journal of Monetary Economics*, 32, 513–42.

King, R. G. and Levine, R. (1993b) 'Finance and growth: Schumpeter might be right', *Quarterly Journal of Economics*, 108(3), 717–37.

Knack, S. (1996) 'Institutions and the convergence hypothesis: the cross-country evidence', *Public Choice*, 87(3–4), 207–28.

Knack, S. and Keefer, P. (1995) 'Institutions and economic performance: cross-country tests using alternative institutional measures', *Economics and Politics*, 7(3), 207–27.

Knack, S. and Keefer, P. (1997) 'Does social capital have an economic payoff? A cross-country investigation', *Quarterly Journal of Economics*, 112(4), 1251–88.

Knill, C. and Lehmkuhl, D. (1999) *How Europe Matters. Different Mechanisms of Europeanization*. European Integration Online Papers Vol. 3, No. 7. Available from: http://eiop.or.at/eiop/texte/1999–007a.htm.

Knoellinger, C. E. (1960) *Labour in Finland*. Cambridge, MA: Harvard University Press.

Kornai, J. (1998) 'The place of the soft budget constraint syndrome in economic theory', *Journal of Comparative Economics*, 26(1), 11–17.

Korpi, W. (1991) 'Political and economic explanations for unemployment: a cross-national and long-term analysis', *British Journal of Political Science*, 21, 315–48.

Kovacs, J. M. (1993) 'Which institutionalism? Searching for paradigms of transformation in Eastern European economic thought', in Wagener, H.-J. (ed.), *The Political Economy of Transformation*. Heidelberg: Physica-Verlag.

Kratochwil, F. and Mansfield, E. (eds) (1994) *International Organization: A Reader*. New York: HarperCollins.

Kristensen, P. H. (1997) 'National systems of governance and managerial prerogatives in the evolution of work systems: England, Germany and Denmark compared', in Whitley, R. and Kristensen, P. H. (eds), *Governance at Work*. Oxford: Oxford University Press, pp. 3–46.

Kubicek, P. (2000) 'Post-communist political studies: ten years later, twenty years behind?', *Communist and Post-Communist Studies*, 33, 295–309.

Kuwahara, Y. (1987) 'Japanese industrial relations', in Bamber, G. J. and Lansbury, R. D. (eds), *International and Comparative Industrial Relations: A Study of Developed Market Economies*. London: Allen & Unwin.

La Porta, R., Lopez de Silanes, F. and Shleifer, A. (1999) 'Corporate ownership around the world', *Journal of Finance*, 54, 200–50.

Labbé, D. (1994) *Tendences de la syndicalisation en France depuis 1945*. Document de recherche. Grenoble: CERAT/IEP.

Ladrech, R. (1994) 'Europeanization of domestic politics and institutions: the case of France', *Journal of Common Market Studies*, 32(1), 69–88.

Lane, D. (2000) 'What kind of capitalism for Russia? A comparative analysis', *Communist and Post-Communist Studies*, 33, 485–504.

Lane, J.-E. and Ersson, S. (1991) *Politics and Society in Western Europe*. London: Sage.

Lange, P. and Garrett, G. (1985) 'The Politics of Growth: Strategic Interaction and Economic Performance in the Advanced Industrial Democracies 1974–1980', *The Journal of Politics*, 47(3), 792–827.

LaPalombara, J. (1964) *Interest Groups in Italian Politics*. Princeton, NJ: Princeton University Press.

Laumann, E. and Knocke, D. (1987) *The Organizational State*. Madison, WI: University of Wisconsin Press.

Lawson, T. (1985) 'Methodological issues in Keynes' Economics: an introduction', in Lawson, T. and Pesaran, H. (eds), *Keynes' Economics: Methodological Issues*. Armonk, NY: Sharpe.

Lee, S.-H. (1989) *State-Building in the Contemporary Third World*. Boulder, CO: Westview.

Leftwich, A. (1994) *The Developmental State*. Working Paper No. 6. York: University of York.

Lehmbruch, G. (1977) 'Liberal corporatism and party government', *Comparative Political Studies*, 10, 91–126.

Lehmbruch, G. (1979) 'Liberal corporatism and party government', in Schmitter, P. C. and Lehmbruch, G. (eds), *Trends Towards Corporatist Intermediation*. London: Sage, pp. 147–83.

Lehmbruch, G. (1984) 'Concertation and the structure of corporatist networks', in Goldthorpe, J. H. (ed.), *Order and Conflict in Contemporary Capitalism*. Oxford: Oxford University Press, pp. 60–80.

Lehmbruch, G. and Schmitter, P. C. (1982) *Patterns in Corporatist Policy-Making*. Beverly Hills, CA: Sage.

Levine, R. (1997) 'Financial development and economic growth: views and agenda', *Journal of Economic Literature*, 35, 688–726.

Levine, R. and Renelt, D. (1992) 'A sensitivity analysis of cross-country growth regressions', *American Economic Review*, 82(4), 942–63.

Levine, R. and Zervos, S. (1998) 'Stock markets, banks, and economic growth', *American Economic Review*, 88(3), 537–59.

Lewis, A. and Pescetto, G. (1996) *EU and US Banking in the 1990s*. London: Academic Press.

Lindblom, C. E. (1965) *The Intelligence of Democracy*. New York: Free Press.

Lindblom, C. E. (1977) *Politics and Markets*. New York: Basic Books.

Lipton, D. and Sachs, J. D. (1990) 'Creating a market economy: the case of Poland', *Brookings Papers on Economic Activity*, 1, 75–147.

Litescu, A. C. (2000) 'Dupa ce au facut galagie electorala senatorii au chiulit de la dezbaterea Raportului RomTelecom: Presedintele comisiei de ancheta, Serban Sandulescu, mai cauta comisioanele', *Cotidianul*, 26 October. Available from: http://www.cotidianul.ro (accessed 16 May 2001).

Lowi, T. (1964) 'American business, public policy case studies and political theory', *World Politics*, 16(4), 677–715.

Maier, C. S. (1984) 'Preconditions for corporatism', in Goldthorpe, J. H. (ed.), *Order and Conflict in Contemporary Capitalism*. Oxford: Clarendon, pp. 39–59.

Majone, G. (1990) *Deregulation or Reregulation?* London: Pinter.

Mako, C. and Novoszath, P. (1995) 'Employment relations in multinational companies: the Hungarian case', in Eckhardt, D., Schmidt, G. and Whitley, R. (eds), *Industrial Transformation in Europe*. London: Sage, pp. 255–77.

Malbin, M. (1979) 'Campaign financing and the "special interest" ', *The Public Interest*, 56, 21–43.

Mankiw, R. N. G. and Weil, D. (1992) 'Contribution to the empirics of economic growth', *Quarterly Journal of Economics*, 107(2), 407–37.

Marin, B. and Myantz, R. (eds) (1991) *Policy Networks: Empirical Evidence and Theoretical Considerations*. Frankfurt: Campus Verlag.

Marquand, D. (1994) 'Reinventing federalism: Europe and the left', *New Left Review*, 203, 17–26.

Martin, A. and Ross, G. (eds) (1999) *The Brave New World of European Labor: European Trade Unions at the Millennium*. New York: Berghahn Books.

Mauro, P. (1995) 'Corruption and growth', *Quarterly Journal of Economics*, 110(3), 681–712.

Mayhew, A. (2002) *Recreating Europe: The European Union's Policy towards Central and Eastern Europe*. Cambridge: Cambridge University Press.

McGowan, F. and Wallace, H. (1996) 'Towards a European regulatory state', *Journal of European Public Policy*, 4, 560–76.

McKinnon, R. I. (1973) *Money and Capital in Economic Development*. Washington, DC: Brookings Institution.

Media Uno (2002) *BNS si Cartel Alfa explica de ce nu au semant Acordul social pe 2002*, April. Available from: http://www.mediauno.ro/bp (accessed 15 May 2002).

Melo, M. de, Denizer, C., Gelb, A. and Tenev, S. (1997) *Circumstance and Choice: The Role of Initial Conditions and Policies in Transition Economies*. Washington, DC: International Finance Corporation.

Mény, Y. (ed.) (1989) *Ideologies, partis politiques et groupes sociaux*. Paris: Presse de la FNSP.

Michels, R. (1962) *Political Parties: A Sociological Study of the Oligarchical Tendencies of Modern Democracy*. New York: Collier Books.

Mitroi, V. (2000) 'Nici nu s-a instituit bine monopolul alcoolului si a inceput scandalul', *Curierul National*, 5 December, Bucharest.

Moerland, P. W. (1995) 'Alternative disciplinary mechanisms in different corporate systems', *Journal of Economic Behavior and Organization*, 26(1), 17–34.

Monitorul Oficial, 169 (1991) (Special issue) 'Privatisation Law No. 58/1991'. Available from: http://diasan.vsat.ro/

Monitorul Oficial, 208 (1992) 'Ordonanta nr.10 din 7–08–1992 pentru aprobarea Statutului-cadru al Fondului Proprietatii Private'. Available from: http://diasan.vsat.ro/

Monitorul Oficial, 156 (1993) 'Hotararea nr.266 din 10–06–1993 privind ramurile si domeniile in care functioneaza regiile autonome de interes national'. Available from: http://diasan.vsat.ro/

Monitorul Oficial, 209 (1994) 'Legea nr.77 din 01 august 1994 privind asociatiile salariatilor si membrilor conducerii societatilor comerciale care se privatizeaza'. Available from: http://diasan.vsat.ro/

Monitorul Oficial, 267 (1994) 'Precizari nr.85535 din 5–08–1994 privind reflectarea in contabilitate a principalelor operatiuni referitoare la privatizarea societatilor comerciale prin metoda MEBO'. Available from: http://diasan.vsat.ro/

Monitorul Oficial, 209 (1998) 'Hotararea nr.299 din 2 iunie 1998 pentru completarea anexei la Hotararea Guvernului nr. 118/1998 pentru aprobarea mandatului Fondului Proprietatii de Stat privind negocierea actului aditional la contractul de vanzare-cumparare a unui pachet de actiuni detinute de stat la Societatea Comerciala 'I.M.G.B.'S.A.' Available from: http://diasan.vsat.ro/

Mukerjee, D. (1986) *Lessons from Korea's Industrial Experience*. Kuala Lumpur: Institute of Strategic and International Studies.

Munteanu, C. (1997) 'Employee share-ownership in Romania: the main path to privatization', in Uvalic, M. and Vaughan-Whitehead, D. (eds), *Privatization Surprises in Transition Economies: Employee-Ownership in Central and Eastern Europe*. Cheltenham and Lyme: Elgar, pp. 182–203.

Murphy, C. and Tooze, R. (1991) *The New International Political Economy*. Boulder, CO: Lynne Rienner.

Naim, M. (1999) 'Fads and Fashion in Economic Reforms: Washington Consensus or Washington Confusion?', Paper prepared for the IMF Conference on Second Generation Reforms, 26 October, Washington, DC. Available from: http://www.imf.org.

Nakano, S. (1999) 'Management Views of European Works Councils, A Preliminary Survey of Japanese Multinationals', *European Journal of Industrial Relations*, 5(3), 307–26.

NAP (1992) *Annual Report 1992*. Bucharest: Agentia Nationala Pentru Privatizare.

National Court of Audit (1995) *Annual Public Report Regarding the Budgetary Account in 1990–1992*. Bucharest: Imprimeria Romana.

NBR (2001) *Comunicat de Presa*. Bucharest: National Bank of Romania.

NCS (1998) *Romanian Statistical Yearbook 1998*. Bucharest: National Commission for Statistics.

NCS (1999) *Romanian Statistical Yearbook 1999*. Bucharest: National Commission for Statistics.

NCS (2000) *Monthly Social Indicators*. Bucharest: National Commission for Statistics.

NCS (2001) *Romanian Statistical Yearbook 2001*. Bucharest: National Commission for Statistics.

Necomm's Privatization in Romania, 1/17/00–1/23/00 (2000) *Review of weekly news from the privatization in Romania, North East area*. Available from: http://privatization.nordest.ro/

NEI (2001) *Raport de Activitate: 1991–2001*. Bucharest: Network Electronica International.

Nellis, J. (1996) 'So far So Good? A Privatization Update', *Transition Newsletter* 7(11–12). Washington, DC: World Bank.

Neustadtl, A. and Clawson, D. (1988) 'Corporate political groupings: does ideology unify business political behavior?', *American Sociological Review*, 53(2), 172–90.

NIS (1998) *Romanian Statistical Yearbook 1998*. Bucharest: National Institute of Statistics. Electronic Version.

Nitu, M. (2002) *Pace sociala – pana cand?* Evenimentul Zilei. Available from: http://www.evenimentul.ro (accessed June 2002).

North, D. C (1990) *Institutions, Institutional Change and Economic Performance*. Cambridge: Cambridge University Press.

Nuti, M. (1995) 'Employeeism: Corporate Governance and Employee Ownership in Transitional Economies', Paper presented at the Conference on Enterprise Restructuring and Labour Markets, Tunin.

OECD (1993a) *Trends and Policies in Privatisation*, Vol. I, No. 1. Paris: OECD.

OECD (1993b) *Trends and Policies in Privatisation*, Vol. I, No. 2. Paris: OECD.

OECD (2002) *Economic Survey – Romania – Economic Assessment 2002*. Paris: OECD.

Offe, C. (1993) 'The attribution of public status to interest groups: observations from the West German case', in Berger, S. (ed.), *Organising Interests in Western Europe*. Cambridge: Cambridge University Press, pp. 123–58.

Okun, A. (1962) *Potential GNP: Its Measurement and Significance*. Proceedings of the Business and Economic Statistics Section of the American Statistical Association. New Haven, CT: Yale University.

Olsen, J. P. (2002) 'The Many Faces of Europeanization', ARENA Working Paper Series, 02/2002. Oslo: Centre for European Studies, University of Oslo.

Olson, M. (1965) *The Logic of Collective Action*. Cambridge, MA: Harvard University Press.

Olson, M. (1982) *The Rise and Decline of Nations*. New Haven, CT: Yale University Press.

Ozawa, T. (1996) 'The new economic nationalism and the "Japanese disease": the conundrum of managed economic growth', *Journal of Economic Issues*, 30, 483–91.

Pagano, M. (1993) 'Financial markets and growth: an overview', *European Economic Review*, 37(2), 613–22.

Paloheimo, H. (1984) 'Distributive struggle and economic development in the 1970s in developed capitalist countries', *European Journal of Political Research*, 12, 171–90.

Panitch, L. (1977) 'The development of corporatism in liberal democracies', *Comparative Political Studies*, 10(1), 61–90.

Papahagi, T. (1999) 'Semnarea acordului stand-by se amana', *Cotidianul*, 22 June, Bucharest. Available from: http://www.cotidianul.ro/anterioare/1999/economic/econ2127iun.htm#22%20iunie (accessed 4 June 2000).

Pastor, M. (1987) 'The effects of IMF programs in the third world: debate and evidence from Latin America', *World Development*, 15, 365–91.

Patapievici, H. R. (1999a) 'Mineriada: radiografia unei institutii', *Revista 22*, No. 5.

Patapievici, H. R. (1999b) 'Un stat slab, o societate fracturata', *Revista 22*, No. 6.

PCR (1972) *Era Socialista: Revista Teoretica si Social Politica a Comitetului Central al PCR*. No. 1. Bucuresti: Editura Politica.

PCR (1975) *Programul Partidului Comunist Român de Faurire a Societatii Socialiste Multilateral Dezvoltate si Înaintare a României Spre Comunism, Partidul Comunist Roman*. Bucuresti: Editura Politica.

Pemberton, J. (1988) 'A managerial model of the trade union', *Economics Journal*, 92, 269–83.

Pendleton, A., Wilson, N. and Wright, M. (1998) 'The Perception and Effects of Share Ownership: Empirical Evidence from Employee Buy-outs', *British Journal of Industrial Relations*, 36(1), 99–123.

Perotti, E. and Carare, O. (1997) *The Evolution of Bank Credit Quality in Transition: Theory and Evidence from Romania*, CERT Discussion Paper No. 2. Edinburgh: Centre for Economic Reform and Transformation.

Peters, B. G. (1989) *The Politics of Bureaucracy*. New York and London: Longman.

Phelan, J. L. (2001) *Renowned US Economists Denounce Corporate-Led Globalization*. Grassroots Globalization Network, 18 November. Available from: http://www.earthisland.org (accessed July 2002).

Piazolo, D. (1997) 'Trade integration between eastern and western Europe: policies follow the market', *Journal of Economic Integration*, 12(3), 259–97.

Pickles, J. and Smith, A. (eds) (1998) *Theorising Transition. The Political Economy of Post-communist Transformations*. London: Routledge.

Pinto, B. and Wijnbergen, S. van (1994) *Ownership and Corporate Control in Poland: Why State Firms Defied the Odds*. Washington, DC: International Finance Corporation.

Pogonaru, F. and Apostol, C. (1999) 'Evolutia pietei de capital', CRPE Working Paper 9. Bucharest: Romanian Centre for Economic Policies.

Poirot, C. (1996) 'Macroeconomic stabilization in an uncertain environment: the case of Romania', *Journal of Economic Issues*, 30(4), 1,057–75.

Polanyi, K. (1944/1999) *The Great Transformation*. Boston, MA: Beacon Press.

Pop, L. (2002a) 'Explaining systemic change: The political economy of post-communist transformations', Working paper 92/2002, Centre for the Study of Globalisation and Regionalisation, University of Warwick.

Pop, L. (2002b) 'Where the domestic meets the international: The role of the IFIs and the EU in Romania's post-communist transformations', *Romanian Journal of Society and Politics*, 2(2), 157–87.

Porte, J. (1999a) 'Court jails Romanian miners' chief for 18 years', *Agence France Press*, 15 February.

Porte, J. (1999b) 'Romanian pitmen routed, firebrand leader captured', *Agence France Presse*, 17 February.

Posen, A. (1998) 'Do better institutions make better policy?', *International Finance*, 1(1), 173–205.

Powell, W. W. (1990) 'Neither markets nor hierarchy. Network forms of organisation', *Research in Organizational Behavior*, 12, 295–336.

Pryor, F. (1988) 'Corporatism as an economic system: a review essay', *Journal of Comparative Economics*, 12, 317–44.

Pryor, F. (1996) *Economic Evolution and Structure: The Impact of Complexity on the US Economic System*. Cambridge and Melbourne: Cambridge University Press.

Przeworski, A. (1991) *Democracy and the Market: Political and Economic Reforms in Eastern Europe and Latin America*. New York: Cambridge University Press.

Przeworski, A. (1996) 'Public support for economic reforms in Poland', *Comparative Political Studies*, 29, 520–43.

Przeworski, A. and Vreeland, J. R. (2000) 'The effect of IMF programs on economic growth', *Journal of Development Economics*, 62, 385–421.

Radaelli, C. (2000) *Whither Europeanization? Concept Stretching and Substantive Change*. European Integration Online Papers, Vol. 4, No. 8. Available from: http://eiop.or.at/eiop/texte/2000–008a.htm.

Radulescu, M. (1996) *Towards a Strategy for Increasing Foreign Direct Investment (FDI). Impact on Romanian Economy*, CERT Discussion Paper 96/17. Edinburgh: Centre for Economic Reform and Transformation.

Reisinger, W., Miller, A., Hesli, V. and Mahler, K. (1994) 'Political values in Russia, Ukraine, and Lithuania: sources and implications for democracy', *British Journal of Political Science*, 24, 183–224.

Rhodes, M. and van Apeldoorn, B. (1997) 'Capitalism versus capitalism in Western Europe', in Rhodes, M., Heywood, P. and Wright, V. (eds), *Developments in Western European Politics*. New York: St Martin's Press, pp. 171–89.

Rhodes, R. A. W. (1990) 'Policy networks: a British perspective', *Journal of Theoretical Politics*, 2, 293–317.

Rhodes, R. A. W. (1994). 'The hollowing out of the state: the changing nature of the public service in Britain', *Political Quarterly*, 65, 138–51.

Rhodes, R. A. W. and Marsh, D. (eds) (1992) *Policy Networks in British Government*. Oxford: Clarendon Press.

Riker, W. and Sened, I. (1991) 'A political theory of the origins of property rights: airport slots', *American Journal of Political Science*, 35(4), 951–69.

Riker, W. and Wiemer, D. (1993) 'The economic and political liberalization of socialism: the fundamental problem of property rights', *Social Philosophy and Policy*, 10(2), 79–102.

Risse, T., Cowles, M. G. and Caporaso, J. (2001) 'Europeanization and Domestic Change: Introduction', in Cowles, M. G., Caporaso, J. and Risse, T. (eds), *Transforming Europe: Europeanization and Domestic Change*. Ithaca, NY: Cornell University Press.

Rodan, G. (1989) *The Political Economy of Singapore's Industrialization: National State and International Capital*. New York: St Martin's Press.

Roe, A., Siegelbaum, P. and King, T. (1997) *Analyzing Financial Sectors in Transition: With Special Reference to the Former Soviet Union*, World Bank Policy Research Working Paper No. 1982. Washington, DC: World Bank.

Rogers, J. and Streeck, W. (eds) (1995) *Works Councils: Consultation Representation and Cooperation in Industrial Relations*. Chicago, IL, and London: University of Chicago Press.

Romania Libera (1990) 'Minerii din Valea Jiului fac ravagii in capitala', *Romania Libera*, 15 June.

Romania Libera (1995) 'Stiri Economice', *Romania Libera*, 29 May.

Romanian Economic Daily (2000) 'Kvaerner still invests heavily at IMGB', *Romanian Economic Daily*, 504, 14 November.

Rompress (1999) 'Miners leaders deny coup accusations', *Rompress News Agency*, 28 January.

Rondinelli, D. A. (1994) *Privatisation and Economic Reform in Central Europe: The Changing Business Climate*. Westport, CT: Quorum.

Ronnås, P. (1996) 'Romania: transition to underdevelopment?', in Jeffries, I. (ed.), *Problems of Economic and Political Transformation in the Balkans*. New York: Pinter, pp. 13–32.

Rose, R. (1991) 'What is lesson-drawing?', *Journal of Public Policy*, 11(1), 3–30.

Rose, R. (1993) *Lesson-Drawing in Public Policy: A Guide to Learning Across Time and Space*. Chatham, NJ: Chatham House.

Ross, A. (1948) *Trade Union Wage Policy*. Berkeley, CA: University of California Press.

Rostowski, J. (1994) *Interenterprise Arrears in Post-Communist Economies*, IMF Working Paper, No. 43. Washington, DC: International Monetary Fund.

Rothstein, B. (1989) 'Marxism, institutional analysis, and working class power: the Swedish case', *Politics and Society*, 18, 317–46.

Rousseau, P. L. and Wachtel, P. (1998) 'Financial intermediation and economic performance: historical evidence from five industrialised countries', *Journal of Money, Credit and Banking*, 30(4), 657–78.

Sachs, J. D. (1996) *Reforms in Eastern Europe and the Former Soviet Union in Light of the East Asian Experiences*. National Bureau of Economic Research Working Paper No. W5404. Cambridge, MA: National Bureau of Economic Research.

Sachs, J. D. and Warner, A. (1995) 'Economic reform and the process of global integration', *Brookings Papers on Economic Activity*, 1, 1–95.

Sako, M. (1997) 'Shunto: The role of employer and union coordination at the industry and inter-sectoral levels', in Sako, M. and Sato, H. (eds), *Japanese Labour and Management in Transition. Diversity, Flexibility and Participation*. London and New York: Routledge, pp. 236–63.

Sala-i-Martin, X. (1997) 'I just ran two million regressions', *American Economic Review*, 87, 178–83.

Salvati, M. (1981) 'May 1968 and the Hot Autumn of 1969: the responses of two ruling classes', in Berger, S., Hirschman, A. and Maier, Ch. (eds), *Organising Interests in Western Europe: Pluralism, Corporatism, and the Transformation of Politics*. Cambridge: Cambridge University Press, pp. 329–63.

Samuels, W. (ed.) (1989) *Fundamentals of the Economic Role of Government*. Westport, CT, and London: Greenwood Press.

Savov, S. (1999) *Economics of Transition*. Sofia: Ciela.

Schadler, S., Bennett, A., Carkovic, M., Dicks-Mireaux, L., Mecagni, M., Morsink, J. and Savastano, M. (1995a) *IMF Conditionality Review: Experience under Stand-By and Extended Arrangements*. IMF Occasional Papers, No. 128, Washington, DC.

Schadler, S., Bennett, A., Carkovic, M., Dicks-Mireaux, L., Mecagni, M., Morsink, J. and Savastano, M. (1995b) *IMF Conditionality Review: Experience under Stand-By and Extended Arrangements*. IMF Occasional Papers, No. 129, Washington, DC.

Schaffer, M. E. (1998) 'Do firms in transition countries have soft budget constraints? A reconsideration of concepts and evidence', *Journal of Comparative Economics*, 26(1), 80–104.

Scharfstein, D. S. and Stein, J. C. (1990) 'Herd behavior and investment', *American Economic Review*, 80, 465–79.

Scharpf, F. W. (1991a) *Crisis and Choice in European Social Democracy*. Ithaca, NY: Cornell University Press.

Scharpf, F. W. (1991b) 'Political institutions, decisions styles, and policy choices', in Czada, R. and Windhoff-Héritier, A. (eds), *Political Choice, Institutions, Rules and the Limits of Rationality*, Frankfurt, pp. 53–86.

Scharpf, F. W. (1993) 'Games in hierarchies and networks', in Scharpf, F. W. (ed.), *Games in Hierarchies and Networks*, Frankfurt.

Scharpf, F. W. (1996) 'Negative and positive integration in the political economy of European welfare states', in Marks, G., Scharpf, F. W., Schmitter, P. C. and Streeck, W. (eds), *Governance in the European Union*. London: Sage, pp. 15–39.

Schmidt, V. A. (1995) 'The New World Order, Incorporated: the rise of business and the decline of the nation state', *Daedalus*, 124(2), 75–107.

Schmidt, V. A. (1999) 'The changing dynamics of state–society relations in the Fifth Republic', *West European Politics*, 22(4), 141–65.

Schmidt, V. A. (2001) *Europeanization and the Mechanics of Economic Policy Adjustment*. European Integration online Papers (EIoP) Vol. 5, No. 6. Available from: http://eiop.or.at/eiop/texte/2001–006a.htm.

Schmidt, V. A. (2002) *The Futures of European Capitalism*. Oxford: Oxford University Press.

Schmitter, P. C. (1974) 'Still the century of corporatism?', *Review of Politics*, 36, 85–131.

Schmitter, P. C. (1977) 'Modes of interest representation and models of societal change in Western Europe', *Comparative Political Studies*, 10(1), 7–38.

Schmitter, P. C. (1979) 'Still the century of corporatism?', in Schmitter, P. C. and Lehmbruch, G. (eds), *Trends Toward Corporatist Intermediation*. London and Beverly Hills, CA: Sage, pp. 7–52.

Schmitter, P. C. (1981) 'Interest intermediation and regime governability in contemporary Western Europe and North America', in Berger, S. D. (ed.), *Organizing Interests in Western Europe*. New York: Cambridge University Press, pp. 285–327.

Schmitter, P. C. (1982) 'Reflections on where the theory of neo-corporatism has gone and where the praxis of neo-corporatism may be going', in Lehmbruch, G. and Schmitter, P. C. (eds), *Patterns of Corporatist Policy-Making*. London: Sage, pp. 259–79.

Schmitter, P. C. and Karl, T. L. (1994) 'The conceptual travel of transitologists and consolidologists: how far to the East should they attempt to go?', *Slavic Review*, 53, 173–85.

Schmitter, P. C. and Lehmbruch, G. (1979) *Trends Toward Corporatist Intermediation*. London and Beverly Hills, CA: Sage.

Schmitter, P. C. and Streeck, W. (1999) *The Organization of Business Interests: Studying the Associative Actions of Business in Advanced Industrial Societies*. Cologne: Max Planck Institute for the Studies of Societies.

Schumpeter, J. A. (1912) *The Theory of Economic Development*. Cambridge, MA: Harvard University Press.

Scott, J. C. (1977) 'Patron–client politics and political change in Southeast Asia', in Schmidt, S., Gausti, L., Lande, C. and Scott, J. C. (eds), *Friends, Followers, and Factions*. Berkeley, CA: University of California Press, pp. 122–45.

Scully, G. W. (1988) 'The institutional framework and economic development', *Journal of Political Economy*, 96(3), 652–62.

Seceleanu, A. (2000) 'Noi file in dosarul "afacerii secolului": Panamaua numita "privatizarea" RomTelecom', *Curierul National*, 2922, 10 October. Available from: http://domino.kappa.ro/e-media/arhive/curierul00.nsf/ (accessed 17 May 2001).

Serbanescu, I. (1999) 'BANCOREX – istoria emblematica a Romaniei postdecembriste', *Revista 22*, No. 38.

Servan-Schreiber, J. J. (1968) *The American Challenge*. New York: Atheneum.

Shafer, M. (1997) 'The political economy of sectors and sectoral change: Korea then and now', in Maxfield, S. and Schneider, B. R. (eds), *Business and the State in Developing Countries. Cornell Studies in Political Economy*. Ithaca, NY, and London: Cornell University Press, pp. 88–121.

Shafir, M. (1985) *Romania: Politics, Economics, and Society*. Boulder, CO: Lynne Rienner.

Shapiro, H. (1994) *Engines of Growth: The State and International Auto Companies in Brazil*. New York: Cambridge University Press.

Shaw, E. (1973) *Financial Deepening and Economic Development*. New York: Oxford University Press.

Shleifer, A. and Vishny, R. (1994) 'Politicians and firms', *Quarterly Journal of Economics*, 109(4), 995–1025.

Shleifer, A. and Vishny, R. (1996) 'A theory of privatisation', *Economic Journal*, 106, 309–19.

SIDEX (1999) *Rezultate financiare la data 30.06.1999*. Bucharest: Comisia Nationala a Valorilor Mobiliare. Available from: http://www.rasd.ro (accessed 21 August 2001).

Siegelbaum, P. (1997) 'Financial Sector Reform in the Transition Economies: What Have We Learned; What Are the Next Steps?' Speech delivered at the 2nd Annual Conference on Bank Credit in Central and Eastern Europe, sponsored by the International Industry Conferences on Bank Credit Risk, IBC UK Conferences Limited, Prague, 2 September.

Skowronek, S. (1982) *Building the New American State*. Cambridge: Cambridge University Press.

Smith, A. (1996) 'Problems of the transition to a market economy in Romania, Bulgaria and Albania: why has the transition proved to be so difficult?', in Jeffries, I. (ed.), *Problems of Economic and Political Transformation in the Balkans*. London and New York: Pinter, pp. 111–30.

Smyser, W. R. (1992) *The Economy of United Germany*. New York: St Martin's Press.

SOF (1996) *Annual Report*. Bucharest: Fondul Proprietatii de Stat.

Solow, R. M. (1956) 'A contribution to the theory of economic growth', *Quarterly Journal of Economics*, 70(1), 65–94.

Spatarelu, S. (2001) 'O guvernare cu doua viteze', *Adevarul*, No. 3269.

Spraos, J. (1986) *IMF Conditionality: Ineffectual. Misguided. Mistargeted*, Princeton Essays in International Finance, no. 166. Princeton, NJ: International Finance Section.

Stancu, A. (2001) *Pacea sociala: o dorinta irealizabila*. Viata Libera No. 3580. Available from: http://www.vlg.sisnet.ro (accessed 16 April 2002).

Staniszkis, J. (1991) *The Dynamics of the Breakthrough in Eastern Europe*. Berkeley, CA: The University of California Press.

Stark, D. and Bruszt, L. (1998) *Postsocialist Pathways: Transforming Politics and Property in East Central Europe*. Cambridge: Cambridge University Press.

Steinmo, S. (1989) 'Political institutions and tax policy in the United States, Sweden and Britain', *World Politics*, 41(4), 500–35.

Stiglitz, J. E. (1985) 'Credit markets and the control of capital', *Journal of Money, Credit and Banking*, 17(2), 133–52.

Stiglitz, J. E. (1999) *Whither Reform?* Annual Bank Conference on Development Economics, April 1999, Washington, DC.

Stiglitz, J. E. (2001) 'Protest and the Secret World of Financial Aid', *The Banker*, October. Available from: http://www.thebanker.com (accessed 3 July 2002).

Stiles, K. W. (1991) *Negotiating Debt: The IMF Lending Process*. Boulder, CO: Westview.

Story, J. and Walter, I. (1997) *Political Economy of Financial Integration in Europe*. Manchester: Manchester University Press.

Strange, S. (1996) *The Retreat of the State: The Diffusion of Power in the World Economy*. Cambridge: Cambridge University Press.

Streeck, W. (1984) 'Neo-Corporatist Industrial Relations and the Economic Crisis in West Germany', in Goldthorp, J. H. (ed.), *Order and Conflict in Contemporary Capitalism*. Oxford: Clarendon Press, pp. 291–314.

Streeck, W. (1992) *Social Institutions and Economic Performance. Studies of Industrial Relations in Advanced Capitalist Economies*. London: Sage.

Streeck, W. (1997) 'German Capitalism: Does it Exist? Can it Survive?', in Crouch, C. and Streeck, W. (eds), *Political Economy of Modern Capitalism*. London, Thousand Oaks, New Delhi: Sage, pp. 33–54.

Streeck, W. and Schmitter, P. (eds), (1985) *Private-Interest Government: Beyond Market and State*. London: Sage.

Swank, D. (1998) 'Funding the welfare state: globalization and the taxation of business in advanced market economies', *Political Studies*, 66, 671–92.

Szalai, E. (1991) 'Integration of special interests in the Hungarian economy: the struggle between large companies and the party and state bureaucracy', *Journal of Comparative Economics*, 15, 290–303.

Tanase, S. (2000) 'Republica de la Weimar', *Sfera Politicii*, 67, 3–4.

Thacker, S. C. (1999) 'The high politics of IMF lending', *World Politics*, 52, 38–75.

The Economist (1999) *Shipyards – Push off, Poles*, 30 October.

Thorelli, H. B. (1986) 'Networks. Between markets and hierarchies', *Strategic Management Journal*, 7, 37–51.

Thorne, A. E. (1993) 'Eastern Europe's experience with banking reform: is there a role for banks in the transition?', *Journal of Banking and Finance*, 17(5), 959–1,000.

Toche, P. (2001) *Is There a Growth–Unemployment Trade-Off?* Department of Economics Discussion Paper Series, No. 62, University of Oxford.

Traxler, F. (1998) 'Collective bargaining in the OECD: developments, preconditions and effects', *European Journal of Industrial Relations*, 4(2), 207–26.

Truman, D. (1951) *The Governmental Process*. New York: Knopf.

Tsikata, T. (1998) *Aid Effectiveness: A Survey of Recent Empirical Literature*. IMF Paper on Policy Analysis and Assessment, March 1998, Washington, DC.

Tudor, R. (2000) 'Guvernul a aprobat stingerea datoriei Petrom catre AVAB', *Cotidianul*, 7 June, Bucharest. Available from: http://www.cotidianul.ro/anterioare/2000/justitie-armata/just0511iun.htm# (accessed 16 April 2001).

Tyler, C. (1988) *The Theory of Market Failure: A Critical Examination*. Portland, OR: Book News.

Ursu, A. (2001) 'APAPS si ISPAT au semnat contractul de privatizare a Sidex', *Adevarul*. Available from: http://www.adevarul.ro.

Vachudova, M. A. (2005) *Europe Undivided – Democracy, Leverage, and Integration after Communism*. Oxford: Oxford University Press.

Vera, N. and Manta, A. (1997) 'Tariceanu nu mai face fata la disponibilizari', *Expres Magazin*, 15 October.

Verdery, K. (1996) 'Nationalism, postsocialism, and space in Eastern Europe', *Social Research*, 63(1), 77–95.

Vitols, S. (1997) 'Financial Systems and Industrial Policy in Germany and Great Britain: The Limits of Convergence', in Forsyth, D. and Notermans, T. (eds), *Regime Changes: Macroeconomic Policy and Financial Regulation in Europe from the 1930s to the 1990s*. Providence, RI: Berghahn, pp. 221–55.

Vittas, D. and Cho, Y. J. (1995) *Credit Policies: Lessons from East Asia*. World Bank Policy Research Working Paper, No. 1458. Washington, DC: World Bank.

Vogel, E. F. (1991) *The Four Little Dragons: The Speed of Industrialization in East Asia*. Cambridge, MA: Harvard University Press.

Voiculescu, L. (2000) 'Jaful RomTelecom: Senatul Romaniei confirma sesizarile Adevarului Economic', *Adevarul Economic*, 43(449), 9–10.

von Beyme, K. (1983) ' "Neo-Corporatism". A New Nut in an Old Shell?', *International Political Science Review*, 4(2), 173–96.

Voszka, E. (1995) 'Centralization, re-nationalization and redistribution: government's role in changing Hungary's ownership structure', in Nielsen, K., Hausner, J. and Jessop, B. (eds), *Strategic Choice and Path Dependency in Post-Socialism: Institutional Dynamics in the Transformation Process*, Aldershot: Edward Elgar, pp. 287–308.

Voszka, E. (1999) 'Privatization in Hungary: Results and Open Issues', *CIPE Economic Reform Today* (2). Washington, DC: Center for International Private Enterprise. Available from: http://www.cipe.org/publications/fs/ert/e32/index.htm.

Vreeland, J. R. (2002) 'The effect of IMF programs on labour', *World Development*, 30(1), 121–39.

Waarden, F. van (1992) 'Dimensions and types of policy networks', *European Journal of Political Research*, 21(1–2), 29–52.

Wade, R. (1990) *Governing the Market: Economic Theory and the Role of Government in East Asian Industrialization*. Princeton, NJ: Princeton University Press.

Wallace, H. (2000) 'Europeanisation and globalisation: complementary or contradictory trends?', *New Political Economy*, 5(3), 369–82.

Wallis, J. J. and Dollery, B. (1999) *Market Failure, Government Failure, Leadership and Public Policy*. New York: St Martin's Press.

Wallis, J. J. and Oates, W. E. (1988) 'Does economic sclerosis set in with age? An empirical study of the Olson hypothesis', *Kyklos*, 41(3), 397–417.

Walter, I. and Hiraki, T. (eds) (1994) *Restructuring Japan's Financial Markets*. New York: Business One Irwin.

Walzer, M. (1992) 'The civil society argument', in Mouffe, C. (ed.), *Dimensions of Radical Democracy: Pluralism, Citizenship, Community*. London: Verso.

Weber, M. (1968) *Economy and Society*, (translated by Roth, G. and Wittich, C.). New York: Bedminster Press.

Weir, M. and Skocpol, T. (1985) 'State structures and the possibilities for Keynesian response to the Great Depression in Sweden, Britain and the United States', in Evans, P., Rueschmeyer, D. and Skocpol, T. (eds), *Bringing the State Back In*. Cambridge: Cambridge University Press, pp. 107–68.

Weiss, L. (1998) *The Myth of the Powerless State*. Cambridge: Polity Press.

Weiss, L. and Hobson, J. M. (1995) *States and Economic Development: A Comparative Historical Analysis*. Cambridge: Polity Press.

Wessels, W. (1996) 'Institutions of the EU system: models of explanation', in Rometsch, D. and Wessels, W. (eds), *The European Union and Member States: Towards Institutional Fusion?* Manchester: Manchester University Press, pp. 20–36.

Western, B. (1991) 'A comparative study of corporatist development', *American Sociological Review*, 56(3), 283–94.

Western, B. (1993) 'Postwar unionization in eighteen advanced capitalist countries', *American Sociological Review*, 58(2), 266–82.

White, G. (ed.) (1988) *Developmental States in East Asia*, New York: St Martin's Press.

Whitefield, S. and Evans, G. (1999) 'Political culture versus rational choice: explaining responses to transition in the Czech Republic and Slovakia', *British Journal of Political Science*, 29(1), 129–54.

Whitley, R. (1998) 'Internationalization and varieties of capitalism: the limited effects of cross-national coordination of economic activities on the nature of business systems', *Review of International Political Economy*, 5(3), 445–81.

Wiarda, H. J. (2001) 'Southern Europe, Eastern Europe, and comparative politics: "Transitology" and the need for new theory', *East European Politics and Societies*, 15(3), 485–501.

Wilks, S. and Wright, M. (eds) (1987) *Comparative Government–Industry Relations: Western Europe, the United States and Japan*. Oxford: Clarendon Press.

Williamson, J. (ed.) (1990) *Latin American Adjustment: How much has Happened*. Washington, DC: Institute for International Economics.

Williamson, J. (1993) 'Democracy and the Washington Consensus', *World Development*, 21(8), 1,329–36.

Williamson, O. E. (1975) *Markets and Hierarchies: Analysis and Antitrust Implications*. New York: Free Press.

Williamson, P. (1989) *Corporatism in Perspective: An Introductory Guide to Corporatist Theory*. London: Sage.

Wilson, F. L. (1983) 'French interest group politics: pluralist or neo-corporatist?', *American Political Science Review*, 77(4), 895–910.

Wilson, G. K. (1985) *Business and Politics: A Comparative Introduction*. London: Macmillan.

Wilson, G. K. (2001) 'The Dual Motives of Interest Group Studies', Paper for the ECPR Research Conference, University of Kent. Canterbury, September. Available from: http://www.lafollette.wisc.edu/research/publications/Canterbury.pdf (accessed September 2002).

Windolf, P. (1989) 'Productivity Coalitions and the Future of European Corporatism', *Industrial Relations*, 28, 1–20.

Winkler, J. T. (1976) 'Corporatism', *Archives Européene de Sociologie*, 17(1), 100–36.

Woldendorp, J. J. (1997) 'Neo-corporatism and macroeconomic performance in eight small west European countries (1970–1990)', *Acta Politica*, 32, 49–79.

Wolf, T. and Gurgen, E. (2000) *Improving Governance and Fighting Corruption in the Baltic and CIS Countries: the Role of the IMF*, IMF working Paper WP/00/1, Washington, DC.

Wolfe, A. (1977) *The Limits of Legitimacy*. New York: Free Press.

Woo-Cummings, M. (ed.) (1999) *The Developmental State*. Ithaca, NY: Cornell University Press.

Woolcock, S. (1996) 'Competition among forms of corporate governance in the European Community: the case of Britain', in Berger, S. and Dore, R. (eds), *National Diversity and Global Capitalism*. Ithaca, NY: Cornell University Press, pp. 178–96.

World Bank (1986) *Progress Report on Structural Adjustment Lending*. World Bank Report R84–150, June, Washington, DC.

World Bank (1992) *Governance and Development*. Washington, DC: World Bank.

World Bank (1993) *The East Asian Miracle – Economic Growth and Public Policy*. New York: Oxford University Press.

World Bank (1994a) *Romania – Financial and Enterprise Sector Adjustment Loan*. Report No. PIC137. Washington, DC: World Bank.

World Bank (1994b) *Romania – Industrial Development Project: Staff Appraisal Report*. World Bank Report No. 11542. Available from: http://www-wds.worldbank.org/se.pdf (accessed 22 April 2002).

World Bank (1995) *Bureaucrats in Business: The Economics and Politics of Government Ownership*. Washington, DC: World Bank.

World Bank (1996) *World Development Report*. Washington, DC: World Bank.

World Bank (1997) *Privatisation and Restructuring in Central and Eastern Europe*. Public Policy for the Private Sector, Note No. 123. Washington, DC: World Bank.

World Bank (1998) *Assessing Aid: What Works, What Doesn't, and Why*. Washington, DC: World Bank.

World Bank (1999a) *Romania – Private Sector Institution Building Loan*. Report No. PID7637, 10 April 1999. Washington, DC: World Bank.

World Bank (1999b) *Project Appraisal Document on a Proposed Loan in the Amount of USD25 Million to Romania for Private Sector Institutions Building Loan*, 17 May. Washington, DC: World Bank.

World Bank (1999c) *Project Appraisal Document on a Proposed Loan in the Amount of USD44.5 Million Equivalent to the Government of Romania for a Mine Closure and Social Mitigation Project*, 6 August. World Bank, DC: Washington.

World Bank (2000a) *Ownership and Conditionality*. OED Working Paper Series No. 8. Washington, DC: World Bank.

World Bank (2000b) *World Development Indicators 2000*. CD-ROM. Washington, DC: World Bank.

World Bank (2001a) *Framework for World Bank Group Support to EU Accession Candidate Countries of Central and Eastern Europe*, 14 September. Available from: http://www.worldbank.org.lv/docs/

World Bank (2001b) *Romania Country Assistance Strategy*. Washington, DC: World Bank.

World Bank (2004a) *Global Development Finance 2004*. CD-ROM. Washington, DC: World Bank.

World Bank (2004b) *World Development Indicators 2004*. CD-ROM. Washington, DC: World Bank.

Wright, V. (1996) 'The national coordination of European policy-making: negotiating the quagmire', in Richardson, J. (ed.), *European Union: Power and Policy-Making*. London: Routledge, pp. 148–69.

Ziegler, H. and Baer, M. (1969) *Lobbying: Interaction and Influence in American State Legislature*. Belmont, CA: Wadsworth.

Zysman, J. (1983) *Governments, Markets, and Growth. Financial Systems and the Politics of Industrial Change*. Ithaca, NY, and London: Cornell University Press.
Zysman, J. (1994) 'How institutions create historically rooted trajectories of growth', *Industrial and Corporate Change*, 3(1), 243–83.
Zysman, J. (1995) 'National roots of a "global" economy', *Revue d'Economie Industrielle*, 71(1), 107–21.

Index